LIVING WITCHCRAFT

MOIRA HODGKINSON

By The Same Author:

Non-Fiction
The Folklore and Magic of Dolls
The Witch's Journey
The Witching Path

Novels
Operation Cone of Power
(With Philip Heselton)
Katy Hunter and the Magic Star
Wild Women
Blue Moon

LIVING WITCHCRAFT

by

Moira Hodgkinson

Published by Fenix Flames Publishing Ltd 2021

Copyright © 2021   Moira Hodgkinson

All rights reserved including the right of reproduction in whole or in part in any form. No reproduction, copy or transmission of this publication may be made without written permission. No paragraph of this publication may be reproduced, copied or transmitted save with written permission or in accordance with the provisions of the Copyright Act 1956 (as amended). Any person who performs any unauthorised act in relation to this publication may be liable to criminal prosecution and civil claims for damages. The moral rights of the author have been asserted.

All names have been changed, except in those cases where individuals are already publicly known.

Published by Fenix Flames Publishing Ltd

Design & Layout: Ashley Mortimer
Cover Design: Chris Hodgkinson

Printed by Lightning Source International / Ingram Spark

Paperback ISBN 978-1-913768-11-9
eBook ISBN 978-1-913768-12-6

www.publishing.fenixflames.co.uk

Living Witchcraft is dedicated to all those, present and past, who have led the way.

With special thoughts for
Sarah-Louise Kay and Sam Langford.

Special thanks to Neil Page for the charming seasonal poems and to my dearly beloved Chris for unwavering support and his uncanny ability to know exactly when I need a glass of wine to unwind.

I am thoroughly indebted to the Fenix Flames team, thank you so much your support: Angela Barker, for much needed sanity-saving conversations, her confidence in me and boundless enthusiasm for my writing; Ashley Mortimer, whose incredible and unwavering support just when I needed it most was so valuable in getting this book published and keeping me going when things were difficult. I could not have done it without you.

Contents

Introduction   viii

January 1
February 25
March 41
April 57
May 77
June 101
July 121
August 137
September 157
October 181
November 201
December 221

Afterword   247

Acknowledgements
About the Author
Katy Hunter and the Magic Star
Operation Cone of Power

Introduction

Living Witchcraft is the (mostly) true account of a year in the life of a busy witch. With a Sabbat festival every six weeks and circle meetings for the full moon, there is always something for pagan folk to be doing, but how does this fit into the daily grind of work, home-life and family commitments?

I work full-time as the administration support officer for a conventional office and as an author and public speaker I regularly attend pagan moots, talks, workshops and festivals. What with developing and leading workshops and classes in witchcraft, giving talks at events, taking part in open rituals and camping throughout the summer at pagan festivals, there's little time left over for much of anything else. Somehow, I manage to squeeze in visits to family and friends, work on assorted craft projects and my writing, and, on rare occasions, I even make sure the minimum of housework gets done. It may sound lot to undertake alongside a full-time job and my writing, but this is normal for me and I love everything that I do. I am never bored, though without my pagan activities and my hobbies to keep me busy, I might have to resort to watching soap operas, something I always do my best to avoid – I have never been a conventional person and I don't intend to change that now.

I have been sharing my knowledge and experience of paganism and witchcraft for nearly thirty years and have worked with a diverse range of groups and individuals, organising rituals for anything up to two or three hundred people at pagan camps, or in private workshops with as few as three or four people. I am invited to present talks and workshops at mind, body, spirit fairs and festivals and pagan conferences. After each event, I'm inundated with emails and calls from people who want to know more.

> *Can you cast a love spell for me? Can I use magic to get my boyfriend back? How do I become a witch? How can I do this at home? Can I join your coven? Will you be my mentor?*

In the aftermath of one psychic fair in Nottingham, I received close to twenty email and social media enquiries, each one taking time to read and reply to, invariably leading to more queries and responses. I do try to give advice when I can, but on those occasions when I genuinely don't have time for a personal reply, I send out details of organisations and events where people can find further information that might help them on their spiritual path.

The number of people with a growing interest in witchcraft and the sheer volume of newcomers at moots and gatherings is, I believe, a clear indication that there is a real need for widely available courses and workshops, more mentors and covens willing to help people develop their path through face-to-face contact with an experienced guide, rather than following rough guides from a Witchcraft 101 book or the internet. People want to be mentored in person, to ask questions, to watch and take part in demonstrations, and to experience the craft for themselves. Open rituals and festivals are one way of bringing pagan and witchy experiences into your life, but these events aren't suitable for everybody and increasingly, questions are coming to me from folk who are looking for ways to bring paganism and witchcraft into their everyday lives. That's one of the main reasons for me writing this book, rather than another instructive or practical guide to the craft. It's more of a diary, a journal, if you like, and I hope it will show you how to work the exercises and techniques learned in workshops or from books into your everyday life, giving you a true feeling of what it means to live and walk the witching path.

It's relatively easy today to find pagan pub moots and talks, but not everybody is able to attend them and it only gives you an outer layer of the craft. To make witchcraft, magic and pagan belief an integral part of your life, to walk the path in heart and soul, it needs to be personal: it has to mean something deep down in your core. Paganism and witchcraft can become an intrinsic part of your life and, instead of being something that you do, it can be something that you are.

You can read this book as simply that; something to read, enjoying the stories and adventures within. But I hope that the events, recipes, crafts and ideas shared in these pages will inspire you to bring witchcraft into your regular life. You see, being a witch or pagan is not something we reserve for special occasions, full moons or Sabbats; it is not about what we do in public at social moots or open rites; it's a way of life, a way of bringing your connection to nature and deity into your home, your life and your heart. Welcome to a witch's world!

Follow me through the wheel of the year as I go to pagan gatherings and festivals, spend time with family and friends, hold healing sessions and witchy workshops, at the same time holding down an ordinary full-time job, being a parent, and creating a life of magic, nature and paganism.

This is what living witchcraft means.

Moira Hodgkinson
February 2021

January

A Song for the Season: January Man, Damh the Bard.

January is a time of waking up, of new beginnings, goal setting, planning and preparing for the year ahead. Outside it is cold and we huddle in front of fires or televisions, avoiding nature unless we are particularly hardy. This winter period is often quiet with little going on socially; we take pleasure in creature comforts, rather than daring to venture out into the wind, rain, sleet, snow and darkness. It is a time of the hearth and home, a period of quiet relaxation, healing our wounds, tending to our families and, importantly, we have time for reflection and planning.

With the winter solstice behind us, even if we are too sluggish to notice it, the world around us is starting to waken, showing the subtle promise of good things to come. When snow and frost are heavy on the ground and my breath forms a cold, white mist in the air, I am content with the knowledge that the seasonal chill has a purpose; many bulbous plants need that cold, hard frost at the beginning of the year to kick-start the germination process. Without coldness and dark, would we really cherish warmth and light?

The first week of January sees the family settling back into the routine, and sometimes bland, world of school and work. I always find this return to normality after the long winter break is something of a mixed blessing. I miss the chance to enjoy activities on the spur of the moment, rather than having to plan around work and school routines, and I miss having free time to visit with friends or family or to head off as the mood takes me into the wild nature of the winter season with long walks. But I will admit, there is a large part of me that quite likes the routines involved in regular life. At the weekend, my daughter, Phoebe, was staying with her dad, as she does every other weekend, so I donned wellingtons and a woolly hat and went off with Chris, my long-suffering husband, for a walk around Sherwood Forest in the snow and cold.

The sun was shining very brightly and all around us people were having fun in the snow. There were snowballs being thrown, snowmen being built and, of course, there were toboggans and sledges a-plenty, along with dog-walkers, couples and families out walking to shuck off the dusty cobwebs of winter. We walked away from the village cricket pitch and the melee of giggles, shouts and flying snowballs, and headed to one of our favourite walks amid the bare branched trees and the chattering of birds, enjoying the sound of fresh snow crunching beneath our boots. The snow was deep in places and I had trouble wading through it as, at the time, I had a chronic pain disorder which was aggravated by walking over rough ground, climbing stairs, or just because it's a day ending with Y. After a while of kicking up fresh snow and throwing the occasional snowball at Chris, my gammy left hip and thigh started to ache, screaming at me to stop and rest. Despite the snow, neither of us felt particularly cold, as we had dressed in warm clothing and the sun was shining brightly, as it so often does at this time of year. Another hour or so later, however, and I really started to feel the ache in my hip settling in, so we circled back and headed home for a warming cuppa. Make mine a tipsy coffee to bring some heat back into my bright red nose!

The house was quiet, our three cats were content, the guinea pigs had plenty of fresh hay, and the fish were swimming quietly in their tank. I put something in the oven for dinner and settled down to work on the proposal for my new book, The Witch's Journey. At this point in the writing process, I had a comprehensive outline, but was still only around half way through writing the content. I had started planning and researching it not long after my first book, The Witching Path, was published, but I was forced to take a long break from my writing while I went through some significant and difficult changes in my life. Finally, there's a place and time for writing again, and I'm glad, because I've missed it. It's always interesting to read my writing after a break. I'm able to look at it with a fresh set of eyes and realise that it's not too bad after all, and I'm quite pleased with it. It's a great feeling. There was a long way to go before it would be finished, but fortunately, non-fiction submissions don't necessarily need to be complete if you want to submit them to publishers. A detailed proposal and a polished sample chapter or two will usually be enough.

Later, I drove over to Nottingham to pick Phoebe up from her dad's and then spent an hour that seemed to last all evening ironing school uniform for the next day. Regular work beckons on Monday morning and although my job itself is not particularly interesting or inspiring, the people I work with are an amicable group. Usually it's only around nine-thirty, often earlier, before somebody in the office has made me laugh out loud. It was lovely to hear how everyone had enjoyed the festivities of Christmas time and to answer a few questions about how I had celebrated Yule. I'm lucky that the team I work with are accepting of my witchy path, even if they don't always understand it and sometimes ask me if I'm late in because my broomstick wouldn't start!

On the first Wednesday of every month I try to go to the Empyrean pagan interest group in Nottingham. Empyrean is the longest running pagan group in the East Midlands and I've been going to the meetings for around sixteen or seventeen years and have given a few talks there myself. My only disappointment since moving to our little village is that I normally need to leave as soon as the talks have finished due to the long drive home, rather than joining everyone afterwards for a drink and a gossip in the Old Salutation Inn next-door. I have been involved in some very peculiar and hilarious conversations in the pub after Empyrean in the past and I miss that aspect of the evening. The two organisers of Empyrean at this time have been good friends of mine for years. Cayt handled the speakers and Ian is the treasurer and host.

This month we were treated to a talk on 'Bows 'n' Arrers' by Dave Howard, a lovely chap who many of the pagan community in the area are familiar with. I first met Dave at an archery event a couple of years ago when I attended my first open competition. He was there with our mutual friend Sue, another pagan-scene regular who, though not an archer, had come along to enjoy the day in the woods. I hadn't seen Sue for ages, so it was great to see her and to meet Dave. For his talk this evening, Dave had brought several bows and arrows with him for us to 'coo' and 'aah' over, including a traditional style war bow with a draw weight of around one hundred and twenty pounds. As archers, Chris and I were impressed by his talk and the primitive, hand-made arrows. I had a go at pulling back the string of the war bow and, as heavy and hard as it was, I managed a full draw. No, I'm fibbing. I think I managed to pull the bow about half-way and that was a struggle. There used be a law across the country stating that every able-bodied man above the age of ten had to practise their archery skills every Sunday before church; they must have had arms like tree-trunks!

Over the weekend, we managed to fit in a visit with our friends Kerry and Brian. This not only gave Chris and I the chance to relax with friends who are also pagans, but Phoebe and their daughter, who is a similar age, get on well together. As soon as the girls get together, even after months apart, we hear them thudding upstairs to seal themselves off into a girly bedroom, and then the giggles begin. I start to worry when it goes silent for a few minutes and Kerry and I exchange glances, slightly nervous about what on earth they might be getting up to, but it's never very long before there's another outburst of giggles and we can relax again. Kerry's family have a veritable hoard of cats and a recent litter of kittens. They are adorable but with three cats in our home already, it had to be a definite 'no' to these little cuties. We caught up on one another's gossip and goings-on and eventually made our back across the county and home again. Two of my friends, Jules and Isabelle, also have daughters who Phoebe is good friends with, and it works out well for all of us when we meet up. We oldies are happy to sit with a cuppa (or a glass of prosecco when I'm with Jules) while the girls re-connect and giggle. I'm very glad that I have a few really good pagan friends whose daughters Phoebe gets on with so well, but it hasn't always been like this.

I've seen things change over the years from me being one of only two or three pagans in the area I grew up in, to being part of a much larger and widespread community that has grown significantly over the last twenty years. These days, nearly every one of my friends is a pagan, witch, medium, druid, crystal healer, Reiki master – the list goes on. I know this isn't the case everywhere of course, and I have spent long periods of time in the past when, for whatever reason, I ended up as a solitary witch, with no access or time to spare for groups. Regularly holding my private practises and rituals is very valuable to me, as well as keeping in touch with witchy research and resources through the internet, books, conferences and magazines.

A few people in our surrounding area had arranged through social media to hold a mid-week pagan social moot. Phoebe wasn't interested in coming along and she's old enough now to stay at home without me needing to worry too much, so off I went with Chris, curious about whom we might meet. I was expecting around ten people or so to turn up and thought they would be easy to spot, as most large groups of pagans usually are. As it happens, we were spotted first. This is probably because I had very recently dyed my hair bright red and I think I must have been hard to miss. We had not met any of the others before, other than a few words on social media in one of the local pagan forums. There were lots of conversations that evening about our different pagan paths and how we came to be on them, the pentagrams and silver jewellery were only on display because the one other woman who was able to make it is a traditional goth, and there was not a smack of pretention or ego to be seen, which makes a nice change. I think these small pagan get-togethers are a great way of making new friends and focusing on sincere pagan conversation. The larger moots and speakers' groups can feel too noisy and impersonal, and the more people there are, the less chance there is for meaningful discussions.

It's not only in pagan-oriented environments where these conversations crop up. I work as an administration support officer in a conventional, corporate office, and although the work itself is mundane and uninspiring, my colleagues are a nice group and we laugh every day. We have a lot of cake and biscuits too, but I'm getting side-tracked. The point of mentioning my job is to reveal how the religious discussions I have with my line manager, who sits facing me on the other side of the desk, really began, and to put it into context.

I've been working for there for a few years now, but when I first started, I was 'outed' as a pagan by one of the team. It was my first week and I was starting to familiarise myself with my new colleagues and realised they are all quite friendly and generally a good bunch. One hot Wednesday in June, only my third day in a new job, I decided to risk wearing a short sleeved blouse. I have tattoos on each upper arm and I'm careful about what I wear in offices, as there is still a lot of discrimination around tattoos in the work place and it's been an issue for me in the past. As it turns out, they were not bothered. Hurray, I thought, I am glad we've got that out of the way. I wasn't quite out of the woods just yet, however.

'That's an interesting tattoo.' Malcolm said.

Oh dear, I thought. He was pointing to my right arm where my pentacle tattoo was half-hidden under the cap-sleeve of my blouse.

'Thank you.' I replied.

'No, I mean that's really interesting, isn't it?' He had moved from his end of the office to lean against the filing cabinet behind my desk (incidentally, this cabinet is officially known as the cake shelf). He stood there with a custard cream in one hand and a significantly raised pair of eyebrows. Malcolm is a rather imposing man in his early forties with a shaved head and multiple silver hoop earrings; an ex-punk with an aura of brusque male authority that he isn't afraid to assert.

Oh dear. Keep quiet, I told myself, just keep quiet. 'Yes, thanks.'

'Your earrings and necklace have got the same symbol.' Malcolm dropped the eyebrows and started to curl his lips at the corner so I could tell that he was trying to wind me up and I hoped it was a good-natured wind-up. But was I ready to admit to being pagan in a brand-new job in a corporate office, working with people I barely knew? No, I was not. Why didn't I realise I'd got that jewellery on? I just smiled and nodded and told myself to say nothing. I didn't know them well enough.

'Is that a pagan thing?' Clearly he was not going to let this drop. He's like a dog with a bone, I now know, always nagging at something to get to the source. 'It is, isn't it? Are you pagan?'

My insides squirmed. Taboos around tattoos are nothing when compared to the taboos and prejudice that some people still have for paganism in its many forms, especially witchcraft, and I hoped the quaking-in-my-boots feeling that overcame me was not too obvious.

'Erm, yes.' I said nervously.

Immediately, I turned around as another voice piped up. My line manager, Andy, bobbed his head over his computer screen and looked directly at me, his face void of all expression.

'Is that Wicca?' he asked, in a voice which was loud and clear. There was no escaping this. I had to say something. Oh heck, what have I got myself into here? Everyone in the office had dropped all pretence of getting on with their work and were openly staring, waiting for me to answer. I panicked for a few long, silent seconds. What I wanted to do was run into the toilets, lock the door and chill out for a few minutes while I took stock of the situation and had time to think about how I should proceed. I took a deep breath and pulled myself together.

'Erm, yes.' I said this in a very small and somewhat reedy voice, desperately hoping I would still have team mates who liked me at the end of the day.

'Oh,' Andy said. 'We've just been talking about that in my church group. I'm an ordained reader.'

What on earth was I supposed to say to that? I had no clue, literally none, as to how I was meant to react to this information. The idea of hiding out in the loo was never more appealing. I have never revealed my faith to the people I work with, even though sometimes I've discussed ghosts or crystals or mentioned that I'm a Reiki healer or a bit of a tree hugger. Being pagan, and especially being a witch, is something I just don't talk about at work. Most people can get on board with new-age crystals, ghosts or meditation, but I've had enough of negative reactions to me being a witch in the past, that I'm always very cautious. At this point, I'm thinking it could go one of two ways. Either we have some really good discussions, or we fall out and never speak amicably again.

As all of this was going through my mind, Andy started to grin and stood up, straightened his shirt a bit and moved around animatedly, pacing behind his desk, a habit of his that he does unconsciously every time he's excited or happy about something unexpected, and the grin turned into a genuinely friendly smile.

'Oooh,' he said, sounding a little excited. 'We're going to have some really good conversations.'

Thank goodness! Now that I could breathe again, I was bombarded with questions. Everyone was interested to hear exactly what this meant and because Andy had said wicca, not witchcraft, I was able to explain everything without the embarrassing stereotypes cropping up once. Quite apart from the relief I felt at the positive response to my faith, it was such a breath of fresh air to realise that I no longer needed to hide any part of who am. A year or so later, they confessed that they already knew quite a bit about me before I officially started in the role, thanks to the internet, and they'd been winding me up from the start. Work was the only place in my life, the only environment, where I had to put on a façade, and now that I don't, I can be open and honest about what I do when everyone else is talking about Christmas or Easter.

Now that that little story is out of the bag, back to this particular week in January, when I noted in my diary a discussion between Andy and myself one late afternoon when everyone else had left for the day. Although the rest of the team will talk about things like this with me, it tends to be light-hearted and I do get quite a bit of gentle teasing about broomsticks, but Andy is openly interested in theology and interfaith dialogue, and if there are only the two of us in the office and time allows, our conversations often take on a much greater depth.

Andy and I were talking quietly about what we had been doing over the weekend. He had been to his church, where he often leads prayers and teaching groups. I had been to the forest.

'Which is kind of like my version of church.' I told him.

'I think I know what you mean,' he nodded, 'God isn't just in the building, the bricks and mortar of a church, He is everywhere.'

'Exactly.' By this time, we had more or less agreed amicably that when he says God and I say Goddess, we are describing different entities or forces, but with a similar meaning for each of us: a spirit or essence greater than ourselves that encompasses all of nature and of which we are all a part. 'It's as if there's no separation between me and the Gods when I'm in the natural environment.'

'And you can feel it, connect with it, everywhere.'

'At the edge of a river or the foot of a mountain.' I said, 'but I do love trees. One of the things I love most about being pagan is that connection to a deeper source of power, and it comes so easily to me among the trees.'

'Yes,' he said agreeably, 'that feeling of a power, a presence greater than us that lingers in the very earth itself.' Then Andy gave a little hum and ah. 'Erm.' He was hesitant now. 'I wonder if... no, oh, it's silly...'

'What is it?'

'Well,' he said, 'a friend of mine runs a group called Forest Church. They meet up in woodlands for prayer and peace and – well, I thought you might like to go. It's a Christian faith group, but you'd be made welcome and I think you'd enjoy it. Just being among the trees, feeling that connection.'

He rummaged for a moment in his man-bag and pulled out a business card, reaching across the monitors between our desks to hand it to me.

I wasn't sure this was quite for me, nor was I entirely convinced that I wouldn't feel out of place, but Andy reassured me that although it may be run by Christians, I would be at home, among friends in the forest, connecting to the higher power in a natural environment. I must confess it sounded okay and it was a genuine offer from a work colleague who I consider a friend, not some kind of conversion attempt. Who cares what we call our religion, what face or name we put to that higher power, the divine source? If it brings us peace, solace, and a sense of the miraculous, why should we not celebrate together in harmony and kinship?

Around the middle of January, our car needed to go to the garage to have the brakes fixed. I always find myself feeling slightly concerned, nay, worried, when something goes wrong with the car and there are quite a few understandable reasons for this, one of the main ones being that I know nothing at all about how they work. I can drive a car; I can fill it with fuel and top up the windscreen fluid and that's pretty much it. I didn't learn to drive until I was in my mid-thirties and only then through absolute necessity. I have never really enjoyed driving, especially when the car is playing up, as this one seemed to be doing with increasing frequency. We had an estate at this point, with a massive boot that we could cram all our camping gear into, and it was starting to get a bit old and temperamental. As I explained, I know virtually zilch about vehicles and what they need to keep them going, but everybody, even me, knows that the brakes are pretty darn important. I don't remember exactly what was wrong with the brakes, except that it was something commonplace, rather than being an urgent issue, however, I do recall that it really bothered me.

I spent a few minutes one evening making a Mexican God's eye as a protective charm to hang from the rear-view mirror. I took two thin twigs, around two-and-a-half inches long, and wound them together in a cross shape with embroidery silks. White in the centre for peace and calm while I'm driving, a pale blue thread next, and then a darker blue to surround them and finish off the charm. The blues remind me of a clear summer's day when everyone has happily and safely arrived at their destination for a perfect afternoon picnic with friends. The shape of the different colours winding in layers round charm itself resembles an eye, hence the name, and it is supposed to repel negative energy and act as a protection against harm.

Mexican eyes, also called god's eyes, are very pretty and can be made to any size you fancy, so this little two-to-three-inch charm is the perfect size to hang in the car.

I made the amulet with things I already had scattered around the house and in my sewing box and I think this is an ideal way to bring magic into your life; it helps to make it personal and using items you already have is practical. Instead of making a trip into the city for special purchases or waiting for the 'right' phase of planetary alignment, I needed a charm right now, so I got on with it using things that were to hand. If I'm honest, this is probably the real reason I ended up making it in blues and white – I had those colours already and knew how they could easily relate to my intentions of creating a charm for safe travel, which is not really about the car or even the journey itself, but about arriving safely at my destination.

I love the way the amulet swings with the movement of the car as I travel and seeing it reminds me that I've done my protection magic and it's okay to relax and let go of anxiety while I'm driving. I can focus on my destination, instead of fretting about the countless little things could go wrong or the annoying new noises the car is making. I have several other god's eyes scattered around the house. Some of them are purely decorative, having been received as gifts or made as part of a demonstration, others hang in my windowsill in the hallway or from the bedroom curtain pole and there more in the windows of the lounge and kitchen, including one which was made for me by Kerry's youngest son. They're a great little project to do with children and I remember one year at the Nottingham Goddess Camp, when Phoebe was only around two years old, we went to a workshop where we made them together. Surrounded by tiny toddlers, teens and happy, hippy adults, we picked out bright colours in textured yarns and spent a couple of hours making dozens of the charms in all sorts of colours and sizes. It was good fun, but not only that, an amulet or talisman that involves any kind of repetitive process, like winding the threads round the twigs, presents an ideal opportunity to charge up the charm with protective, magical thoughts as you go along.

With every twist of wool, with every few stitches of the needle or stroke of a paint brush, you can repeat a key word or phrase that fits in with your intention.

Safe travel, arrive happy.

The week was as busy as usual, with work, gym, archery club on Tuesday evening, and dying my hair again to cover the encroaching grey and replenish the red which fades far too quickly. I managed to get some more writing done and finalised the proposal for the new book I was working on, The Witch's Journey. With twitchy nerves I pressed the send button on my email and, as I don't yet have an agent, off it went to an independent publisher who specialise in pagan and witchy subjects. Although I was pleased with the proposal and the three completed chapters I had been working on, the market is flooded with writers submitting their books and all I could do was sit back and wait with crossed fingers, hoping that my book proposal would stand out from the rest. It could be anything from a few weeks to a few months before I heard back from the publisher. In the meantime, I had to try and forget about it and carry on with my life instead of checking for a reply to my submission every five minutes.

One evening in the middle of January I wanted to hold a solitary ritual for the year ahead. I like the idea of goal setting, striving to achieve a specific outcome, even if I never reach it or change my mind about what I want, and I did a short ritual around this and then read some articles from OBOD on Druidry. An unexpected advantage of my daughter spending regular time away with her dad is that it leaves me with the opportunity to do my practical magic, meditations and rituals in peace and quiet. When she was very young, I always made sure she was sound asleep before I set out my altar and created my circles; if we were going out to an open ritual her dad and I would take it in turns to stay at home with Phoebe, so that at least one of us could concentrate properly on the ceremony.

Bunches of lavender in a child's bedroom, sleep sachets filled with hops and a small dream catcher over the bed, along with a pagan prayer to the Goddess to watch over them, helps to keep children oblivious to the goings on as you move the lounge furniture about to make room for your rituals. Another trick that worked well for me was having a well-established bed-time routine that we never wavered from.

I ran a successful coven in Nottingham for seven years when I was with Phoebe's dad, but after we separated, it was difficult to keep it going for several reasons and unfortunately it fizzled out. Solitary rituals and working small rituals with Chris, once we came together, kept me going, but there is that special something about rituals with a group of close-knit witchy companions that I really missed. I had started to invite some of the pagan friends I had made since moving to the village around to the house for circles on the full moon or the Sabbats. Gradually, this evolved into a regular development group of sorts.

Most of the people who came were either very new to the path or were not used to practising with others and, due to the difficulties of finding reliable babysitters, one or two children came along to about half of the meetings, which really hampered things. This is very different to the Linden Wood Coven I was used to, or the Gardnerian coven I have joined since, where each of us had a good deal of experience and practise under our belts. This group, the Sherwood Oak Circle, was more of a teaching circle than anything else. The presence of the children was distracting and meant planning things that are suitable for them as well, so nothing with any real focus or intent behind it. Those who had children initially agreed it was better not to bring their kids along unless we were having a social evening, but things didn't work out that way. If we ended up with a sleepy toddler one night, I would have to switch from a pathworking session to something more appropriate, like making seasonal cards with glitter and glue or watching Postman Pat.

The full moon meeting with the Sherwood Oak Circle this week was based around planning for the Imbolc ritual that would take place at the end of the month. Eight adults, two giggling teenaged girls, and a toddler. Collectively, they can be quiet for around ten minutes at a time, if the teens are willing to occupy the toddler. That was the plan, but our house isn't big enough to set a room aside for them to use while we carry on elsewhere. Although it wouldn't be appropriate for us to do any real circle work with the kids, they do like to join in with simple invocations for the elements and any chanting or drumming. We set up a simple sacred space and took turns to call in the elements with invocations and then welcoming in the Old Ones. After blessing assorted new crystals on the altar, we went over the ritual I had come up with for Imbolc – this was going to be a strictly child-free event as it would take place outdoors and at night. Although we are right on the edge of Sherwood Forest, it's a well-known tourist area and not very private, so the ritual would take place slightly further away in a more secluded woodland with plenty of thick trees and very few dog-walkers or passers-by to ogle at us. Once the arrangements were made and the ritual outline agreed upon, we said goodnight to everybody and headed up to bed. I crawled under the covers, loving the scent of sandalwood incense that lingered throughout the house.

One of my big loves is being creative with textiles, I'm nearly always knitting or sewing something. Towards the end of last year, Phoebe and I had been to visit my friend Jules and her daughter, and Jules very kindly let me sleep in her room while she took the sofa downstairs. On her bed was the most beautiful quilt I have ever seen in my life. Jules is a big fan of pumpkins, fairies and all things orange and fantastical. Her entire house is filled to the rafters with delicate fairy lights, dozens of pumpkin decorations, fairies, tiny red toadstools hiding on the picture rail, pumpkin coloured cushions, pumpkin-shaped baking dishes, pumpkin ornaments, and she even has a pumpkin coloured split-screen VW camper van. Jules keeps up this theme in the bedroom with a double-sized quilt that she designed. Her own sewing skills weren't up to the task of making it, so another friend of hers did the needlework, but Jules spent a long time designing the pumpkin themes, picking out exact shades, textures and patterns of fabric. It's truly a work of art. Sleeping under this gorgeous bedspread was inspiring and I suddenly decided I was going to have a go at making a quilt myself. I've never done any quilting, unless you count a cot quilt that I made in textiles class at school when I was fifteen.

This month seemed as a good a time as any to start the project and after sketching a design for a two-foot square quilt that I would make to start with before launching into anything larger, I rummaged through my fabric stash for suitable materials. It quickly became evident that this wasn't going to work; I had lots of fabric scraps, but nothing which would suit the quilt I'd designed.

'Stuff it, I'll just chop up all of these fabrics, sew squares together, and make a double-bed sized quilt instead.' Thoughtfully planned, eh? Phoebe and Chris watched with puzzled expressions over the course of the next couple of evenings as I patiently chopped up dozens of twelve-by-twelve-centimetre squares of random fabrics and sewed them together in long strips. The dimensions were probably the only thing I really worked out in advance; the twelve-centimetre squares gave me a centimetre all around for the seam allowances. Make a note of that: carefully measured squares.

I had vague ideas of knitting or crocheting leaves and branches, adding appliques and sequins and sewing things in place to make a three-dimensional tree of life on the quilt along with a moon, sun, pentagram and awen and maybe symbols of the Lord and Lady too. As I put the squares together in a random order, it started to look lovely and even better than that, I realised that many of the fabric remnants in my stash were important to me in one way or another. That piece of emerald green satin was left over from something my mum had made for herself years ago that I had then made into a blouse in my early twenties; the orange-and-brown camouflage fabric was a once-loved pair of jeans I used to wear all the time at Rock City; a few pieces of duchess satin were left over from my hand-fasting dress; some gothic red-and-black fabric scraps were remnants of the material I made into waistcoats for Chris and his best man to wear at our hand-fasting. As I worked on it, I very quickly realised this quilt was: a) a long-term project; b) filled with pagan and personal symbolism; and c) would make me curse and sweat and jab my fingers until they bled. With all this history sewn into it, I was at least reassured that the darn thing was going to be worth it. When this quilt is finally finished (like I said, it turned into a long-term project) it will be nowhere near as cleverly designed as the pumpkin masterpiece, but it should last a life time and will be a constant reminder of my family and some of the good times I have been through with them all. Those first couple of evenings spent working on it led me to create new and inventive swear words specially designed for the craft of quilting!

Remember me carefully cutting hundreds of squares out to my specific dimensions with enough material for a seam allowance? It didn't quite work out that way and most of the seams didn't match up. That wasn't the real problem, though. I could put up with a few wonky lines, but the practical matter of fitting a double-bed sized quilt under the arm of my domestic sewing machine was something else altogether. The quilt is henceforth and eternally known as The Beast!

I have a bad habit of leaving far too many things to the very last minute and I kept up this tradition as Imbolc approached, when I finally got around to making little dolls to represent Brighid for the ritual. I had done a little advance thinking about this and bought a packet of white pipe cleaners, white ribbons and strips of thin lace. I twisted pipe cleaners into body shapes and tied white ribbons and lace around them to make the symbolic dolls, around thirty in total, and put them all to one side while I got on with putting the final touches to the ritual.

Ritual planning doesn't always come easily, even after years of doing it, but the basic format is always the same. I start with a cleansing of space and participants, create a sacred space, welcome in the elements and deity, give blessings, provide time for personal thoughts on the seasonal theme, share something to eat and drink, give thanks to the elements and the Old Ones and then close the sacred space. The real planning involves writing invocations, deciding which poem or story relates to the season and what people will do during the ritual as a focus. Whenever possible, I call on volunteers in advance who are confident enough to call in the elements in public, and I like to make rituals as inclusive as possible, so that participants don't feel bored, disappointed or left out.

Once the ritual was written, I printed off several copies of it to hand around and asked Chris to put on his tech-guy hat and figure out what was wrong with the printer. There always seems to be something wrong with the wretched thing when I'm in a hurry and I curse myself for always leaving everything to the minute. Next time, I will plan and prepare everything well in advance. Honestly.

Chris has a level of patience normally known only to saints and Buddhist monks, and while he worked on getting my ritual printed off, I dashed into the kitchen where a significant amount of baking was in order. Crescent moon biscuits and a batch of fairy cakes would go down well with bottles of fresh apple juice as our libation for the ritual. I know the traditional offering is cake and wine, but I like to offer a soft drink too. I had already checked with the people who are coming to make sure nobody had any allergies. Baking, ritual, Brighid dolls...

All I needed now was a good weather forecast, after all, it was still the middle of winter and the snow had only just cleared.

Crescent Moon Biscuits

Ingredients:

4oz butter or vegan margarine
8oz plain flour
2oz sugar
Optional flavourings or white chocolate chips

Rub butter and flour together in a large bowl until the mixture resembles fine breadcrumbs, add sugar, stir. Add a small amount of milk or water and mix to create a firm dough.

Roll onto a floured surface, use a moon shaped cookie cutter and lift the biscuits onto a greased baking tray. Alternatively, use round cookie cutters to create the crescent moon shapes by taking a piece out of each circle with the cutter.

Bake in a medium to hot oven for 5-10 minutes until just golden. Leave to cool and decorate.

Icing:

Mix approximately 4oz of icing sugar with a spoonful of water or lemon juice and drizzle over the biscuits. Children might want to decorate further with silver confectionery, rainbow sugar strands or sugar flowers.

Brighid Dolls

Young children will love the simplicity of the Brighid dolls I made for Imbolc. It should only take a few minutes to make a large bundle of these for your own ritual. Younger children might like to decorate the garden, dotting the little Brighid dolls among the flowers and grass. They could even go a step further and lay out a small box lined with a white handkerchief as her bed, putting the doll inside and inviting her to wake up and bring light and good tidings to everyone as the plants start to grow.

Make it into a game of hide-and-seek by hiding the dolls yourself; kids can collect them in a basket and hand them out during the ritual.

You will need:

White pipe cleaners
1m of white or cream lace and ribbons

Take a pipe cleaner and wrap the centre of it around your finger to make a loop for the head. Twist the rest of the pipe cleaner together for a short 'body' and separate at the bottom for each of the legs.

Wrap a length of white ribbon, lace or scrap of white cloth around the centre and tie into a bow for a make-shift dress.

Mexican God's Eyes

Another easy project and one that even very young children can manage with a little assistance. There are plenty of video tutorials and diagrams on the internet if you can't grasp it from these instructions.

You will need two straight twigs or sticks, approximately 2-3 inches long, and various lengths of wool, ribbon, string or embroidery silks in an assortment of colours. Beads, feathers, sequins, leaves, and flowers can be threaded onto the yarns or tied on afterwards to decorate. A glue gun will be useful, if available, and if you can't find suitable sticks, try blunted cocktail sticks as a substitute.

Lay the twigs in parallel next to each other and tie in the centre with a long piece of wool, string, embroidery silk or ribbon. Twist the twigs to form a cross and wind the yarn around the centre several times to secure them in this crossed position.

Hold the cross in one hand and wind the yarn over the top and then underneath one of the arms of the cross, returning to the starting position. Rotate the cross clockwise and repeat the yarn winding: over the top of the next arm of the cross and underneath it. Rotate again and repeat, each time turning the twigs in the same direction and always passing the threads over the top and then under. You will notice a pattern emerging in the yarn as you wind it from one arm of the cross to the next. The reverse side will look very different so see which side you prefer.

Add new threads, colours, beads and other decorations as you go along if you wish. On reaching the top of the twigs, you will need to secure the yarn with a tight knot, leaving a long tail to hang it up with. My knots usually come undone after a while, so I tend to use a glue gun to stop the whole thing unravelling.

Circle Work – Solitary

Find a place and time where you will be undisturbed for a short while, lock yourself in the bathroom if you really must, just make sure you will be able to sit comfortably. Prepare your space with candles, incense, pen and paper, wine and cakes if you want them, and a suitable container to catch any ashes from the paper.

Light a candle and incense, put on some meditative music if you like, and sit comfortably as you start to relax.

Think about what the previous twelve months have brought you, all the achievements you've reached, the high points and the lows. What could you have done differently? If faced with some of these situations again, would you like to react in a more positive way? How did your plans for last year work out or not? Could you have done more to improve things, to look after yourself better or make more productive use of your time? Do you wish you'd done things differently, worked harder or had more free time? How might you have done things differently to have less worry and stress and more in terms of love and laughter?

Now think about what you would like to achieve in the coming year, the goals you want to reach, how you want to conduct yourself, what learning or adventures you want to have. Make up your mind now that you will be all those things you long to be, that you will move forward with your life, develop worthwhile friendships, be more sociable, or whatever else you want. Think of how you'd like your relationships with family and friends and work colleagues to be, how your summer will be spent, what you will work on to progress spiritually.

Choose one specific thing that you really want to work towards over the next year; something you've always wanted to do and are perhaps starting to work on already, or a new goal completely.

Maybe you want a career change, a new home, to improve at sports, have a more active life, a better loving relationship, or simply to carry on being a kind person in your interactions with others.

As you watch the candle flame flicker and glow, write down your goal and hold the paper above the flame so that it catches the glow and the warmth. Don't burn it yet, just see that bright fire energy and focus on your goal. Visualise the things you need to do to achieve this goal. See yourself doing it and succeeding, be very specific. What do you want? See yourself a year from now with exactly the result you want.

Now let the flame slowly consume the paper with your wishes written on it and say aloud or in your mind:

I allow good things to come into my life, I allow myself to grow and develop. I treat myself with kindness, as I would treat others. May the Lord and Lady bless me with all I need to achieve this goal. Bless me with grace, friendship and love. Lady of the silver moon, Lord of the green forest, grant me this, my heart's desire, as I do will, so mote it be.

Finish by giving thanks, clear away your ritual tools and keep a note book by your bed to write down any further thoughts, intuitions or dreams you might have.

February

A Song for the Season:
The Host of Seraphim, Dead Can Dance.

After the dark nights of winter, it's always nice to welcome Imbolc and the returning sun. The first white snowdrops begin to poke their heads through the frosty ground, bright green shoots are starting to bud slowly on the trees and the mornings are lighter, the evenings longer. Yet it is still cold, the ground is hard with deep frost, our breath is misty in the air as we gather in the woods for the Sabbat.

Imbolc evening finally arrived and having only finished the preparations the previous day, I felt rushed and frantic, as if there simply wasn't enough time for everything. I had packed everything I'd need for the open ritual, which gave me the rest of the day to work on The Beast, wrestling with it and the sewing machine, followed by a quick tidy up of the house before heading off to the woods. Our meeting point was a large layby on the road near to the forest and it was already fully dark by the time we got there.

I took my magical kit bag, frame drum and all my bits and bobs, including dozens of candles and jars, out of the car boot, and waited for the guests to arrive. It's a short walk through ancient oak trees to the ritual circle in the woods, where everybody struggled to light candles in the wind. I handed out the printed ritual sheets, set up a cloth on a small portable table with the basket of dollies in the centre and all the usual ritual items, including something to eat and drink. There was only torchlight to see by, the evening was cold and windy, and the candles wouldn't stay lit.

With nearly twenty of us gathered in robes, thick coats and scarves, I cast a circle and we held peace with one another in the quiet of the dark forest, feeling the call of the earth under our feet, the wind of air blowing a chill around our hands and faces, the light of the torches and the reflected sunlight bouncing off the moon as the element of fire, the moisture in the air and the frost of water. Being in circle with other pagans and witches, no matter what we do, no matter how well or how long we've known each other, always gives me a warmth in my heart and my soul cries out. Several people were shivering as the woodland at night, without a cloud in the sky, was very cold and a frost was beginning to form. I'm not the sort of pagan who dresses up in fancy robes at the slightest hint of moonlight, but I did appreciate the blessing of a very warm winter coat on this occasion.

The focus of the ritual was for each of us to call out or silently say what we wanted to achieve this year, burn our wishes, written on a slip of paper, in the flame of the one candle that managed to stay alight, and then take one of the little Brighid dolls from the centre to represent our wishes for a new start. Some of the group called out loud and others were silent in their reflections, but everyone took part in some way, and I set aside a couple of the little dolls for a friend who had not been able to make it.

At the end of the ritual, the group gathered closer together, holding hands for the traditional blessing:

> May the circle be open, yet unbroken, may the peace of the Goddess be forever in our hearts, merry meet, merry part and merry meet again.

Swinging our hands in time to the chant and finally sweeping upwards with a cheerful cry to merry meet again, the circle closed, and I looked round happily at all the smiling faces. Some of us were old hands at this, others were attending their first ritual, yet the smile was the same across the board; contentment, a sense of family, of celebration.

Afterwards, we invited the group to our house just down the road for a chat and a cuppa and it was not until very late that night that the conversation finally died down and the last visitor had driven off.

As a slight aside to the ritual, I'll mention a minor non-event that was noticeable to Chris and myself by its absence. In our open-plan lounge, the staircase leads up behind a small sofa, and it is here that our household spirit travels from one end of the house to the other. Almost everyone who has sat on this sofa, whether psychic or not, has at some point turned to look behind them with the distinct feeling that somebody was on the staircase or standing right behind them. Our three cats regularly sit and watch as this spirit passes through. This Imbolc night, one of our guests, a woman who has often professed to be a medium, proved to be the one person who didn't pick up any kind of psychic vibes at all from that part of the house. Was I right all along in thinking this person was not anywhere near as psychic as they claimed or was our spirit just not active that night? Whatever the case, I was highly amused by it.

The day after the ritual, I was joined by a few pagans for a walk around Sherwood Forest and the day was beautiful and sunny. The frost of the previous day had cleared up and we had a leisurely walk through the trees. One lady, an archery acquaintance with pagan leanings, had brought her toddler along and for some reason the little guy seemed to latch onto me. Small children often do and I honestly have no idea why: I really don't look like the natural earth-mother type that kids usually go for – you know the sort of person I mean, I'm sure. They have long, wild hair which is in the process of turning grey beautifully and they wear flowery dresses that make them flow instead of walk, they possess soft, kind-looking eyes, gentle faces, and pockets full of tissues and treats. Anyway, this little tyke insisted on holding my hand as we walked around the forest, tugging me first this way and then that way to look at this tiny flower or that pretty stone on the path. He encouraged me to try tree climbing but I settled for sitting on a log, as my tree-climbing days are over. After a few hours of pleasant conversation and a gentle stroll, we went our separate ways and I returned home with a few oak apples for the altar. Later, the long walk took its toll on my hip, so it was time for a long, hot bath, filled with bubbles, pink rock salts and lashings of lavender oil.

Over the course of the next week or so, I spent a few evenings working on the new book and a few more tackling The Beast. Several pricked fingers and broken machine needles were the result of my attempts to tackle the quilt, as the batting I'd chosen for the inner layer was far thicker than I'd realised and getting the centre of the wretched thing under the arm of my puny sewing machine was a nightmare. I invented a few more new words to describe The Beast – words which are best not repeated here!

My writing, on the other hand, was going very well and I thoroughly enjoyed the research I was looking through. Some of the things I learned while investigating lunar and solar magic were especially interesting as I stumbled onto NASAs website for a scientific view of the moon. Edgar Mitchell, one of the first astronauts to walk on the moon, conducted experiments in telepathy and psychic ability during his time in the lunar orbit. He later founded the Institute of Noetic Sciences to further scientific research into the unknown realms of ESP and psychic abilities. It's a subject I've found fascinating ever since I was a young girl, but I won't go into it here; the details are in the book, *The Witch's Journey*, if you're interested.

Empyrean's speaker this month was Ross Parish, a local folklorist and historian who works with the Nottingham Hidden History Team. With a talk entitled 'Pagan Holy Wells of the East Midlands', it was bound to be full of interesting facts and stories, pieced together from local historians, residents and assorted literature. Ross's enthusiasm for his subjects is always engaging and he was on top form this month with a well-researched account of local sites. A thoroughly enjoyable evening. Once again, we had to dash off straight after the meeting as Phoebe was at home on her own and I don't like to be back too late. Checking up on Phoebe last thing at night is a real treat for me. She doesn't like the fuss now that she's older, and I don't like to disturb her sleep, but the odd times when I do look in on her at night, I can't resist adjusting her covers, stroking her hair and planting a little kiss on her forehead. I love how cosy and sleepy and warm she is, her gentle murmurs if she wakes up and gives me a quick hug before drifting back to sleep, and I feel very lucky.

Another week full of work, a couple of sessions at the gym, and the usual run of the mill housework: cooking, cleaning and all those sorts of mundane tasks that make me wish I could magic it all away with a simple twitch of my nose or the click of my fingers. Sometimes, being a witch is not nearly as much fun as it ought to be. I like to pretend that I live in an alternate reality where magic is cast with a few simple words but when I open my eyes the washing up still needs to be done. At the weekend I did yet more work on The Beast and finally managed to finish stitching through all the layers and between each square and the backing fabric. Thank Goddess for that. I put the dreadful thing away in the box room upstairs, determined not to look at it again until the autumn. when I would have more time to start on the next stage, which will be all the appliques and pagan motifs to overlay the patchwork background. Saturday evening was spent with a couple we had met at the pagan pub moot recently, for more pagan-oriented chat and friendship. I did more research and writing for my book on Sunday, along with family time watching a film with Chris and Phoebe before she went off to bed. My crafty fingers don't stay still for very long – after putting The Beast away for the night, I grabbed some knitting wool and needles and sat working on a cabled cardigan while Chris and I watched a late night horror movie.

When I was a kid, my mum brought three of us up single-handedly and to make us feel special, she started a tradition that we call a Nice Night. Mum would buy a bottle of lemonade and a few quarters of sweets, rent a video, and then we would all cram together on the sofa, having a Nice Night together. The sibling bickering would come to a halt, we'd cuddle up with each other on the sofa, share the sweets out evenly, and Mum's choice of film was always spot on. Unknown to either of us until after we'd been doing it a few years, my brother and I both carried on the tradition of having a Nice Night with our own kids. Though Phoebe has grown past the stage of Nice Nights now, we do still enjoy having a movie night and pizza: home-made cheese and tomato with a stuffed crust.

I always like to put a bit of kitchen witchery into practise when I can and as I kneaded the pizza dough, I poured my heart into it. When I stir anything in a pan or bowl, I turn the spoon clockwise, and even the spoon itself is magical, in a way. Years ago when I was running a workshop and camping at a Pagan Federation gathering in Derbyshire, a few stalls were set out with the obligatory hand-made pagan goodies. I'm as much of a sucker for pagan goodies as the next witch, but when I saw these expensive spoons carved with a simple pentagram in the bowl or words like 'blessed be' or 'kitchen witching' along the handle, I was shocked. A fiver each for a spoon that probably cost fifty pence from Wilko? Honestly, did it really take that much effort to etch and burn that pentagram into it? If I did this myself I would – oh, wait. I can't do this myself. I would need to buy equipment to do it with, go to an evening class to learn some neat pyrography skills, spend a small fortune on practise pieces, and let's not talk about the endless hours of patience it would take me to learn how to do it well enough to make it worthwhile. Somebody else has already taken the time and effort to go to Wilko, paid parking fees for the car while they shopped, used their time, electricity and equipment, paid their stall holder fees, not to mention their creativity and the fact they have put their own energy and magic into it, as well as using their skills in pyrography, skills that are well beyond me. I bought two. Like I said, I'm a real sucker for witchy paraphernalia. I also believe that we should value our crafts-people who put their time, effort and care into making beautiful things we can't do ourselves.

Back onto the subject of pizza dough and kitchen-witching, I'm no expert chef and I'm not a qualified herbalist, but I do enjoy making magic work for me and with every twist of dough, I plough my energy into it.

> *Let all who eat my dishes feel the power of my good wishes.*

Kneading dough, stirring soup or a casserole, mixing a jar of store-bought spaghetti sauce – whatever you do in the kitchen, you can do it with magic. Fill yourself with good intentions, positive vibes and energy, and channel this into your cooking. If you're feeling angry you can vent those feelings, bashing them into bread dough as an offering; not something you would eat, but a focus to bury or burn in a ritual. The earth is a great recycler and burying something like this in the ground lets nature take away that angry energy you no longer need, breaking it down into something new and pure again.

It's easy to incorporate simple spells, charms and witchery into the things you do in your everyday life and it shouldn't take any special, magical spoons. One that I got myself for fifty pence and keep unadorned will work just as well as the more expensive ones decorated by others, because it is your intention that counts. Your energy, your sense of happiness for your family, your positivity and good wishes are what makes the magic work, no matter if it's a simple home-cooked pizza or a complex candles-and-cords magical spell that takes you hours. It's your intention, your energy and magic that makes it happen, not the tools that you use, no matter how much they cost or who made them. That's not to say the tools don't help, especially at the start of your magical journey. They are a good starting point and a way of focusing and channelling energy. Gradually though, the wands and athames soon become secondary and you'll find that, although you probably still use them, you don't *need* them. Your pointing finger is far more powerful than any crystal encrusted wand.

The following week brought us another pagan moot with people I had made connections to on social media but had yet to meet in person. I enjoyed it in a quiet sort of way. There were around eight to ten people gathered in a very small and traditional pub, complete with a little brown dog scrounging crisps under one of the tables. Once we had all the introductions out of the way the conversation started to take some interesting turns. Jo is a lady I always think of as a real kitchen witch, using the herbs and plants that she grows herself to make her magic shine. Gary was a complete beginner and wanted to know what books he should be reading, what events he should attend, where local pagans meet up for rituals and how could he get involved himself. There were also a few others like me, who were part of a small group of friends who gathered at full moons or the Sabbats for rituals. Like many newcomers to paganism, Gary wanted all the answers straight away, but there are no quick fixes in the craft. He would have to do the reading, the research and the practise himself in order to learn and experience anything meaningful. Moving forwards on our path, no matter how long we have been travelling, is something we should all be striving for. Even people who are a public authority on the subject are still learning. That's very much the case with me, I'm no expert by any means and the more I learn, the more I realise there is to learn and how very little I really know.

Having put away the mega-quilt, no longer The Beast now the worst of it was over, I had twitchy fingers at the weekend and some remnants of orange and brown fabric with a pumpkin motif called out to me to be used up. I drew up a quick and easy pattern for an A-line knee-length skirt. Ruffles at the bottom, zip at one side, job done. I made the skirt on Sunday evening and wore it to work in the morning. Every time I wear a garment that I've made myself, I get a little buzz of pleasure and any compliments on my handicrafts make me grin with inner pride. 'Thanks, glad you like it, I made it myself!'

As the February half-term came around, I booked a few days off work to spend some family time with Phoebe. We went to our regular Tuesday evening archery session and took part in one of the work-days in the woods. This mainly involved setting out target faces, checking the shooting positions were clearly marked with coloured pegs, and lifting and shifting the 3D targets into position, ready for our upcoming open competition in March. Phoebe and the other teens in the group work quite hard for the club and they enjoy it; once all the work is done, they can usually shoot the course together. However, it can often leave Phoebe feeling physically drained and on several occasions, she's had time off school. This doesn't seem quite right to me, a bit of exertion like this at her young age shouldn't leave her feeling so worn out, with aches and pains, headaches, a general lethargy and tiredness. As she'd been a feeling unwell a fair bit lately, I decided to book her in with the doctor. We had been before several times about this over the last couple of years, but previous doctors had been dismissive, claiming she had nothing more than growing pains. One doctor in the village suggested we try paracetamol, as if this wasn't the first thing I would think of as a mother. This time I wouldn't be taking any of that nonsense and insisted she have a blood test to see if she was anaemic. Luckily, the doctor on this occasion agreed and we booked a blood test with the practice nurse.

I managed to squeeze in a trip with Chris to one of my all-time favourite places in Derbyshire on a rare day off together. A small stone circle, not far from the more well-known Nine Ladies circle at Stanton, Doll Tor is gorgeous, quiet, uninterrupted and peaceful. Just sitting there for a few minutes is enough to restore my soul and somehow, the energies of the place remain constant. The atmosphere of some sacred places can change with the seasons, the weather, the time of day or even the mood that I'm in, but this place is always the same – restorative, calm, solid. I had brought incense with me, a few cotton ribbons to use as clooties, a rug to sit on and a warm jumper to stave off the February chills, and soon I'd set up a simple circle. A surge of energy came pulsing through my body, from the soles of my bare feet and up through the finger-tips of my outstretched hands, as I held incense and feathers to the sky to greet the beautiful day. Chris held hands with me in the centre of the stones, adding his subtle, quiet energy to the circle. I love simple rituals like this, that reconnecting of my soul and spirit to the deeper, vibrant spirit of nature that I am part of.

A good friend of mine got in touch with me through social media and although we never lost contact as such, it had been a while since we'd seen each other in person, and she had some news that she was keen to share. Liz lives on the sweetest little narrowboat in the world and I drove to see her at her current mooring, a picturesque riverside village not far from Newark. On the way there, a robin flew out from the hedges only a metre or so in front of me and went straight under the car tyres with a small thud. No!

This can't have just happened. I was absolutely horrified. The poor little robin didn't stand a chance. It was the first time, and the only time to date, thank goodness, I'd ever run over anything and I was just heart-broken. I pulled over briefly and cried for the poor little bird who had done nothing wrong and yet still I had killed it. I know. I can hear you saying it, just as I do in my own head: there was nothing I could have done; it wasn't my fault. I know this. But still I wonder: are we the most despicable species on the face of the planet? Every time I see an animal or bird lying dead by the side of the road, I could weep a river of tears for what we have become, for what we have done to the earth, the way we have carelessly destroyed so many natural habitats in the creation of our own. My visit with my friend would be marred by the sadness inside me if I didn't put it aside and, as time was ticking on, I got back into the car and carried on driving through tear-blurred eyes. I was more relaxed and feeling much better when I was greeted by Liz with her natural cheerfulness and exuberance. I was thrilled to see her after what must have been a year or more and keen to hear what she had been up to lately.

Aloe Vera, famed for its valuable healing properties, was not new to me but now I learned more its many uses as Liz revealed her new business venture and how selling aloe vera products with Forever Living had pretty much transformed her way of life. All the products contain aloe vera; from toothpaste to drinks, cosmetics to house-hold cleaners. As part of a larger organisation, Liz thought I might like to get on board with promoting these products. I was glad that she was enjoying her new job but I'm no sales person and I just don't have the spare time to dedicate to it and can't risk leaving my secure and reliable job. After the aloe talk was over, we enjoyed a fantastic, giggly afternoon together chatting about our respective goings-on and reminiscing over coffee.

I met Liz through the Nottingham Goddess Camp community and we had both been heavily involved in running the camp at different times. We've had some amazing times with the pagan community that sprung up around the Goddess Camp and with the other organisers. I remember one fantastic ritual when we'd planned something around the theme of Baba Yaga. Liz had dressed up as Baba Yaga with a dark shroud over her head and a heavy staff in one hand. Everyone was invited up to meet with her to share their secrets, ask for their hearts' desire and receive her blessings. A couple of the youngest camp children had actually been a little scared of her, which seems ridiculous, as she is one of the most approachable and friendly people, so this reaction was testimony to her role-playing, rather than any reflection of Liz herself.

Another time and another ritual, several of us were calling out invocations to the elements on a beautiful, hot summer's evening. Liz called in water and within minutes, completely without warning the heavens opened and it rained heavily for over an hour. It was the source of much amusement for years afterwards every time it rained. A raised eyebrow, a head tilted towards Liz with a questioning glance.

'No,' she would declare adamantly, 'it wasn't me this time, I called earth.' This would then prompt somebody else to ask if we should be expecting an earthquake any time soon.

The Sherwood Oak Circle met up towards the end of the month, this time at Paul and Sarah's house so that it wouldn't interfere with their toddler, Jack's, bedtime routine. John was already there when we arrived and Brian and Kerry couldn't make it, so there were only five adults present and most of the evening was given over to keeping little Jack occupied. I really don't know what had happened to the bed time routine, but we all went ahead and played with Jack and watched Postman Pat, ending up with a half-hearted discussion on crystal healing while Jack played up and refused point-blank, with protesting cries, to go to bed.

I'm so glad that Phoebe had a regular routine at bedtime when she was young and would settle easily at night. She'd sometimes stay up late enough to say hello to everyone if I had visitors round, but when I put her to bed – wham – pillow, head, sleep. I should point out if you're thinking 'lucky so-and-so' that luck had nothing to do with it. This was the result of lots of hard work on the part of myself and her father insisting on a routine. Not only did this work in our favour, it was better for her too; like most little kids, she was incredibly active and a decent night's sleep was restorative. I don't dislike children; the hugs and kisses and their playful, innocent natures are precious things that I enjoy, most of the time, but if your child is happily asleep or being taken care by someone else, it leaves you free to focus on what you're doing, gives you a bit of 'me' time and there's no need to worry about children getting bored while you try and meditate or carry out a healing spell.

Having had more of a social circle than a ritual one, I couldn't help feeling I'd missed out and decided it was time for another solitary ritual. I was also still feeling awful at having accidently killed the poor robin and I hadn't had a chance to do anything much around that, other than lighting a candle for the bird. I had to plan everything to fit around mundane work, going to the gym, cooking and cleaning and helping Phoebe do some research for her homework. It would be another late night, but one I very much needed to keep myself grounded as regular life went on around me.

In the meantime, I grabbed some sage and fanned it around the house straight after work. It only takes a few minutes and leaves the house feeling fresh and clean. I love that about sage bundles; they work as a kind of instant magic. No need for casting a circle or long and poetic invocations. I don't particularly like the smell of sage bundles, it reminds me ever so slightly of bad body odour, however, it is very effective, and using it in the house leaves the place feeling fresh. Sage also works well to get rid of any animosity, stale atmospheres or unhelpful energies that may be lingering. A thorough house-cleansing every now and then will help your energies stay grounded and calm.

A handy tip to make your witchiness accessible and bring it into your everyday life, is to keep at least some of your magical items in a place where you see them every day. I have an old bureau that used to belong to my gran; the drop-down leaf opens to reveal a useful space with a couple of small shelves and plenty of room for a large pot, where I keep a few biros, note books and stamps to one side. The rest of the bureau houses most of my incenses, oils, candles, crystals, one of my small cauldrons, smudging bundles, cleansing sprays and so on. Having this right in front of me when I come into the house means it's immediately accessible. I don't need to think about it, I can simply chuck my handbag down and delve straight into the bureau, where the aura sprays I make are kept. I can quickly cleanse my aura after a hectic or stressful day at a moment's notice. Keeping some of my witchy items in a well-used place means every that time I open the bureau, I'm putting energy into the little spell boxes that are stored in there after a working. I see the box or a candle or a photograph on top of the bureau and it reminds me to send a little more energy or healing to the spell's recipient. I love having this easy way of making witchcraft and magic so immediate. It helps to make my pagan practice a true part of my life, instead of something I need to think about and make time for. My small blessing with a candle for the robin is included further below, but I also took a bit of time to ground and centre myself first.

A Poem for Imbolc

Long nights, short days, all in slumber, silent, still.
The Cailleach dwells in the forest deep.
Hoary frost, deep snow, frozen soil, all is quiet, calm.
Foraging hard, Squirrel scampers, seeking, rarely finding,
Trees bare, no seed or fruit on the ground.
I scatter nuts to Squirrel's delight, timidity forgotten with the feast.
Cold air on skin, each footfall leaves trails on crisp snow.
Squirrel darts away and Bird arrives.
Bird spies me, as if in silent thanks, then chirps and is on his way.
Cold air on skin. Trees bare.
Yet there – and here – and yet there
A bright shard of green grows bravely above the white.
Brighid's herald, the snowdrop, is dawning.
The Cailleach dwells no longer here, bright sunlight fills the sky,
And the world will warm again, wake again, live again.
Bringer of spring time joy, Brighid arises.

> *Smiling, content, I scatter nuts, friend Squirrel scampers*
> *again to collect.*
> *The circle, never ending, begins anew.*
> *Reflection is over, the new year lies ahead.*
> *Amid snow and frost, new life surges*
> *To continue the cycle of life and death and life.*

Blessing for a Beloved Animal

It's always hard to lose an animal we love and to see wild animals lying lifeless at the side of the road. This blessing can be altered to make it personal to your family and your pet or it can be used as a blessing for wild animals. A ceremony of farewell can be useful for children, as well as adults, to mark the passing of a beloved animal companion.

Set up your sacred space with a white altar cloth, several white candles, salt, water, a plain stone, and a photograph of the animal. For wild animals, you can use a photograph or picture from a nature book to represent the animal. For a family pet, you can lay out any collars, toys, or a photograph of you and your beloved animal companion.

Cleanse your space and set up your circle in whatever way you prefer. Spend some time remembering the animal and all it represents to you. Tell your pet what made them special and that you will always remember them fondly. Don't hold back on expressing your tears and emotions. Say out loud anything that comes to mind and then light your candles.

> *I bless you, dear (animal), with love and peace. I honour your time on this earth with us and give my thanks to you for sharing it with me.*
>
> *I wish the free spirit of the air for you, I wish the bright spark of the fire for you, I wish the deep peace of running water for you, I wish the soul comfort of the earth for you.*

Take a small stone, hold it over the candle flame and ask for the animal's soul to be looked after and loved in the next world.

> *With this rite I mark your passing, dear friend, and release you to care of the Old Ones.*
>
> *I call to Lord Herne of the forest, who watches over all animals, to join this rite, to take the soul of this beloved animal on its final journey to the Summer Lands.*
>
> *May we remember, and know and love them again, in this world or the next. May they be loved and be at peace, free to soar and run and jump for joy.*
>
> *Lord Herne of the forest I give this soul to your care.*
>
> *Farewell dear beloved. Blessed be.*

Put the stone in your garden as a memorial or take it to a place in nature where you feel your animal would have been content.

At Samhain, put a photograph of your beloved pet on the altar and take time to remember them again.

March

Awaken! Awaken! Fur and feather,
Brimstones in the air, hares in the heather,
All creatures rejoice and sing with joy,
North of Lizard and South of Hoy.

The world spins along, equinox is here,
A momentary balance, a special time of year,
When night matches day and nature takes note,
A signal of progress and a change to the rote.

Winter chills are forgotten once more,
As hidden beasties fling open their door,
To build and create, new paths to forge,
From high in the hills, to deep in the gorge.

Spring strolls in, timed by the sun,
Nests to build, errands to run,
Food for the taking, babies to make,
A busy time of year with urges to slake.

The balance tips inexorably on,
For here, for now, the sun has won,
To lengthen the days and shorten the night,
To cheer in the warmth and relish the light.

(Neil Page)

March is an awakening time of year. The fresh green shoots and bright yellow of daffodils in the garden are reaching for the sky, the diary is getting booked up with events after the solitude of winter, and there is a sense of expectation and hope in the chilly air as the sun shines gloriously through fluffy white clouds. Though wind and rain visit often in March, the increased activity of wildlife and the high-pitched chatter of birds are a heartening call to life, now that the days are longer and brighter.

The archery club we belonged to were holding an open competition and I drove over to the club woods with Phoebe to join the rest of the gang, and the day was spent checking over score sheets and bookings in the cabin and making around sixty or so bacon and sausage sandwiches for our hungry volunteers, who were busy lugging around heavy targets, cutting back brambles and doing other bits of manual labour to get the course set out. Now the hard work of setting up was done, we were ready to have a go at the course ourselves before the competition the next day. Neil, our club vice-chairman and all-round top bloke, was in the same group as me. Easy to get along with, Neil has a likeable and happy disposition and a great appreciation of nature and the wildlife within it. He has an endearing love of nature in all its forms and beauty, like listening to a breeze making the leaves rustle and whisper or hearing the call of a chaffinch.

From the conversations we'd had on the subject so far, I was aware that Neil leans more to paganism than anything else. Every time a bird twittered in alarm at the sound of our arrows making their loud 'thwocking' noise as they pierce the targets, Neil was the one who instantly said, 'Ooh, did just you hear that goldfinch?' I just nod and smile. I can only identify a very small handful of birds based on their calls – blackbirds, crows, pigeons or owls. As we walked, he and Phoebe fell into their routine of gentle teasing. 'Come on, Phoebe, this is an easy shot, even you can nail it.'

She stepped up to the red peg that marks out the first shooting position and nocked an arrow, eyeing up the target, a life-sized poly-resin tiger. Carefully, she pulled back the bow-string to full-draw, paused, and then released the arrow. A second later that dull thud reached us, and Phoebe's arrow hit its mark. As we wandered from target to target, we all had several good shots and one or two poor ones and finally I had to admit that this was enough for one day; my gammy leg needed to rest. Back at home, I ventured into the kitchen to prepare dinner for the family. I think I may well have cheated for dinner and shoved something frozen and ready made in the oven and made a quick salad. I am not the sort of person who slaves away for hours in the kitchen. I do most of the cooking in the house, but only because I am normally at home in the evening much earlier than Chris.

The morning of the competition rolled around and it was a very early start, packing things into the car and heading down to the woods so that I could hand out score cards and collect entry fees from the competitors. A couple of hours later, it was time for a coffee and a sit down. My gammy hips and legs had started to really ache after standing up for so long in the cramped admin cabin. The rest of the day was spent selling a few raffle tickets and walking round the course to see how everyone was getting on, looking for lost arrows and generally chatting to the competitors. Three o'clock saw me back in the admin cabin to check scores as people finished the course and the next two hours were busy as we prepared a list of winners and handed out trophies.

After coming home and putting our various bits and pieces away, I was hoping for nice relaxing week. No such luck. We finally had to admit that one of our cats was starting to get old and I was worried about her eyesight. Kitty has always been needy and anxious and often has trouble jumping even small distances, preferring to climb onto low surfaces and gradually make her way to a higher point that any other cat would jump straight up to. She sometimes can't see little treats that I put right in front of her nose, she follows me about like a lost puppy and had been getting even more nervous and neurotic than normal. Time for a check-up. My main concerns were that she might be developing cataracts, her fur was getting shabby and dry and her anxiety and quirky behaviour were getting slowly worse. The vet gave her a clean bill of health, though she needed some minor dental work to clean her teeth. We did find out, however, that Kitty has a birth defect in her eyes which accounts for her poor eyesight and the vet explained that cats with this condition often have neurotic, unpredictable behaviour and are very anxious and needy – check that! We booked an appointment for the pussy cat dental clinic and took Kitty home for a bath. Yes, she did need one. After weeing in the cat basket on the way to the vet and again on the way back, Kitty did not smell pleasant. For those of you who don't own a cat of your own, I can assure you that the rumours are all true. Bathing a cat is like a short trip to hell and you're lucky to make it back alive with all of your limbs still attached.

The rest of the week was filled with more writing, working out at the gym and the usual routines of going to work and doing a bit of cleaning. Writing The Witch's Journey involved a lot of research and I've already mentioned how easily I get side-tracked. For example, while looking up some of the facts and figures for a section on moon magic, I was staggered by the huge distance between us and the moon. This led me to wondering how long it took to travel there in the 1960s and how long that same journey would take with today's technology. NASAs website is full of very interesting things and while doing my research, much of which didn't make it into the final version of the book, I was distracted by some information I did include that involved astronaut Stuart Roosa and redwood tree seeds. Col. Roosa, who used to work for the US forestry service, took hundreds of tree seeds with him into lunar orbit. The seeds were planted back on Earth and the resulting trees are called moon-trees. Deciding what research is both relevant and interesting enough to include in a book is not easy and I had a hard time with it. Writing a book is a solitary task and the people who I'm around most of the time don't have a clue what I'm writing about at any given point or how hard that process can be.

'How's the writing going?' This is probably the most annoying question I get asked as a writer. I'm sure the expected answer is something like this: 'Three books finished so far this week and you won't believe the twist at the end. The film will be out next month.' The reality is more on the lines of: 'Hard, actually. Not had time, I'm only half way through, I don't know what happens next in the story, my hands ache after three hours of typing, I deleted more words than I wrote, only coffee and chocolate are keeping me going.'

Most of this week was spent researching, writing up the research and editing out bits that didn't quite fit. There was a lot of editing; after all, I was writing about the moon as it relates to witchcraft, not focusing on the science. It hurts a little bit on the inside as an author when you have to cut out huge chunks of precious words that you've put time and effort into. It can be lonely work though it is rewarding as the page count gradually creeps slowly and surely towards to the projected target.

Chris took Kitty to the vet for her dental work and gave her the necessary bath afterwards. The vet had to put her under anaesthetic to clean her teeth properly and I was really worried about how she'd be feeling, but when I got home from work, Kitty was acting as if nothing untoward had happened at all. I still gave her lots of fuss and pussy cat sweeties and told her she what a good girl she is. I like to think that I'm one of those spiritual types who can really communicate with their animals and know exactly what they are thinking, but with Kitty, one can never really tell. She's not a witch's familiar, she's just a cat with a few issues. Shibby, on the other hand, is a cat of a different kind. Chris had Shibby long before I met him and she is very definitely his cat. Anyone else's lap will only suffice if Chris is at work or away from home. She's an old white and tabby cat with very long fur that sheds in fuzzy piles all over the house as soon as I've cleaned up. She seemed to be limping one morning, but as she spends a lot of time sleeping or out of doors, it was difficult to assess exactly how bad it might be or if she was really limping at all. The next day it was clear that she was struggling to jump and there was definitely a limp in her back legs. She'd recently taken to sleeping on a narrow window sill at the foot of the stairs and it was possible that she'd fallen off at some point in the last few days. Now it was her turn to visit the vet. Thankfully, Shibby doesn't normally wee in the cat carrier, but she does meow and protest loudly for the duration of the twenty-minute drive. The vet gave her a good check-over and thought she'd very likely had a fall and sprained her legs or hips. Anti-inflammatory drugs were prescribed along with an injection. Hopefully she would recover fully in a week or two, but we were to bring her back if she didn't improve.

One of my favourite ways to get rid of stress and have a bit of tranquillity in my life is to visit my friends, the trees. I feel so lucky to live on the edge of Sherwood Forest – so close to so many trees, and most of them oak. Tucked away in the forest is an ancient meeting place named Thynghowe, and shame on us, we were some of the only folk in the village never to have visited the site. We decided to put that right and set out for a long walk, kitted out in raincoats and chunky walking boots. We followed what turned out to be a dreadful map of how to find the mound. We seemed to have been walking for hours before we reached the track where the mound of Thynghowe was marked on our dodgy map. Alas, Thynghowe was not there.

'Check the map, Chris,' I said. 'Again.' He held it up and we looked blankly at the tracks on the map and the woodland paths we were on for a few minutes with several hums and aahs. Not a good match. By this point I was getting a lot of pain in my hips and was glad I had brought along my walking stick. I didn't need to use it regularly, but it was essential on long trips over rough ground like this. Although Sherwood Forest is quite large, it's fairly flat and we hadn't needed to climb any steep hills or slopes and I was grateful for that.

'If we go down there,' Chris pointed, 'it should lead us back here,' his finger indicated a spot on the map, 'and then we can take this path which should take us straight to Thynghowe.'

We did some back-tracking and side-stepping through unknown paths to find the trail that we must have missed earlier. For another hour we went along several more winding tracks through the trees, following fences and pathways and plodding through bracken and heather and spiky brambles and listening to the birds. I swear they were laughing at us. We hadn't made very good progress, but we were quite close to one of the main paths back through the area known as Birklands, a well-known part of the forest. We decided to give up and go home, partly because we were getting cold and hungry and partly because my pain was getting much worse. We could hear voices just up ahead and as we stepped out of our tree-shaded path into the open heathland, we came across one of Chris's oldest friends, sat on a bench chatting to his companion. With his rough collie sat patiently by his feet, Rob welcomed us warmly and introduced us to his friend. This was a true synchronicity, for we had been talking about him and meaning to get in touch just a week or two ago.

Rob is a druid and had been the priest at our hand-fasting a few years before. We had a lovely time catching up with him and fussing his dog. Shame about the lolling tongue that insisted on leaving my face damp and stinking of dog-breath. Once the dog-kisses were over with, we left Rob and his friend and tramped through the forest for a while longer until we finally made it back home. Hot chocolate, warm clothes and heat-treatments for the hip pain have never felt so welcome. I was disappointed that we didn't manage to find Thynghowe and wished I'd been able to find a better route planner, but I did find several large and golden oak apples on the trees and, after asking Brother Oak nicely, I had brought them home to add to my collection for making a garland.

I had a routine check-up at the opticians and my prescription had changed slightly. I went back at the weekend, wearing my contact lenses, so that I could see properly to choose new glasses. Chris and Phoebe went to the local leisure centre for a swim and Chris managed to break one of his toes. It was quite funny when his mum telephoned for a general chat out of the blue one evening. I listened to Chris's end of the conversation as he told her he'd managed to break his toe while swimming. I could hear, quite loudly, my mother-in-law saying, 'And when did water become hard enough to break toes, my son?' He had jumped straight into the deep end, fully expecting to sink and bob up again, but managed to catch his foot against the side of the pool on the way down. I don't know what to do with him sometimes. I gave him some sympathy and TLC in the form of Reiki and he felt a bit better.

Around this time, I was part of a discussion on social media about local pagan happenings and where and when any events or pub moots were taking place. There wasn't a regular pagan moot in the North of Nottinghamshire at that time, which was why several of us had decided to meet up at a neutral venue earlier in the year. Other than this, being part of a pagan social scene meant travelling into Nottingham, across to Chesterfield or up to Sheffield, all of which are towns with a large and public pagan presence. All very well for those of us who can travel around easily, and the few Mansfield pagans who I knew of were in a good position to get public transport to any of these venues. For those of us living a little more in the sticks, however, if you don't drive, it's not easy to get around as the buses and trains are few and far between and less than reliable. This wasn't much of a problem for Chris and me as we both drive, but a young woman who declared herself very new to paganism and witchcraft had no easy way of getting around. She asked if there was anybody near to her who might be able to meet up and say 'hi'. Lisa is only a ten-minute drive away from me and we arranged to meet after we had both finished work one evening.

Lisa has a quiet, almost timid, persona that hides a kind heart, a whacky sense of humour and a few endearing quirks. Her favourite animals are reptiles and she's a big fan of heavy metal while being a gentle soul. With this alternative mix in her personality, she and I were bound to get on well from the start. She seemed quiet and shy, but thoroughly interested in paganism and asked me to explain a few things to her. We talked about the Wheel of the Year, the Goddess and God, and how to integrate simple pagan practise into daily life. We arranged to see each other again soon. I wrote a bit about our chat in my book of shadows and one of the things that stands out as I read it now is that I instantly liked her and she had a sense of familiarity to her, though we'd never met before. She seemed very witchy and pagan already: she didn't quite understand it all yet, but it was already there, living inside her.

The weekend was taken up with a practise shoot around our club woods. A large pine forest half an hour's drive away, on loan from the Forestry Commission, has a course laid out where we can shoot all year round. Following our course of thirty to forty targets through the pines, we talked and laughed with other archers, with hearty teasing if a stray arrow hit a tree instead of the paper face targets. I always feel guilty if it's one of my arrows that ends up piercing the bark of a tree. Sorry trees. Occupied with my bow and arrow and the constant banter of other people, I still made time to breathe deeply of the fresh air and run my hands over the bark of the trees, appreciating the sound of the birds and the feel of the earth all around me.

We spent one evening with Angie and Pete, who we'd met at the pagan pub-moot, and had a pleasant time getting to know each other. We talked about what had drawn each of us to paganism, recommended books, and the conversation flowed easily. My diary was starting to fill up with more meetings and events and it was a clear sign of the wheel beginning to turn again towards the light of the summer solstice, now only three months away. Ever since I started my pagan path, I've found this time of year, heading towards the warmer and brighter days of mid-spring, to be the real start of the social year.

I did a lot of writing over the next few weeks, constantly surrounded by books for reference and inspiration. Our dining table was covered in them, chairs too, as I did research and reading and writing. Along with this creativity, my mum dropped in for a brief visit. Mum's an incredible artist and attends regular classes at nearby Cuckney, so she'd called in to visit on her way past at the weekend. She wasn't just coming for the sake of it though, she said she had an ulterior motive. I wondered for a second if I'd done something wrong and then remembered that although she is still my mother, I am now an adult. As I served up a pot of coffee and slices of cake, Mum presented me with a gift. I opened the small jewellery box to find my late gran's engagement ring, which Mum wanted me to have. The ring is beautiful although far too big for me and it has a tiny diamond missing that needs to be replaced, so I put it safely away for now.

Mother's Day came around and after a long walk in the countryside, I was treated to a box of chocolates, a bottle of wine and a new book to read. Every year I tell Phoebe she doesn't need to get a gift for me on Mother's Day. I don't like the overt and pointless commercialism of it, but every year I end up with chocolates, wine and a new book, so I can't complain.

The next day was uneventful, though Phoebe missed a day of school as she was not very well. This is often the case after a long and busy day for her, that general lethargy and weakness, aching limbs and headaches. Well, I'd done what I could to investigate and checked with her that nothing was bothering her about school. Missing school seems to be a big deal for Phoebe, she makes sure she always meets her homework deadlines and has some good friends at school to hang out with, so I was satisfied that there were no problems there. We would have to see what the blood tests showed up.

I went to visit one of my friends after work and I was looking forward to seeing her and her partner. Wendy is a spiritual medium and used to run a small holistic therapy centre and shop in the village, which was where we met. Luke, her partner, is a transfiguration medium with a magnetic, charismatic personality. We talked at length over copious amounts of coffee and slices of an enormous chocolate cake Wendy had made. I had attended one of their short courses on spiritual development the previous year, part of which included the use of the technical equipment used by paranormal investigators. EMF detectors, voice recorders and infra-red monitors, and a spirit box. The spirit box is a modified radio which scans different frequencies, picking up each one for only a second or two, resulting in a garbled mixture of static noise with the odd word being broadcast across a range of stations. According to Luke, the melee of sound can be manipulated by spirit entities to give answers to the questions asked by paranormal investigators. Some of the jumbled words did seem to be relevant to the questions the group were asking; it was very eerie. I quite liked it.

As we talked this evening, Luke offered to show me his transfiguration at work. Their country cottage on the boundary of the village is full of creaking wooden floorboards and heavy oak doors, and as he led the way to his study, the old property seemed to creak every in one of its wooden bones in anticipation. I didn't know quite what to expect, although I'd seen glimpses of his transfiguration during the course and already knew a little bit about the ability. At the height of spiritualism's popularity during the Victorian era, transfiguration mediums were highly sought after. Transfiguration involves channelling spirit in order to produce a complete change in appearance of the medium.

Luke's spare room was adorned with comfortable chairs, a low table, plain burgundy walls and soft lighting. We sat facing each other and Luke asked me to clear my mind and watch his face carefully. Before long, there visible changes in the face I was looking at. I glimpsed behind me to check the wall for a hidden projector, so convincing was the image.

I could see very plainly a second face overshadowing Luke's own features, giving the impression of a hologram or projection. The face I saw was distinctive, dark skinned with a neat black goatee, and possessed piercing dark eyes that seemed to be reaching out to me. I know some people pooh-pooh mediums and spiritualists, but I cannot think of any possible way this could have been faked, either in this setting or on the other occasions I had seen glimpses of Luke's transfiguration at work.

'Do you see something?' His voice was completely his own.

'A different face laying over your own,' I said. 'He looks oriental, an elderly gentleman.'

'Is it someone you recognise? You can ask him questions.' Luke said. 'The answers won't come through me, but you'll be aware of them.'

'I'd like to know who this is please.' I could hear a reply, but it wasn't aural, it was internal, more like a sense of knowing the answer myself as soon as it was given to me. After establishing that this spirit was not a relative or anyone I'd known while he'd been alive, I started to get more specific information. All through this, the ethereal face remained clearly overlaid on top of Luke's own features. The entire episode had taken perhaps fifteen or twenty minutes and, with all honesty, those twenty minutes are among some of the weirdest I've experienced. The weirdest and most exciting moments to date, however, are probably some of the things I've seen with Chris when we have been on overnight ghost hunting expeditions, but that's another story!

There was still a large slab of chocolate cake left, so Wendy wrapped a large slice for me to take home for Phoebe and Chris. I slept heavily that night and woke up tired. I should take this as a sign that more relaxation and meditation, coupled with early nights, would be useful for me right now. Hmm, with working full time and planning talks and workshops and trying to run my little teaching circle, chance would be a fine thing. Time to see what April has in store.

Spring Equinox Dragon Eggs

These cute little dragon eggs are easy to make and look extra fantastical with the addition of glitter and sparkles. You will need several regular hen's eggs, a glue gun, or string and PVA glue, and a range of paints and brushes. I adore the fragile and delicate nature of the finished decorations but if you prefer, use polystyrene craft eggs.

Prick each end of the egg with a pin and blow out the insides, saving the eggs for making cakes or omelettes later. Rinse the empty egg shells under cold running water to clean and leave to dry out completely. Using a glue gun or tubes of puff-up glue, make a trail around the egg in swirls, scales, stripes or spots. Be creative! Alternatively, create raised patterns on the egg by soaking string in the glue and winding around the egg and leaving it to dry. When the eggs are completely dried, decorate them in pretty colours. Try blues and greens mottled together, or purple and lilac, whatever takes your fancy. Add sparkles or glitter on the raised surfaces and you will have a beautifully decorated dragon egg.

Kids love getting a box of eggs filled with these and if any of them break, maybe the baby dragon must have been ready to hatch out and has flown away into the sky!

Dragon eggs can be threaded with cotton and hung up in a window for children or they can adorn your solstice tree at Yule. A simple and effective craft that can be as creative as you want.

Oak Apple Garland

Oak is my favourite tree and corresponds with the Ogham Duir. The popular name for the spirit of oak trees is Dryad, from the Greek druas or druad, 'tree nymph'. One of the trees of the Celtic Ogham, Oak represents solidity, a place to stand, emotional maturity, the home and hearth, comfort, strength and endurance.

What we commonly call oak apples are wasp galls: small, woody, and a rich chestnut or warm brown in colour, these galls are formed when gall wasps lay their eggs on the tree branch. The tree forms the woody galls to protect itself and eventually the insect's larvae hatch out from the gall, making a small hole as it does so. These little holes are easy to pierce all the way through and can then be strung into a necklace, a charm bracelet or hung in the house as a garland for good luck and prosperity. May 29th used to be known as Oak Apple Day and some rural areas, including Castleton in Derbyshire, still have an annual festival around this time. Castleton's Garland Day, one of the most well-known, has historical links to Oak Apple Day, with the King and Queen of the day parading through streets with flowered baskets on their heads.

I love to have an oak apple garland strung up in the house, its warm golden beads offer protection and stability, especially when combined with the deep red of dried rowan berries.

When collecting oak galls, or anything else from living trees and plants, it's good manners to ask permission first and then – and this is the important part that people tend to forget – wait for that permission to be granted before cutting or harvesting your wand, twigs, seeds or galls.

To make your garland, gather around twenty oak apple galls and look for the small holes left by the hatchling insect as it crawled its way out. Use this as a starting point and push a bradawl or metal skewer through to the other side. Use string, embroidery silks, wool, wire, or ribbons to thread the oak galls.

Dried rowan berries between each woody brown gall looks effective and adds to the efficacy of the garland as a protective charm. Add other items onto the thread in whatever design you like: beads, feathers, charms, dried hazels, hawthorn berries.

Hang the garland above the hearth, in the window, or above doorways for strength, a stable home and protection.

April

A Song for the Season: Newgrange, Clannad.

April sees the year's early flowers bursting into bloom, pastel pink cherry and apple blossoms create dreamy clouds of colour on their trees and gently drift to the ground in the slightest of breezes, a comforting snowfall of petals. The forest is alive with the signs of wildwood creatures waking from their winter slumber and in trees and hedges, under the eaves of houses, birds can be seen, sticks and leaves in their beaks, building nests to house their young. Early mornings are blessed with light and even in crowded cities the pavement cracks are filled with fast growing weeds and buzzing bees working hard in back gardens and along the grass verges of busy roads, gathering sweet nectar.

The first week of April was quiet at work and limped along slowly, fortunately my evenings made up for it. On Monday, I'd been to see Luke and Wendy, and on Tuesday we had our regular night at the archery woods. It was a nice evening, teamed up with a few other club members to traipse around the archery course for couple of hours, listening to the birdsong and the constant susurration of leaves stirring in the breeze. I managed to get to the gym this week, with a couple of long sessions which included a lot of weights, and although my legs ached like mad, I persevered.

Phoebe returned home from school with piles of homework and scurried off to her bedroom to get on with it while playing loud music. Chris hadn't come back from work yet, so I did some boring house work and then got on with a bit of writing before making dinner. I was really starting to feel my hips getting worse after the long day walking round the archery competition at the weekend and I poured a deep, hot bath, the hottest I could stand without scalding myself, and hung a bag of lavender from the garden under the tap as the water ran. It didn't help much with my pain levels, but it was relaxing and my hair smelled lovely. Lavender is one of my favourite plants and when I visit my in-laws, I miss the huge lavender patch that used to adorn the large front garden of their old place and the dozens of plump bumble-bees who used it as a playground.

Lisa came over one evening and was particularly interested in learning about runes. I'm not a fan of working with runes, they have never appealed to me, but I was able point her to a few books that might be useful. Lisa was curious about the rituals of witchcraft and as I had nothing else on I explained some of the principals to her.

I set up a simple altar and circle, describing how I visualise the boundary of the circle and what some of the tools are for. She lapped it all up with quiet enthusiasm and carefully worded questions, making mental notes of what I was doing and saying. We meditated for a short while before giving thanks and putting things away.

Lisa picked up a bundle of smudging feathers and smiled. 'I like this.'

'It's just a twig I found in the wood with some feathers from a bird of prey sanctuary, held together with a bit of ribbon.' I told her. 'It's only a prop though, you don't really need it.'

Lisa frowned, uncomprehending, and I showed her how to use her hands in place of the fan, smudging us both with a bunch of smoking sage. I waved my hands about in a circular, fanning motion and she joined in.

'See? I'm doing the same thing, but without the feathers. And it doesn't have to be sage – there are plenty of herbs and flowers that work as powerful cleansers.'

'Do I have to get some?'

'No,' I smiled, knowing she's on a tight budget. 'You don't have to get any of these things. Witchcraft shouldn't cost you a penny. But if you do use them, the tools will help you make a start. They give you a focal point until you start to get a real sense of the energies you're working with.'

Later, Phoebe and Chris and I sat together to watch one of our favourite programmes, MasterChef Australia. Phoebe has made some fantastic dishes at school and took an interest in the recipes on the programme with a view to making some of them. Unfortunately, these cookery shows don't tend to show all the cleaning up that's involved afterwards, so I have to make sure she realises that it's not all up to Mum!

This week brought me a telephone call from one of the nurses at the village surgery with news about Phoebe's blood test results. It was not anaemia after all, but a vitamin D deficiency, and a prescription for a course of supplements was already waiting there for me to pick up. Apparently, it's a very common deficiency in both children and adults and often misdiagnosed. Even with supplements, it would take at least six months for her vitamin D levels to get back to normal. I looked it up on the internet – whatever did we do in the days before Google? The symptoms of debilitation, fatigue, muscular pains and headaches, were ones that poor Phoebe was all too familiar with. Vitamin D is often called the sunshine-vitamin as the sun is our main source of it and spending time outside with your forearms uncovered for around half an hour two or three days every week is usually enough for most of us. Not only will spending time outside increase our vitamin D levels, as pagans, it's a way of reconnecting to the earth, the skies, the wildlife and the natural world all around us.

Chris and I had arranged a pagan pub moot in the village for several people I knew locally. Since moving out of Nottingham itself I had lost contact to some extent with the pagan community and I was looking forward to having something on my doorstep. Turning up early, and pleased that I'd been able to walk there instead of driving, we found a quiet table outside in the early evening sunshine. We soon were joined by Luke and Wendy, Carla, and Lisa, who had cadged a lift from her dad. Carla and I had met each other back when I'd only been in the village for about six months and was regularly taking a bus for work. We are both quick to smile at friendly seeming strangers and after a week or so of saying hello, it was not long before we were sitting next to each other to pass the time on our long bus ride, chattering merrily away. She has a sense of serenity around her amid the hustle and bustle of ordinary life, so it was easy to like her straight away. After a week of inconsequential chatting, we were firmly into the territory of paganism and spirituality. She invited me to a monthly meditation session that she regularly organises and I promised to let her know of any events or rituals I had coming up. On hearing my full name properly and finding out I'm an author, Carla squealed excitedly.

'Oh my God,' she had exclaimed, 'are you that Moira? I've got your book.' I probably blushed at this point, but she wasn't done yet. 'I can't tell you how much that book means to me.'

The Witching Path was the first book on witchcraft she read that spoke to her soul. 'It just felt like I knew this was what I should be doing. I can't believe it, Moira, that book changed my life, made me realise I've been a witchy-witch-woman all along. I can't believe this, I feel so lucky to have met you.'

Well, I don't get praise like this every day. I was, and still am, tickled pink that Carla had got so much out of my first book.

Wendy, who had stocked copies of the book when she'd run her spiritual shop in the village, already knew Carla and they were both pleased to meet Lisa. Conversation ranged from discussions of ghosts and poltergeists to UFOs and unexplained phenomenon and Carla invited us all to her meditation group.

A special highlight this month was 'A Day for Patricia Crowther,' organised by the Doreen Valiente Foundation and the Centre for Pagan Studies. As luck would have it, the event coincided with Phoebe's regular weekend away with her dad, so Chris and I wouldn't have to rush off early to get back home for her. I'd booked my tickets in advance and was very excited, as rumour had it that Patricia herself would be attending for at least some of the day. Having been to a lot of pagan conferences in the past, I had high expectations for this event, and it did not disappoint. With good quality witchy traders selling everything from robes to protective floor washes, an exhibition featuring the magical tools and texts of both Doreen Valiente and Gerald Gardner, and a full programme of speakers, it was bound to be a cracking event. There wasn't anything truly unexpected going on, except for Patricia herself giving a stunning poetry recital at the end of the day. The only very minor disappointment about the whole day was that there was only one speaker at any given time rather than two or three at once to give a bit of variety and which previous events and conferences had led me to believe was the norm. The speakers, however, really were worth listening to and it provided an opportunity to hear talks I might not have heard otherwise.

Vivianne Crowley, Wiccan author, lecturer and psychologist, was one of the esteemed speakers. She has a vast knowledge and experience and her voice carried across the hall in a beautiful, relaxing way while keeping everyone interested in her subject. Planetary magic is a fascinating area, one Vivianne had chosen for her talk as Patricia Crowther herself is very interested in it, having shared a lot of her own knowledge and experiences in her writing and other works. Vivianne explained what each of the seven planets used in magic are associated with; relevant deities, days, times, influences, emotions, spheres of interaction, and much more. We were given suggestions of how to work spells and rituals utilising the qualities each planet, how to build a ritual with preparation, planning and forethought being the key to success. Vivianne recommended several weeks or even months of focus on a specific planet, setting up the altar well in advance, using appropriate herbs, colours, scents, photographs and so forth. An explanation of the seven-pointed pentagram and each planet and day's position around the points of the star was also useful. Not only was Vivianne's talk full of detailed information, she was an eloquent and erudite speaker who made the subject come alive.

I had planned to attend the witch's question and answer panel and had a few questions I would have liked to ask, but somehow, I managed to miss almost the entire session. I admit, I was rather distracted by the pagan goodies and conversations on offer in the hall. The merchandise stalls were incredibly varied. There were community stalls and information stands mixed in with the expected displays of silver jewellery, velvet cloaks, crystal wands and hand-made crafts, and you already know my appreciation of hand-made items as opposed to those that have been mass-produced. I snared myself an oak hair barrette with the Ogham symbol for Oak, Duir, burned into it, and an oak wand decorated with dark blue strips of leather and copper wire. The stall holder had made these wands himself and although I was put off by the high price initially, after talking with him and listening to his tales of growing up in the countryside, learning the trees and plants and spirit of the forest, I was enchanted by how much knowledge and insight he possessed and his deep and obvious connection to nature. The time he had taken to make these wands, along with an honest spirituality that he put into each one, swayed me over, so I parted with the cash and tucked the wand into my bag along with the hair slide.

Not only was I busy listening to the talks and eyeing up the trinkets, I was talking virtually non-stop all day. Gathered from all over Nottingham and much further afield were people I hadn't seen for a long while. My friends Ian, Donna, Jane, Sarah, Ashley, Cayt, and so many more I can't honestly remember. I was in my element and Chris tagged casually along, quietly sitting beside me as I talked. He is a very patient man, especially as he isn't always very confident around large groups of people. I started chatting to the people who were running the Children of Artemis stand and picked up a leaflet on the organisation and another one with information about their annual pagan camp. The Artemis Gathering, held over a full weekend in early August, sounded to be good to be true. The Children of Artemis also host Witchfest each November and membership of the organisation would entitle me to significant discounts at both events, so I went ahead and signed up, receiving two copies of the latest 'Witchcraft and Wicca' magazine in return. The Children of Artemis team were very friendly and made their gathering sound amazing and I decided to get tickets straight away. I do love a good pagan camp and judging from the look of last year's line-up this was going to be a very good one. Coupled with the charm and friendliness of the people tending the stand, The Children of Artemis as an organisation seemed like a good place for me to belong, along with my ongoing membership of the Pagan Federation.

The day was rounded off nicely with a raffle, and Patricia Crowther, to a rousing round of applause, handed out some of her own witchy memorabilia to some of the raffle winners. My friend Donna won a small prize and was delighted with a set of psy-cards that Patricia had donated. I don't know whether Donna has used these cards at all – I must ask her one day. After the raffle, Patricia gave a short speech followed by a poetry recital that she didn't seem able to stop. Seeing this wonderful lady on stage was like a watching a metamorphosis as she shifted appearance from elderly, slightly frail looking woman sitting demurely and restrained, to become an outgoing, lively, energetic and passionate woman who was going to have her say and damned be anyone who wanted to get in the way! Her stage presence, nay, charisma, was magnetic, and she gave so much energy and drama to her poetry that the organisers couldn't reign her in. And quite rightly so, this was, after all, a day in her honour.

Patricia was honoured with short speeches of appreciation from the people closest to her and she received a rousing standing ovation by way of thanks from all at the conference for her outstanding contributions to the rise of modern witchcraft. Presented with a framed portrait of herself and the obligatory bouquet of flowers, Patricia bowed gracefully and then sat patiently and elegantly as a long queue of fans formed to have their books signed by her. I hadn't taken one with me, but I queued anyway and spent a couple of lovely minutes with her. Patricia Crowther is one of the early writers whose work helped to shape my fledgling witch-hood and influence some of what I still practise today. She very kindly let me have a photograph taken with her, and, as my hair was still looking like a post box and matched her beautiful red suit, she laughed that we must have planned psychically for the colour co-ordination. What an amazing lady. I was grinning from ear to ear as we took the usual hour to say goodbye to everybody I had seen over the course of the day.

Another average working week followed the event, filled with trips to the archery woods one evening and a few sessions at the gym where I ran into Lisa, both of us exhausted and red-faced after our respective work outs - I thought there was something about her that I recognised! I was determined to make it to Carla's meditation in the village hall this week. Phoebe didn't fancy it – no surprise there – and Chris stayed home too. The two of them settled down to watch a film together and I walked into the village for the meditation. I've already written about this in one of my previous books, but I'll give you an outline here, as it was a deep and touching experience.

After the usual catch-up over a cuppa, the group sat in a circle and Carla took us through her unique meditation. She played a series of chants on a CD and we joined in, not caring about tune or tone, just chanting out to the music. After half an hour of chanting, the music changed to a long instrumental track for a silent meditation. I sat and let my mind wander as I focused on my breathing and conjured up images in my mind of my favourite place in the forest, which had become the starting point for much of my journey work. Walking from this woodland spot, I started to take unexpected twists and turns and soon came to a clearing by a vast lake with a large wooden house on the shore. Around a massive fire on the shores of the lake, with a gargantuan bubbling cauldron hanging over the flames, were sat a young boy of around twelve years old and an elderly blind man. This is a familiar scene as part of the tale of Cerridwen and Taliesin and as I watched the flickering flames of the fire, the story came to life in front of me.

I saw the Goddess Cerridwen come over to the fire, knowing her brew in the cauldron was finally ready to give to her dim, ugly son, Afagdu. Just as she arrived, however, the boy, Gwion Bach, stirred the brew and a splash of the hot liquid spat up from the cauldron, burning his hand. Instinctively, he stuck his fingers into his mouth to soothe them. The full power of the magical potion was held in that single drop of the potent liquid, the rest of it spoiled and poisonous, and Cerridwen began to wail with rage. She tipped the vessel over in a fit of anger. The young boy, Gwion Bach, was granted all the power of the Awen. He realised his mistake straight away and knew he had to run. I watched as the Goddess flew into a violent temper and the chase began. Cerridwen chased the boy in magical journey of transformation that only ended when he turned himself into a piece of corn. Cerridwen, as a hen, gobbled him up. Nine months later, just a flash of time in this trance, she gave birth to a son. Still enraged with the boy but unable to harm the new-born infant he had now become, she him cast into the river. What I saw did not end with

Cerridwen watching that little bundle float down the river. She turned back to the cauldron, now full of a crystal-clear liquid, and she saw that I was watching. She bent to retrieve a goblet, dipped it into the cauldron and offered me a drink. In the original tale, of course, Cerridwen's brew is spoiled and the cauldron turned over, its contents spilling and flowing to the river, poisoning the white horses of Garanhir. I can't explain how I felt when I drank from her cauldron, but it gave me a feeling of peace, contentment and a sense of *knowing* myself. Knowing that I'm capable, strong, independent, sure of my inner beauty and vitality.

When I left Cerridwen's fireside and strolled through the woods, I saw a young fawn grazing nearby. The fawn was startled by the sounds of hunters, just outside the boundary of the trees, and Cernunnos, the Horned God, appeared, complete with shaggy beard and great antlers. He turned to the hunters and roared with a thunderous bellow, scaring them off. The fawn, petite and delicate in the face of the mighty forest Lord, trotted nimbly away, Cernunnos faded out of view and, rather abruptly, I was aware that of Carla asking if everyone was all right. I grounded myself and joined the others for a coffee.

Carla had brought some dubious smelling herbal teas with her and tempted me to try one. It smelled herby and bitter, like a mixture of yeast extract and dried rabbit food. While we talked, I sipped the bitter tea; it was okay, but I wouldn't have it in my cupboard at home. I was still overwhelmed and grinning from the meditation I'd had when Carla asked me: 'What do you think?'

I answered with, 'Amazing. The most vivid and clear journey, such a story.'

'Huh?' She looked puzzled.

'Yes,' I said, and told her animatedly about the journey I'd been on and it took me a minute or two to realise why she started laughing.

'That's awesome, Moira, thanks for sharing that with me, but I was asking about the tea!'

A few days later, I'd just about returned to planet earth with the help of mundane things like work and helping Phoebe with her homework. Phoebe rarely needs help with her homework and when she does, it's usually maths. I confess I'm dreadful with numbers, so Chris gets stuck with this one even if he can't understand the odd ways in which maths is now being taught at schools. Our guinea pigs were fit and healthy and put in their run on the back lawn every day now that the weather was picking up. It was adorable to hear them squeaking with delight and watch their powerful jaws reaching for the grass before their little legs have even touched the ground. One of the cats, however, was not doing so well.

Shibby, the old girl who'd been limping, was not getting any better and the anti-inflammatory medication prescribed by the vet was having very little effect. Another trip to the vet. He was disappointed that Shibby hadn't improved and it seemed that whatever knock or bump she'd had had triggered early onset arthritis. He gave her another week or two of anti-inflammatory drugs. She wasn't as agile as normal, preferring to take longer routes to get to places if it meant she didn't have to jump as high, nor was the poor thing prowling and playing as much as normal and she spent a lot of time curled up asleep.

'Oh, for goodness sake,' I thought one day, 'why on earth don't I give the cat some Reiki?'

I have no idea why this had not occurred to me before, but there we are. It was around seven-thirty in the evening when I made myself comfortable on the sofa and called her over to me. Shibby wandered into the lounge and hopped up to my lap, meowing at me and settling down in a furry ball, ready for some fuss. I petted her for a few minutes and then started to channel my Reiki. I have never seen her move so fast! She shot off my lap and dashed straight for the cat flap in the kitchen door, leaving it swinging behind her as she scarpered.

'Okay,' I mused. 'Shibby doesn't like Reiki.'

However, the next night, I was sitting in the same place at roughly the same time in the evening, and along she came. I put my hand out to her to smooth and scratch beneath her chin and encourage her onto my lap but instead, she sat in the space between me and the arm of the sofa. I carried on fussing her fur, but she kept nudging my hands with her face. Nudge, nudge, very insistent. Hmm... I wonder. I started to channel waves of Reiki healing, holding my hands away from her slightly and, sure enough, she dived straight for my palms and nudged at me. Okay, this was unexpected. I put my hands around her face and tried to picture where a cat would have chakras and sent Reiki into those points along her spine. That was all it took. Shibby flopped down into a puddle of fluff and spread herself out, nudging my hands into the positions where she obviously felt she needed the most healing. She was now a Reiki addict and demanded it every few days when her legs start to play up again. Virtually every night for the next two weeks solid, she plonked herself down in the same spot and meowed until I came over and gave her Reiki. About twenty minutes later, she'd get up and wander off.

'I have had enough Reiki for today.' Shibby would say with her loud meows after each session. 'You are dismissed, Human Slave.'

So that's how I spent the next couple of weeks; sorting out laundry, taking Phoebe for another blood-test with the practice nurse, writing my new book, going to work, and being a cat Reiki-slave. I must say though, the Reiki did me good too, always very relaxing: one of bonus effects of Reiki is that as you give it to another person, you receive it yourself too.

I had an unexpected phone call one night from my brother. He would be exhibiting at Kelmarsh County Show at the weekend.

Phoebe, Chris and I were, for once, all free that weekend, so we jumped at the chance to go and see my brother. Kelmarsh is nearly a two-hour drive from us, but the opportunity to see my brother for the first time in over eighteen months was priceless, so off we went.

My brother and his family live in the middle of nowhere, in the county of Caithness, around thirty miles inland from John O'Groats in Scotland. That's not the highlands, by the way. Caithness is what the locals call the lowlands beyond the highlands. To put it another way, it takes around fourteen hours to drive there from Nottingham. Hence, we don't see him very often and never in the winter: the roads that far north are regularly closed due to the mountains of snow that makes driving treacherous, with sheer cliffs at the sides of the impossibly steep and winding roads.

It didn't take long to find the stalls near the arena where my brother was pitched up with his stand of country goods. It was fantastic to see my brother, he gives strong hugs and never fails to make me laugh. We caught up with gossip, swapped stories about our kids and generally grinned and hugged a lot while Phoebe played with my brother's little Bedlington terrier, Scruff. Three or four large cages contained bundles of furry ferrets, who my brother and his friend show to raise money for their local ferret rescue charity.

The cluster of sleepy ferrets included Stumpy, a young ball of fluffiness who had to have one of his front paws amputated as a kit. I'm not a big fan of ferrets, but even I love Stumpy with his beautiful golden coat and his dark red eyes. He's very docile and likes to be held, but Stumpy's patience was tested when a crowd of visitors and their multitude of slightly rude children wouldn't stop poking at him. My brother handed Stumpy to me and put a few drops of ferret pheromone on Stumpy's belly. Immediately, the ferret started to lick himself all over, curling and twisting and nuzzling, rubbing his little face into my hands. Adorable, a bit like watching cats when they've had too much cat-nip! Scruff the dog is even more amusing.

'Now, this dog is a highly trained piece of traditional machinery,' my brother tells the audience during his demonstration. At this point, Scruff is sniffing a cooling pile of horse poo left over from an earlier equestrian display. The audience, of course, titter a little bit at this.

'Honestly,' my brother carries on, 'he may look all cute and fluffy and butter wouldn't melt but trust me.' He picks up a stick to mark a spot where Scruff has left a little offering of his own, which dear bro' will have to clean up later. 'All I have to do is say the word, and he'll be off like a shot. Of course, it's the end of the day, he just wants to go to the truck and his bed. BED!'

He points over to a dog bed beside his truck across the arena. Scruff runs the other way. This charade carries on for a few minutes until finally, my brother wanders over to Scruff.

'This time,' he says, 'I'm going give him the command again and he *will* go to his bed. Watch carefully, this is how it's done. BED!'

Just before the dog can scamper off again, he is scooped up under one arm and my brother marches him across the arena to his bed and the show ends with a round of hearty applause and laughter.

Country fairs are always full of interesting displays of falconry, dog agility, pony scurry races and to my delight, at Kelmarsh this year were the Knights of Middle England, a jousting troupe who put on a fantastic performance. Proud horses and knights in colourful costumes and shining armour galloped into the arena in a remarkable display of jousting and tomfoolery. I've always been passionate about horses and enjoy the thundering beat of galloping hooves across hard earth that sends shock waves through the ground and into your feet.

There are several horse deities and creatures in folklore, mythology and legends. Horses can be a symbol of travel, courage, strength and fortitude, and the Goddesses Rhiannon and Epona are both closely associated with horses.

Folklore and mythology of horses include stories of beautiful unicorns and winged horses, great beasts who charge across the night-sky pulling the chariots of the Gods, our landscape honours this magnificent beast with the white chalk horses of the Salisbury plains and Wiltshire hills, hewn from the earth by our ancestors. Horse brasses and shoes are hung in homes to ward off evil and farriers have a special magic of their own, with their highly guarded 'horseman's word' and the chants that ring out in the forge.

All in all, it was a brilliant day and it was so good to see my brother after such a long time. He was heading back to Caithness that evening, so we gave a hand helping him and his friend pack up and stow all their camping gear, equipment, cages, ferrets and dog into the van and I had a bit of teary moment saying goodbye, not knowing when we'd see each other again this year, if at all.

The next gathering of the Sherwood Oak Circle was an adult only event, at last. We cast the circle, invoking the Lady and Lord and taking turns to call in the elements. I'd been thinking about what to do for this session, as the rest of the group are still new to it all and it falls on me to organise and plan the rituals. I invited everyone to sit quietly and comfortably and took up my frame drum, starting up a slow, rhythmic beat.

The guided visualisations I lead tend to be unscripted, often with very earthy themes. Pathworking journeys should ideally be individual, unique and meaningful for each person so I will explain beforehand that we'll be journeying to meet the ancestors or the Salamanders of fire, for example. I lead the group into a relaxed state, setting the scene, and guiding people to a certain point. After this, I usually let the beat of the drum or a long silence take over so that people are free to explore the other realms without being influenced by whatever I'm saying. The rest of the

Sherwood Oak Circle didn't have much experience of journey work and Paul especially struggled to visualise, so I kept the session short to keep him focused.

'Be still.' I spoke quietly, timing it with the beat of the drum. 'Listen to the quiet, still voice inside you.' *Boom, boom.* 'Feel your connection to the ancestors.' *Boom, boom.* 'Your connection to the earth, (*boom, boom*) feel yourself completely relaxed, at peace (*boom, boom, boom*) rooted in the soul of the earth, connected to the energy all round...'

The quickening of the drum, the deep bass and boom, took over as I led the group along the path and then I stayed silent, carefully watching everyone else while remaining in a slightly trance-like state myself, as I beat the drum. An important point to remember if you are leading any kind of visualisation or pathworking is to keep a careful eye on the participants. You need to be aware if anyone is cold, uncomfortable or is getting upset, making sure everybody is thoroughly grounded afterwards. After a short while, I spoke quietly to gradually guide everybody back along the path to the here and now. After checking everyone was feeling alert again, we talked for a while about their experiences and there was a lot of frantic note-taking.

We shared cake and fruit juice that John and I blessed on the altar, gave thanks to the elements and deity, and took down the circle. It was then that we had the chance to catch up with each other, finish off the cake, and socialise a bit. I mentioned my meetings with Lisa and everyone else was keen to meet her, so we organised a couple of potential dates for an early summer barbeque. If Lisa expressed any more interest in coming to the group, it would be a good opportunity for us all to get know her. After everyone had left, I checked up on Phoebe. She was snuggled up under her duvet and her sleepy eyes creaked open a fraction as she stirred and murmured. I gave her a kiss, loving that warm, cosy feeling of a happy, sleepy child after another long day.

Charm Bracelet

Pagan festivals and conferences are awash with merchandise stalls selling wonderful witchy wares. Sometimes the budget just won't stretch far enough, and even inexpensive things can be out of our price range. To counter that and to fill you with a sense of achievement, why not make your own witchy charm bracelet? You can pick up everything you need from a craft shop or jewellery supply store, repurpose old jewellery or charity shop finds, along with things you already have.

Start a collection of small trinkets, tiny keys, beads, buttons, the remaining one of a pair of earrings, crystal beads that came off your last broken gem-stone bracelet, and any other small items that might look nice on a charm bracelet. A quick trip to your local craft store or haberdashery to pick up any more charms or beads, a short length of leather cord, jump rings to attach the beads and a jewellery clasp if you want to use one.

Thread your trinkets, charms and beads onto a thin strip of leather, cord, ribbon or thick cotton. You can use jump rings to attach the charms, tie a knot in between to separate them, and then fasten the cord with a clasp or simply knot the ends together. Now wear the bracelet, stand back and admire your freshly adorned wrist.

You can bless the charm bracelet for a specific purpose in your circle if appropriate.

You'll get a buzz out of it when you have this conversation:

'Ooh, what a lovely bracelet, where did you get it?'

'Why, thank you very much. I made it myself!'

Pathworking with Earth

Find a place where you won't be disturbed for the next half an hour and make sure you will be warm enough. Switch off the telephone and shut out the dog. Lie or sit comfortably, without folding your arms or crossing your legs. If you want to use a meditation track in the background, you can do so, but make sure there aren't any words to distract you.

Start by using an aura cleansing spray or smudging with incense. Open your chakras one by one, keeping your breathing rhythmic, and your eyes closed. Breathe in, breathe out, slowly and unhurried. Tense your body and then relax. Feel yourself getting more relaxed with every breath.

Sink deeper into a calm state, relaxed and peaceful. Visualise a white mist surrounding you that gradually clears. As the mist dissipates, you are sitting on a gently sloping hillside. The grassy hill feels safe and peaceful. Grass moves softly in a slight breeze that touches your face. You can feel the sun warming your skin. Reach out with your hands and touch the ground beneath you.

A path to the side of you leads up to the top of the hillside, where you see a copse of trees. Step onto the path and feel the grassy earth beneath your feet. The hill slopes gently up as you tread along the path, walking towards the trees. As you near the crest of the rise, you can see the trees are a mixture of oak, beech, elm and ash.

You follow the path through the trees, noticing the temperature is slightly lower here, under the shade of the green canopy above you. The ground changes from dry earth to a more compacted soil, strewn with fallen twigs and small pebbles. Listen to the sounds of the forest all around you; the susurration of leaves, the chirping of birds, rustling sounds in the undergrowth as small creatures scurry about.

The path leads you onwards, past thick growths of bushes and shrubs, the air feels cooler, but not uncomfortable, as you walk deeper into the trees. Ahead of you, the path splits around a large tree, roots twisting out of the ground.

The bark is thick with grooves and crevices and dappled with patches of shade and sunlight. Reach out a hand to touch the tree, feel the rough skin of the bark under your fingers. Lean up against the tree and be still and be silent. As you stand calmly with the tree, the atmosphere changes, welcoming you with warmth. The tree opens itself up to you. Ask for the tree spirit, its nymph or dryad, to make itself known to you.

Do you have questions you want answers to? Do you have dreams to dream or knowledge to learn? What happens now is for you alone. After a time, give thanks for your experience.

Give thanks to any spirit or elemental you have spoken to and slowly, slowly, draw yourself away from the tree. Your fingers leave the bare bark with a parting caress, your feet finding their way back to the path. Walk slowly, noticing how or if, your surroundings have changed. It grows lighter as the canopy of leaves overhead begins to thin.

The path leads you to the boundary of the forest, where once again the sounds of nature are all around you. The light of the sun warms you and the breeze picks up slightly as you emerge from the trees and walk slowly back along the path.

Return to the spot you started from and see once more a white mist. The mist begins to curl around you, shrouding you in comfort and peace, bringing you back.

Slowly start to waken in the here and now, feeling your surroundings change. Become aware of your breathing, in and out, in and out. Feel the clothes on your body, gently move your hands and wiggle your toes.

In your own time, start to stretch and move and sit up. Take all the time you need and, when you are ready, have something to eat and drink to ground yourself. Take note of anything you saw or touched – insects or tree creepers on the bark of the tree, an animal darting out of your way. Was there a small pebble, an acorn or some other object that found its way into your hand and what, if anything, did the spirit of the tree say to you?

May

A Song for the Season:
Under a Beltane Sun, Damh the Bard.

Summer is fast approaching now. The sun's warmth has begun to shower the land with its golden glow. My skin tingles with anticipation of long, warm nights ahead. Hawthorn blossoms display their creamy white flowers, and wild creatures can be seen and heard in the woods and fields that surround our village. The hedges are full of calling birds, welcoming the start of summer with their eager, seductive songs.

I've met a lot of pagans and witches who say they couldn't possibly choose a favourite time of year or one Sabbat over another, but I can. It's Beltane all the way for me. I love crisp winter mornings and misty autumnal days, but Beltane heralds the start of the year's camping season and camping is one of my favourite activities.

Beltane is the real beginning of summer, with warm sunny days, light evenings and blooming flowers. I normally celebrate Beltane with Chris and Phoebe camping, either at a festival or a long weekend away, and combine it with a celebration for my birthday at the beginning of May. The first Monday after the weekend is always a bank holiday, so it's a three-day weekend. This year it was a weekend in Derbyshire with the Sherwood Oak Circle.

We pitched up at the campsite in Birchover, known for its excellent facilities, a good playground for children, and where, at all hours of day and night, peacocks strut across the fields and between the tents, showing off their glorious colours. I've been visiting this campsite for decades and once, after a particularly late night, I was woken up very early in the morning to the queerest sound.

A scraping, tapping, slightly tinny noise was repeating loudly and sounded as though it was right next to my head – what on earth was it at this time in the morning? I wearily and somewhat cautiously crawled out of my warm sleeping bag and unzipped the tent just enough to poke my head out of the opening. Despite it being a well-populated campsite, thoughts flashed through my sleepy head of recently watched horror movies.

It was still very dark, only the barest hint of dawn above the horizon, and no human noises could be heard, just this tap-tap-tap, right outside the tent. Instead of being confronted with a flesh-eating axe-murderer, I caught one of the peacocks pecking at left-over pasta in the saucepan I had left out. I reminded myself that washing-up while camping is a chore I ought to take more seriously in future. Who would have thought that peacocks were fond of pasta?

This year, there were five of us camping plus Sarah and Paul's toddler. Phoebe was spending time with her dad this weekend so couldn't join us. The weather was superb for camping. Lovely and warm with not a breeze or cloud in sight and the sky was a pure, bright blue. Summer was well on its way and I looked forward to a relaxing weekend of doing nothing much in particular. We pitched up our tents on the Friday evening, followed by a glass of wine and cake to celebrate my birthday.

Our tent is a tunnel design, with a large seating-cooking area at the front end and a small overhanging canopy. It takes no time at all to set it up, but I do spend a fair amount of time making it really feel like home from home. There are rugs on the floor, a thick duvet and proper pillows on the airbed in the bedroom area and table and chairs set up in the living area. Colour-changing solar lights are strung up around the canopy that overhangs the front and I use clothes pegs to secure the lights and several lengths of pagan-themed bunting. The bunting, left over from our hand-fasting, is hand-decorated with fabric paints and hand-stitched Awen symbols, pentagrams, oak leaves, ogham, and other pagan symbols. The sunset brought on a stunning array of colours and the moon shone brightly overhead in the clear, star-studded sky.

After a peaceful night of chatting and catching up with each other, we were joined for the day by John, who couldn't camp due to his work schedule. We made our way to the Nine Ladies stone circle, within easy walking distance of the campsite. There were plenty of dog-walkers and hikers at the circle, so it wasn't an ideal place for a Beltane ritual. However, it was John's first time there and his excitement and enthusiasm for the ancient monument was infectious.

The Nine Ladies circle is in a wide, open area of grassland with views out across the sprawling countryside. An English Heritage site, the standing stone circle is part of a larger complex of prehistoric circles and standing stones on Stanton Moor. The Bronze Age stones of the Nine Ladies are rumoured to be a group of women who were turned to stone as a penalty for dancing on a Sunday and a tenth standing stone known as the King Stone, now fallen, was allegedly their fiddler. The stones themselves have a lovely feel to them in some ways, but there is something very open and wind-swept about the site and I have never done a ritual here. It doesn't appeal to me that way and I have heard a couple of people saying that the stones are sometimes used by groups who don't portray witchcraft in a favourable light. Rumours like this sometimes have a basis in fact and this year, whether it was related or not, the local news channel had reported vandalism yet again on and around the stones in the form of graffiti and the scorch marks of fires. It's heart-breaking and disappointing that some people seem to think this kind of behaviour is acceptable.

Still, we admired the many brightly coloured clooties, ribbons, dream catchers, twiggy pentagrams and other decorations and offerings in the trees. I could spend a long time just looking at these; there are literally hundreds of offerings here; photographs, letters, crystal bracelets handing from branches, posies of flowers, postcards left in memory of the Beloved Dead, written petitions to the Old Ones for help or comfort.

John had never visited any kind of sacred site before and he was overwhelmed by the Nine Ladies. We were walking together and quietly talking when a woman and her young family trotted past us.

'Oooh,' cried out a small child, clambering over the stones while their mother watched on. 'Like Stonehenge.'

'Yeah,' replied the woman, her voice loud and discordant among the peace. 'Let's dance round 'em like they did in the old days.'

John was horrified. 'Excuse me?' He muttered under his breath. The lady and her little brood must have heard him, because she immediately changed direction and herded the young ones away from us. I can only guess at what she was thinking, but John was clearly annoyed that she'd been making light of what he, as a newly proud pagan, revered as an ancient site of reverence and awe.

After spending a while at the Nine Ladies, we headed across the heathland, dotted with soft swathes of purple flowering heather and sweet-smelling gorse, making our way to Doll Tor.

Within easy walking distance of the Nine Ladies, this stone circle is a much more intimate and friendly place. To access Doll Tor, you pass first through a large- open field with a large, solitary standing stone to the right near the boundary wall. This giant monolith, named the Handle Stone, has iron footholds set into it and Paul and John went straight up, me and Sarah trying to convince them to come down so that little Jack didn't keep trying to come up after them. It's very high and I've never been tempted to clamber up there, though I'm told the view is spectacular.

Once past the standing stone and across the field, an old, moss-covered stone wall, around four feet high, encloses an area of dense woodland with cow pastures on the other side. It is here that the stone circle of Doll Tor is set in a thick copse of trees, mainly oak and silver birch. The circle of stones is not large and the stones themselves stand only knee high or slightly larger at their tallest. I like to think of it as a Stonehenge for Sindy dolls, though I'm sure this is not where the name really comes from. Doll Tor may not have the impressive stature or scale of Stonehenge and Avebury, but it holds its own special charm of magic and mystery. Aside from the occasional dog-walker or hiker, one could almost be entirely apart from time and modernity, nestled among stones that are thousands of years old, held secure in the bower of oaks overhead.

We set out a blanket with our picnic on it, after giving little Jack a bit of time to run around and get that three-year-old energy out of his system. Giving thanks to the spirits of the place for welcoming us, we set up our sacred space and held our Beltane ritual. As part of the focus for the ceremony, we each collected a twig or branch to decorate with the ribbons and threads that I had brought along in my witchy tool kit, winding them together into miniature maypoles. After blessing the maypoles with a wish, we leaned them up against the stones, taking care not to disturb the other offerings and clooties left by previous visitors. We wished for the usual things – good health, stable finances and happy relationships – and ended with a chant and closed our sacred space.

Having had such a glorious, warm and happy day, it would have been a shame not to capture the moment. As Chris was taking a photograph and the rest of us smiled and pulled funny faces for the camera, he suddenly went stonily quiet and pointed behind us. We turned to see a herd of cows with their calves walking calmly along the path to one side of the stone circle. I watched with a small measure of trepidation. These mothers would see us as intruders in their territory and would surely want to protect their young, just as Sarah and Paul were now suddenly on high alert for little Jack, who cowered behind Sarah's legs while peeping out for a good look at the cows. We needn't have worried: the cows walked nonchalantly passed us on their way to the other end of the copse and whichever field they were visiting next.

They were very curious as they came past us, but they were good natured animals and the calves, with their large, wet noses and patched brown and white fur, were just beautiful. I was close enough to touch them and imagined how soft their faces would be – I left it at imagination, though, just in case. It took a good ten minutes or so for the cows to pass by and we watched the last of them disappear through the open gate at the end of the long track. A few minutes later, a lone straggler came clambering up the path, looking for her grass-munching friends. Chris pointed to the left, into the woods.

'They went that way,' he said. The cow looked over, followed his direction, and headed off that way to catch up with its friends. Of course, he'd pointed completely the wrong way as a joke, not expecting the cow to pay him any attention, but she didn't see the funny side of it when he called out and apologised.

'Wait. They really went this way.' Too late, Ermintrude was well on her way through the trees and no feeble human was going to distract her. After she was out of sight, we finally managed to get a photograph. We took a final walk round the circle and I took a few moments to touch the roughened surface of each stone in turn before we packed up our belongings, checking the area for stray litter, and headed back to the campsite.

Once we had cleared up a good amount of fried food and pastries between us for breakfast the following morning and packed away tents and awnings, we paid a quick visit to Matlock Bath before heading back home to the mundane routines of regular life.

I adore Matlock Bath, that lovely walk by the river, so many new-age, hippy shops (although as I write this, a year or two later, I am more than a little disappointed that most of these have now closed and re-opened as charity shops or cafes). It's a lovely place, and with it being a bank holiday weekend, we couldn't park for all the bikers. Why is it, I wonder, that some places attract massive groups of bikers? There is a pub in Avebury which has the same draw and bikers flock there in droves, and to Matlock Bath, from quite some distance away. We took a slow tour around the shops, browsing the goodies and inevitably coming out with shopping bags full of new clothes and jewellery and Sarah found a nice range of crystals to add to her collection. Sarah has hundreds of crystals and her knowledge of them is extensive. I think she is secretly planning on opening her own crystal shop one day.

Once we were settled back at home, Chris and I lugged the camping gear back up to the box-room for storage once more. I was glad the following day was a bank holiday, as sleeping in the tent had done my hips no good at all. It was good to be able to stretch and lounge about in the garden for a barbeque, instead of being cramped up over a computer in the office all day. Lisa had voiced interest in my small development group and as everyone had been open the idea of her coming along, the barbeque would be a relaxed way of introducing everyone. Once again, the weather was just perfect, sunny and bright, and the afternoon went well, with everyone being very welcoming towards Lisa.

I had gathered a couple of large, flat stones over the weekend and I spent one evening this week with Phoebe painting and decorating them. Although some of my family are talented when it comes to art, that part of our gene pool must have missed me out and drawing is not one of my strong points. Phoebe painted intricately designed mandalas and I cobbled together a reasonable looking fairy door, complete with a latticed window and vines growing up around the sides. It wasn't too bad an effort and I put it in the bay window of the lounge where we have an unreasonably large window sill. Full of witchy trinkets, two large dragon statues left over from Chris's bachelor days, a growing collection of ornamental witches, three of my crystal balls, a crow sitting on a log and much more besides, the window display is a work in progress. My problem with this is not my trinkets, it's that trio of pesky felines who insist on curling up there to watch the birds on the roof tops and overhead street lights outside.

Holly, the youngest of our cats, sounds like a cross between a cat, a hyena and a car engine when she spots a pigeon; she bunches up and growls at the birds before rushing outside to get closer. The birds aren't bothered, they're far too high and too fast to be worried by the cat. What a mess, though, muddy paw-prints and scraps of fur all over the place when she returns to the windowsill after scampering outdoors, and I get the job of cleaning it up. Guess how I spent the rest of this week? Housework is an unrewarding chore and one day, when my novels are made into films and I win the Booker Prize, I dream fondly of employing a housekeeper and never again having to lug a heavy hoover upstairs.

We did run of the mill things for the rest of the week; making dinner, stirred clockwise with good wishes; coming in from work to open the bureau and unwinding instantly with the aura spray; archery practice night; laundry.

I received an email from the publisher to whom I'd submitted The Witch's Journey. Rejected. Very disappointing, especially as they had been so keen initially, but I had another publisher in mind and decided to dedicate some time to the proposal package to see if it could be improved. I really wanted to make a good impression and painstakingly spent hours poring over the proposal, sample chapters and submission letter, checking the grammar, the spellings and improving the overall impression of the initial text. It's one thing writing an entire book, it's something else entirely to sum that up in a few short pages and paragraphs to make it sound outstanding.

My in-laws visited for dinner with us one evening and I made vegan carrot and lentil burgers, as my mother-in-law has coeliac disease and these would be suitable for her diet, which also has to be dairy free. We had a good time talking and hugging and eating together and Phoebe was happy spending time with us, rather than acting like a typical teen and retreating to her room. A lot of my spare time this week was devoted to archery as our club were hosting another open competition. Chris was busy working and unable to attend, but Phoebe was determined to camp with a few other club members for the weekend. After a busy day, she and I set up one of our smaller tents in the archery woodland and settled down with the other club members for conversation around the campfire.

The rustling and bustling of the forest came to life as the temperature dropped and people started drifting away to the camping area across the track from the cabins. Phoebe decided to call it a night and knowing there were plenty of trustworthy people within metres of the tent, I decided to venture off for a short walk in the darkness. Being a witch, after all, doesn't mean very much if you don't get to enjoy the woodlands at night. The gibbous moon was bright and glorious and the hidden shadows and pathways of the midnight trees were too tempting to resist.

Darkness in the forest is not like the darkness of the city, where the orange glow of street lights and the small noises of human habitation are never far away. In the night forest, shadows spring to life with possibility: every sound is a sign of the rough, wild and untamed life that watches; listens; waits. Under every leaf, behind every tree and high up in the branches overhead, creatures are stirring, predators lying still in wait, prey lying still in hiding.

Setting off down the track at the side of the cabins, I soon found my feet veering off the beaten track of their own accord. I followed my senses and wormed my way past trees and over roots that were barely visible in the near-perfect darkness. Though the moon was high and nearly full, little light managed to penetrate the heavy canopy above me. I felt drawn by some unseen hand towards an area of the woods I don't normally visit, and there I found a gnarly old oak tree. The woodland is owned and maintained by the Forestry Commission and the majority of the trees here are coniferous with areas of birch, sweet chestnut and oaks dotted here and there. The oaks in this wood are relatively young and don't have those thick and sturdy trunks of the oaks found in Sherwood Forest, so this specimen felt rather grand. I breathed in the cool night air, exhaling a fine mist, and put my bare hands onto the bark.

> *Brother Oak, I greet you with friendship and peace. I ask you to give me your blessings, your strength and stamina, to help me through the day tomorrow. Give me confidence and energy, give me grounding and peace. Brother Oak, I give you my love and my peace, my blessings and friendship. Blessed Be.*

While I'm on the topic of talking to trees, I'd like to take a moment to encourage you to do the same. I know it's a cliché for alternative, new-age, pagan types to talk to trees, and for that reason a lot of people shy away from it or only admit very furtively that it's something they do themselves, but this seems a real shame to me: trees can give us so much if we take the time to listen. Some years ago, on a weekend away with the Goddess Camp organisers, in a beautiful private forest on the outskirts of Edwinstowe I had an incredible experience that will always stay with me.

My then-husband and I had been going through a very rough patch; arguments and disagreements had turned into hardness and animosity. We spent the day with good friends and in the evening, the group began to gather around a roaring campfire with djembe drums and pagan chants. I had conflicting emotions to contend with; I was deeply sad and unhappy, and I drifted silently away from the circle to ask Brother Oak for some guidance. The tree I settled down with was surrounded by thick brambles, heavy with darkening blackberries, thorns and spider webs. I pushed past the vines and stood with my back firmly against this tree, my friend in the forest, silently imploring for comfort.

Standing still, feeling apart from time and place, I felt my arms starting to move gently, almost like a tai-chi move. Back and forth, a flowing cloud floating, gradually moving in a figure-of-eight pattern in front of me. I could feel the spirit of the tree moving through me, directing my movements. My hands reached down and slowly moved up, lifting above my head, collecting calm energy and pulling it down, soothing it into my aura. This carried on for about ten minutes as I silently spoke to the tree spirit, asking for comfort, strength and guidance.

> *What should I be doing with my life, Brother Oak? I feel lost and so unhappy. Where am I going wrong and where is my path leading me to? I feel as if I have lost my way.*

I heard the tree spirit, the tender dryad, speaking back to me with emotions and feelings that are hard to put into words, but the meaning was clear.

You know yourself what needs to be done. You know you should be asking these questions of yourself because you know the answers are within you. All you need to do is realise it. Your path is clear, you know what direction it needs to take. Do what must be done. Your belief in yourself has waned. Recapture it, care for yourself, listen to your intuition and you'll see the way more clearly.

I asked a few more questions and received insights and guidance in this ethereal realm. I gave my silent thanks to the tree and the dryad, putting my hands against the wide trunk. I became aware once more of the rough bark, the breeze all around me that stirred the branches and vines but left my long skirt and hair untouched. My time with the oak was over and I looked upwards into the branches. Thin twigs and branches crossed and wove around each other, forming the very distinct outline of a horse's head. There were silver birch branches among those forming the shape, giving the horse's head a faint white glow. White horses symbolise that I'm on the right path; right here and right now, things are going the way they are supposed to go. I turned to leave but when I took a step away, I was confronted by the most enormous spider web and I swiftly turned to the other side where, immediately in front of me, there was a small cluster of perfectly formed oak apples. I asked Brother Oak if I could take them. Well, duh, what do you think? would be a good interpretation of the feeling I got from the dryad. I gave my thanks and picked the golden globes from the branch and went on my way, bumping into bramble bushes full of juicy looking berries. I wasn't tempted, however, all the berries I'd picked so far that weekend were sour. Nevertheless, still feeling as though I'd been guided here for a reason, I picked a few and popped them into my mouth, pleasantly surprised that they were juicy and sweet. I thought long and hard about the emotions, feelings, and guidance I'd been given by the spirit of the oak tree that weekend and it did give me a lot of comfort. Over the next few weeks, I meditated some more on my journey and the path my life was taking and everything tied in with what the oak had told me.

Tree-hugging is not a meaningless hippy cliché; it can give you genuine peace and help. I think of it as akin to visiting a close friend and sharing your troubles; even if nothing is resolved, the peaceful stillness presents an opportunity to take stock, to see things more clearly, or simply to spend time in quiet reflection. When I find myself going through a trying time, when I feel out of sorts or sad or lonely or confused, visiting an oak tree in this way makes me feel better and I do it often. It's useful to remember, though, that building up a deep rapport and connection to tree spirits, or indeed any elemental, can take a lot of time and patience and we must maintain that connection with regular visits when we don't want advice and guidance too. Like this night, back in the archery woods, going to the trees to offer my friendship and asking the Old Ones for strength to get through a busy day is a good way of keeping my friendship with Oak up to date and meaningful. Friends are there for the good times as well as the bad and the sad times.

I had a rough night, tossing and turning in the confines of a sleeping bag on hard ground, kept awake by the perpetual, nagging pain in my hip and the small noises of night creatures ferreting through the undergrowth, the shrill piercing cry of owls screeching overhead. And let's not talk about the elephantine snoring coming from another club member who shall remain anonymous! I packed away the tent and attempted to make myself look presentable at an unearthly hour on Sunday morning in order to start taking shoot fees and handing out score cards to the visiting archers, the first of whom arrived at only seven-thirty. Yawn!

I hadn't packed anything herbal to help me with a bit of morning energy, so coffee would have to suffice. Lots of it. I did have lavender essential oil and applied it liberally to my hip area. The good weather was interrupted by a light drizzle in the afternoon and at the end of the day, when the archers started to bring their score cards back to the admin cabin, they were all looking happy. Tidying the cabin and packing away the score cards, medals and equipment was an onerous task and luckily, our club has plenty of capable people willing to drag all those bulky and heavy targets back into the stores. At last the day was done and I was very happy and relieved to get back home for a long soak in a hot bath. Bubble bath, candles, rosemary essential oil, reading a few pages of my current Phil Rickman novel. Chris returned home from work and we had all missed each other, so there was a good deal of hugging and we spent a couple of hours together with Phoebe before she went up to bed.

I couldn't sleep as I had not finished altering the proposal for my new book and was annoyed with myself for putting it off. I decided to practise some relaxation techniques to try and help. I lay still, centred myself and focused on my breathing. In, out. In – relax, out – let go. Breathe in, hold the breath, breathe out, relax. Every time an unwanted thought cropped up, I started counting my breathing too. In – one, two, three, four. Out – one, two, three, four. I did this for around fifteen minutes and gradually began to feel better. There are other techniques I sometimes use when I can't sleep, especially when something is milling round and round in my head and it's hard to shut out the thoughts. One of my favourite methods is a variation of the rainbow countdown. I've written about this before so I won't bore you with the details, but there's more about it at the end of the month if you want to try it yourself: don't restrict it to bedtime, as this simple visualisation can be used any time of the day or night when you want to de-stress and feel peaceful, deep in your core.

I was woken by a peck on the cheek as Chris leaned over me to say goodbye before he left for work. It was another hour later that my own alarm went off, though it only felt like minutes. How had morning happened so quickly? At least I had eventually managed to relax enough to get some sleep. I was not surprised that Phoebe, after all her hard work trekking over rough ground with 3D targets, rushing backwards and forwards on little errands, was not feeling very well. She looked very pale and worn out and ached everywhere, so we sat down together for a few minutes to talk. She decided she'd probably manage a full day at school but promised to let the teachers know if she felt too horrible. I rushed to get ready for work with a quick shower, hair stuck up in a plain band, a customary lick of black eye-liner. Monday morning and the daily jaunt to work and back, followed by a ten-minute meditation to unwind at the end of the day.

I went again to Carla's mid-month meditation class in the village hall and had a thoroughly good time. It's a very easy and laid-back group and it was probably the only witchy-oriented thing I would get done this week as I had camping gear to clean and a tent to air, along with working on the proposal for the rejected book to see if I could really make it shine. I took time to answer emails, telephoned the members of the development circle to arrange our next meeting and I planned a talk that I would be doing in June at one of the local esoteric fairs. I had the usual amount of dish-washing, great hillocks of laundry and vacuuming to be done, most of which I put off for as long as humanly possible. Phoebe did a mountain of ironing without being asked to and I argued with Chris over something insignificant. Being a witch does not make me perfect, far from it!

Chris and I have our ups and downs and there had been a few more downs than ups for various reasons lately and we decided it was good idea for us to spend a bit of quality time together, just the two of us with nothing particular to do and nowhere particular to do it. Phoebe was scheduled to spend a weekend with her dad over in Nottingham, so I booked us a pitch at a campsite in Cannock Chase. I was looking forward to being close to Chris and having time alone together.

Honestly, there was no ulterior motive involved on my part at all. Having grown up in a house where Dennis Wheatley novels and books on divination lived on my mother's book case nestled happily alongside Agatha Christie and the Bible, I had an early interest in mysteries, ghosts, vampires, unexplained phenomena, UFOs, and the supernatural in general. I remember being very young when I first learned about fire-walking yogis, the Mothman and Chupacabras, vampires, unexplained phenomena and things that go bump in the night. I was a fan of Stephen King, James Herbert and Edgar Allan Poe at an age when my peers were reading Enid Blyton or Roald Dhal, so how on earth had I not heard of Cannock Chase until recently?

Chris's closest friend, Dave, grew up in and around Cannock Chase. He casually revealed one day the previous summer that he had once seen a UFO land there. I've known Dave for years; he knows I go mad for this kind of weirdness and why, oh why, had he not thought to tell me this before now? Google is my best friend. It turns out that Cannock Chase is very possibly the UFO, vampire, werewolf, black-eyed demonic child and pig-man capital of the UK. I have no idea how I had failed to come across this before now. I read up on it avidly and found out there are several campsites dotted around the area.

There was no ulterior motive for me wanting to visit the place, it was simply a romantic break that would bring us closer together after recent arguments. We would have a peaceful weekend alone together and go for some nice walks. At night. In a spooky forest. Under the full moon. Was it even a full moon? I didn't care. Off we went, ulterior motive and all.

Cannock Chase is an area of Outstanding Natural Beauty with three sites of Special Scientific Interest and several nature reserves. There is a diverse range of flora and fauna, including some rare species, and there is a variety both of flat and hilly terrain. The sun was shining beautifully all weekend and we pitched our tent overlooking a slight valley surrounded by lush greenery.

We arrived late in the evening to set up our tent, complete with colourful bunting and solar powered fairy lights, and then went for a short drive to the nearest village, ostensibly to obtain chocolate rations for the weekend, but really, I was UFO spotting. We found a tiny little corner shop about a ten-mile drive away and the surrounding area was perfect UFO territory, with long, flat stretches of road, nary a house in sight and a complete lack of traffic. Did they come and abduct me? No, they did not. I was not treated to a single suspicious looking light in the sky and nor was I woken in the middle of the night by strange noises or the fall of sinister footsteps or the snuffling noises of werewolves outside the tent. Still, I was having a good time and our first day in the area was sunny and bright. As we washed-up our breakfast dishes and talked about the day ahead, the sun was already hot and bright. We donned sunglasses and shoved bottles of water and a few sandwiches into a rucksack and set off on foot, walking for about an hour to a small visitor centre for further maps and information on the area.

What a stunning environment we passed through on our walk. Cannock Chase, I decided, is the perfect location for monster hunting and I was keen to read about some the local folklore and legends. Lee Brickley's book, UFOs, Werewolves and the Pig-Man, was the one of the resources I stumbled across prior to our visit and though I didn't see any signs of the pig-man Brickley describes, to this day, I remain hopeful. Vast stretches of open land and huge swathes of forest provided plenty of potential werewolf nesting places and alien ship landing sites. I kept a close eye out for anything untoward or slightly suspect but instead, I saw families taking their kids on day trips, dog-walkers and pony-trekkers.

Further along on our ambling walk, vaguely following a path we had picked from one of the guides and, bearing in mind my gammy hip and walking stick, we sat and rested for a while with a bite to eat. Common lizards and wild rabbits could be seen all around us as we sat enjoying the warm weather and pleasant views. As the path crossed a small stream, we paddled bare-footed in the refreshingly cool water as cyclists, ramblers and dog walkers came and went. The water was delicious on our hot feet. By noon, the sun was at its height and despite layers of sun-cream, my shoulders were starting to zing with the heat. We let our feet dry out, shoes and socks went back on, and we carried on with our stroll, Chris marvelling at the peacefulness of the environment, and made our way to one of the many visitor centres dotted through the chase, where we stopped for a welcome ice-cream.

On the way back to the campsite we became disoriented and ended up far from the trail we had intended to follow. We found ourselves walking through a densely wooded area surrounded by barbed wire fences and a 'no trespassing' sign indicating we were already inside the off-limits zone, though neither of us had seen any other warnings. I vaguely hoped that this was the top-secret military base frequented by the alleged pig-man of Cannock Chase. Alas, it was not. We hiked uphill through dry bracken and over rough hillocks to a ridge where a wide dirt track led out of the forest, taking us back to the more populated areas of the chase, and soon we were heading in the right direction once more. At the campsite, we eyed with envy a small fire pit one family had brought with them. Chris went over to talk to the guy in the morning while he was emptying the ashes out and found out where it came from. It's a surprisingly sturdy collapsible fire pit with a grill tray to double up as a barbeque, and folds completely flat to store and transport. We decided to get one ourselves when we returned to civilisation, as it would come in handy for future camping adventures and outdoor rituals.

We spent another long day walking through Cannock Chase, taking in different paths and scenery, including a stunning lakeside and hilly glades. Eventually, however, it was time return to the campsite to pack down to set off for home. Before we left the area, we drove across to Castle Ring and I'm glad we hadn't walked there as it was quite some distance. My hips were giving me a lot of pain by now and to be honest, I couldn't help but feel a little disappointed with Castle Ring.

An iron-age hill fort in an area of outstanding natural beauty, dating to 500 B.C. and just over 800 feet above sea level, I had imagined a beautiful, atmospheric site, full of history and wonder. Instead, we were greeted with a slightly raised, circular hill fort set within a back drop of trees and despite the sultry early summer heat, there seemed to me to be an atmosphere of dampness and darkness to the place. It was almost oppressive. I felt clouded and uneasy within the boundary of the circle, perhaps because of its relative proximity to civilisation with a busy road nearby, perhaps because of the tourists, ramblers and dog mess. Whatever it was, there was something about Castle Ring that left me feeling uncomfortable, and I was pleased to be back in the midst of civilisation in the evening, where a hot bath and lavender oil massage took my mind off the uncanny atmosphere.

We had a meeting of the Sherwood Oak Circle this week and Lisa had been invited to meet the group again. After the usual half-hour of catching up, we made a start, with John and I setting up a simple sacred space and everyone else taking turns to invoke the elements and then moved on to a series of energy sensing exercises. The focus of these was auras: how to cleanse the aura, how to see an aura, how fill it with bright, shining energy as a form of protection. I thought it would be a good way of introducing Lisa to the subtle energies of auras as well as a good reminder to the others. I showed everyone how to use a candle to see your own aura – you can try this yourself at home, it's easy to do and works for virtually everyone almost instantly.

Light a candle and place it in front of you with your hands on the other side of it, palms facing towards you. Do this against a dark background if possible and spend a few minutes relaxing, looking at the space between your fingers. Keep your finger tips an inch or two apart, your eyes slightly unfocused, and, with a bit of time, the area around your fingers and hands should start to take on a soft glow all the way around them. Think of the Ready-Brek advert, if you're old enough to remember that! Some people describe the aura as akin to a mirage, the twinkling heat haze seen in the road on very hot days: there's nothing physically there yet it still has a visible presence. If you can see this glow or light around your fingers, try moving your hands around a little, back and forth towards each other, circling around. You will hopefully start to see lines or threads of that mirage-light connecting one hand to the other, one finger to the next.

Although this is a very easy exercise, I always love people's immediate reaction to it. John, excitable as ever, especially loved this, and as well as his hands glowing from the orange-yellow light of the candles, he could see his aura clearly in other colours too. We closed the circle and consulted diaries to plan our next meeting.

During the middle of that last week of May, I heard on the pagan grape-vine that an old friend of mine had moved to a hospice very close to where I work. Sheila had not been well for some time and in the autumn the previous year, the local pagan community had put on a charity cabaret event as a fund-raiser so that she and her husband could afford to have some modifications added to their home and buy a few other essentials to make her life more comfortable. Sadly, her cancer was still advancing, and the diagnosis was very bleak. As the priestess of a long-running open group in Nottingham, Sheila was well-known and loved by everyone who had ever been part of that group and, until very recently, she had been a familiar face at Empyrean and Sabbat meetings. As she was now down the road from my office, I arranged to visit her one afternoon after work.

I was shocked at how poorly Sheila was. We hadn't seen each other since the fund-raiser the previous September, where I'd been running a cake stand with a couple of friends, and we weren't good at keeping in touch, but at one point she and I had been close, so it was a real mixed bag of emotions I felt that sunny afternoon at the hospice. Cancer had spread through her body so rapidly it had left her desperately ill, but her indomitable spirit shone strongly through it all and we had a good, though heart-breaking, afternoon, reminiscing and sharing stories, catching up on one another's gossip. It was so good to see her, Sheila's hugs are worth diamonds, we laughed and cried and laughed again to brighten her up – anything that brightens up the day of a terminally ill woman has got to be a good thing.

A forest walk was in order at the end of the month, accompanied by a couple of friends who are part of the Mansfield pagan scene and for once, Phoebe came with us too. We met in Sherwood Forest and spent time rambling through the woods in the sunshine. There is a particular junction where four paths meet with a fence surrounding the woodland on one side and it is here that several bird feeders are placed, always full of nuts and seeds provided by visitors to the forest. It fills me with joy and warmth to see so many blue-tits, coal-tits and sparrows swarming around the feeding stations here. Our friends didn't seem particularly overwhelmed by them, but Chris and I could have sat watching the fluttery little guys for hours. Phoebe was at that age when nature walks are so boring she could cry, but even she was impressed at the multitudes of robins, tits, goldfinches, jackdaws, treecreepers, goldcrests and chaffinches.

Mundane life returned with work and another meeting, this time purely a social gathering, of the Sherwood Oak Circle. Chris and I spent an evening visiting Brian and Kerry and, once again, she and I were listening with equal measures of anxiety and amusement, for the sounds of our respective daughters giggling manically from upstairs. I have no idea what they get up to and perhaps that's not such a bad thing. We brought both teenagers back with us for a sleep over with Phoebe. There were giggles all weekend along with a fair amount of screeching and screaming. We took them ten-pin bowling and took great delight in snapping pictures of them both wearing ludicrous checked bowling shoes and eating gigantic ice-creams. They had a brilliant time and thankfully neither of them ended up with ice-cream headaches.

Mini Maypoles for Beltane

An easy activity and one especially good for letting your child's imagination take over. Whenever I've done this with very young children, they get carried away and make dozens of them. Maypoles for Beltane can be used as a magical meditation, a decorative craft activity, or as part of a larger spell working for fertility and growth. Go off for a long ramble out into the countryside if possible and find somewhere nice to spend a while. Make a day of it and take a picnic and blankets and enjoy some fresh air. With lollypop sticks and ribbons, you could do this inside if you can't easily access the natural environment.

You will need a stick for each person, a plentiful supply of natural objects like long grasses, reeds or flexible twigs, stems of plants, pretty flowers and vines. Ribbons, twine, string, wool, cotton, buttons, beads, feathers and scraps of fabric will also be useful, as will a pair of scissors.

To make your maypole, find a decent sized stick. Knobbly and branchy and twelve inches long with a forked end, or something short, smooth and straight. Length and thickness are not important, providing you can tie things onto it. Start by knotting long wild grasses onto the stick or wrap it with brightly coloured ribbons that trail down the shaft of your stick. Red and white are the most appropriate colours for a maypole. It shouldn't take long to finish this little craft project, so try doing it as part of a ritual or as a tool for active meditation. For fertility magic, use red and white ribbons and focus on the overt symbolism of the maypole: the long, phallic shaft and the feminine red and white winding around it.

If you want to hang the maypoles up in the trees or leave it out against a standing stone, please use biodegradable, natural or organic materials such as cotton, silk, woolly string or vines, twigs and leaves.

Rainbow Countdown for Sleeplessness

This visualisation doesn't rely on a good imagination; it's based around thinking of a wave or light moving over you like the waves on a beach, ebbing and flowing. This isn't about seeing yourself on a beach or trying to imagine the colour is an actual wave of water, because it isn't. It's just a wash of light that soothes you and takes your worries and stress away with it each time it comes over you and then recedes.

Switch out the lights and turn off your phone, make sure you're completely comfortable, neither hot nor cold, and lie still without crossing your arms or legs.

Close your eyes. Breathe slowly. Relax.

Visualise a wave of colour and light and imagine it slowly coming towards you. A soft wave of rainbow red. Just as the waves of a beach would come gradually further up your body, so this wave of colour reaches your toes and feet first. It washes you completely in calm red waves and slowly recedes, taking away with it any tension or stress you're holding in your feet.

The wave returns, it is still red, and it washes gently over your feet and comes a little higher up this time to cover your ankles before retreating, taking away with it all the tension stored in your ankles. As the wave slowly ebbs and flows up your legs, past your knees and then over your thighs, it leaves you feeling more relaxed each time. The red wave takes away all your stress and tension and worry. Visualise this as slowly as you can, keeping calm and breathing gently. With each breath you draw in, the wave comes a little higher up your body, as you exhale, the wave retreats a little. Take plenty of time with this, there's no hurry and the more gradually you do this exercise, the more relaxed and peaceful you will start to feel. Focus only on the red wave of light until it comes up as far as your root chakra, let it linger for a short while, soothing red around your chakra and your lower abdominal area.

Now the light retreats and comes back as an amber or orange colour, very gently soothing you and retreating, covering you in an orange light and retreating again. The orange light wave passes gradually further up to the next chakra, the sacral chakra just below your navel, and it sits there swirling lightly around the chakra and your abdomen. As it recedes, any tension stored here goes with it and floats softly away. Let the orange wave return and gradually come higher with each ebb and flow until it comes to rest for a moment around your solar plexus chakra. Gradually the light becomes yellow and slowly washes over you again, gently, softly.

Take your time, letting the yellow waves wash over you, each one leaving you more and more relaxed and calm. After a while, go through the rest of the rainbow colours for each chakra – green waves around your heart, blue for your throat area, indigo for the third eye chakra at your brow and finally violet or white for the crown chakra at the top of your head. Let each colour ebb and flow, just as you visualised with the first ones; see it swirl around each chakra in turn, finally finishing with a white light coming to rest over your crown chakra. Imagine you are completely bathed in this rainbow of light, utterly peaceful, all worries pushed aside, calm and content.

With practise, this routine may have you falling asleep before you can get all the way through the rainbow of colours. Take note of your dreams when you carry out this exercise.

June

Sun-bleached meadows buzzing with life,
Bees seeking nectar, movement is rife,
Hoppers in the hedgerow, damsels on the wing,
Sounds and scents only summer can bring.

Fledglings flitter in the sun dappled glade,
Following mum foraging in the shade,
Bountiful food there for the taking,
Bugs and grubs for muscle making.

Another solstice arrives at last,
Long hours of day a thing of the past,
As the still warm nights stretch out in their turn,
Bringing the changes all things discern.

Summer moves on to swell the fruits,
As saplings strive to sink their roots,
These cycles are now and forever will be,
The clockwork that runs all we can see.

(Neil Page)

June is the month of the summer solstice, long warm nights nestled beside an outdoor fire and walks through the countryside surrounded by the vibrant colours of summer flowers. There are blue skies, bountiful flowers in gardens and hedgerows, swifts nesting beneath the eaves of the house. Working hard across the country, bees collect sweet nectar from the rich blossoms of lavender stalks in the garden and lazy cats spread out to absorb summer warmth.

This month, I'd been invited to give an introductory talk on witchcraft at a psychic fair and was also looking forward to meditations, drumming, and of course, the solstice ritual.

To start the month off, Chris and I headed off to visit some of his family for the weekend, staying at his sister's home with her family in the old terrace house that had once belonged to their grandparents. I often end up talking with Chris's mum about our joint addiction to knitting, discussing various techniques and patterns and admiring the new soft yarns we both have to play with. She has an amazing collection of knitting patterns and I usually manage to coerce her into parting with one or two of them. We had a good day on the Sunday with family, joined by sister and brother-in-law, assorted nephews and nieces and Mum. Chris's family, both the Middlesbrough and Nottingham branches, are very good at putting on Sunday lunches and there were countless dishes of assorted goodies for everyone to tuck into. I volunteered myself and Phoebe, much to her disgruntlement, for washing-up duty before heading back home for work and school the following day.

It's always worth a visit to see families whenever we have the chance, and not only our biological families, but our spiritual ones too. These different families are equally important, built of bricks forged through friendship and trust and love: these are the people who matter in our lives, the people we love and care about. I treasure all our family and friends, my pagan community and its many members, however spread apart we are across the country, however rarely we may see each other: it lifts me up to spend time with them all.

So that was the first weekend of June out of the way already – it seemed as though time was flying by without me really noticing and I still had to finish preparing for the upcoming talk. I did the usual routines of working during the week, cooking for the family and a couple of work out sessions at the gym. On the Tuesday evening we had our regular archery session at the club woods, and it was lovely to come home after work and head straight out with Phoebe for some practise in the warm and peaceful forest. Another day after work I saw a locum GP at the local surgery about my hips. I was only there for some more pain killers, but having never seen this doctor before I had to give a rough account of the issue I was having. Despite various tests, scans and x-rays, there was no clear diagnosis after more than ten years and having to go through it all again was wearing me down.

'Hmm, you'll probably never know what the cause is,' he said. He hummed a little more. 'These trochanteric pain syndromes can be hard to treat. I'll give you something for it.'

Hang on. That was a medical term, wasn't it? My jaw dropped to the floor. Did this gentleman just give me a name, a diagnosis? I asked him what he meant. Greater trochanteric pain syndrome. I finally had a name for my disorder. Of course, it doesn't mean much – I have a pain syndrome in the trochanteric area of the hip. But even though this tentative diagnosis was a description of the symptoms, not a cause, I was staggered by the fact that I now had a name for it. Unless you've been through this yourself, you'll have no idea how difficult it is to have a disorder that can affect you severely one day, but not so badly the next; to have people see you with a stick one moment and not needing it the next week. All you are able to say is: 'I have something wrong with my hips', and it seems that this isn't good enough for other people.

'It must be this condition. My Auntie had that. Have you tried this treatment?'

After explaining that I've been suffering for over ten years, do you think I haven't already tried everything I could lay my hands on?

At last I'd be able to tell people what's wrong with me. It took a while to sink in and once it did, I requested referral to a specialist in similar conditions, which the locum doctor was happy to arrange. In the meantime, I could do my own research into possible causes and treatments so that I would be armed with information by the time the appointment came through.

I spent a few hours planning and putting together the witchcraft talk, as well as working on my new book and the accompanying twenty-five-page proposal. The week shot by like a bullet and suddenly, Saturday had arrived. Chris and I went to Nottingham for the mind, body, spirit fair at the Galleries of Justice. Arriving just after lunch, I made my way to the admin desk to show my face and check-in with Erick, the brains behind the whole operation. As usual, I'd misplaced the tickets he'd given me, but it wasn't a problem and Chris and I started to make our way through the crowds. Looking at the programme, I was delighted to see a slight change to the schedule. One of the speakers had unfortunately had to drop out and Erick had asked Carla to step in at the last minute.

She cobbled together a talk on fractals and brought a few things along with her to demonstrate what fractals are – everything from pictures of crop circles in the Julia set right, through to the patterns formed in the florets of a giant Calabrese broccoli she was using as a prop.

This was the first time the venue, an old gaol and former court house, had been used for a fair like this, but despite a few problems with access, it turned out to be a good location with dozens of large rooms and halls available for talks, workshops, stalls and readers. My eye was drawn to a set of lapis lazuli stones with the four major Reiki symbols etched into them in gold. After holding them in my hands for a short while, I thought they might come in handy for Shibby's ongoing Reiki treatments, and I also picked up a very beautiful crystal skull in opalite, which glows with a warm golden colour in daylight.

When Chris and I first met, we took part in an over-night ghost experience at the Galleries of Justice and had a few hair-raising experiences there, so it was great to come back here for the show, this time in daylight. We listened to one or two talks and browsed the many merchandise stalls before I went into the old court room for my own talk. I was slightly surprised to run into a woman I know vaguely through work. We chatted briefly before my talk and I found out that she belongs to a spiritualist church and has quite an interest in spooky happenings. The hall started to fill up with a massive queue of people all waiting to go in to my talk. I went into the court room, Erick showed me how to use the microphone, and off I went. I spoke about the Wheel of the Year, how we celebrate the turn of the seasons, the Goddess and God and the elements of nature that make up the core of pagan beliefs. I gave a few personal examples of how spell crafting can work, with the use of props including poppets and mojo bags, as well as giving out a bit of information on how and why I believe spells work and what situations we might use them for.

I always leave a good ten-or-fifteen minutes for questions at the end of any talk and the usual ones came up, which I was able to answer with ease.

Does magic really work? What crystals would you recommend for a love spell?

After the final question, I thanked my audience to a round of applause and as I turned away from the podium to leave, I found myself blocked in by a long line of people who wanted to talk to me privately. I was able to take a few of their questions, but time was ticking by and I quite literally had to push my way past the rest of the group with an apology so that the next speaker could come in for their talk. I felt guilty that such a large portion of the audience followed me out of the courtroom instead of listening to the next session. Erick had kindly let me have space to sign my books and take a few more questions in a less busy area. It's events like this and the appreciation of others that makes me feel that what I do is worthwhile. I am truly grateful for the warmth and friendliness of the people I meet at events.

One lady asked me to sign a book for her, asked a few brief questions, and then gave me the most wonderful hug. Her beautiful curling hair smelled of strawberries and her sparkling eyes lit up with a little tear as I hugged her back. Another lady asked for advice on a spell to find out if she was following the right path. A man in his early-twenties and an older woman who had come with him posed the most interesting question that day.

'Do you know who Matthew Hopkins is?' he asked me, looking very nervous. I assured him that I did indeed know of the gentleman in question. What witch doesn't know who Matthew Hopkins was?

He took a small step backwards and gulped. 'I was Matthew Hopkins in a past life.'

Well, there's something a witch doesn't hear every day. I had no idea how to react to this and felt very awkward. It seemed farfetched: but who am I, who has flown on the back of a unicorn in spirit journeys, to judge, ridicule or disbelieve anyone else's experience?

I stepped forward and smiled and we patted each other somewhat tentatively on the back before turning it into a proper hug. He explained his circumstances to me.

'I was at a past life regression event, we just happened to be sitting next to each other.' He turned to his friend.

'And it turns out,' said his female companion, 'that I was a witch who he put on trial and put to the stake all those centuries ago. We've been friends ever since and started working together in alternative healing.'

It was a strange conversation, though not one of the strangest I've ever had, and I tried to suspend my disbelief as I listened to them.

After all, if this young man truly believed he was the reincarnation of Hopkins, self-appointed Witch Finder General, then it was courageous of him to come and seek me out. We chatted for a few minutes before another of my audience jumped in to change the subject. I shook hands warmly with 'Hopkins' and his friend before moving on.

All this time, I was aware of some of the Sherwood Oak Circle and my oh-so-patient husband lingering in the background and, gradually, the crowd filtered away. I always enjoy speaking events, even though they can be exhausting: for months afterward, I have a deluge of emails and messages on social media as people continue to request advice and guidance. Some of them seem to expect me to give them all the answers, while others are happy to get a quick bit of advice. I don't mind this kind of contact to an extent, but I can't be a personal mentor to everyone simply because they saw me once at a talk in a crowded hall. Working full-time, having various crafts as a hobby, writing books and articles in my spare time and having a family life, holidays and going to moots and talks myself, on top of the events I speak at, means I genuinely don't have enough time to go into long email exchanges with strangers.

It was an exhausting but exhilarating day and by the time we arrived home I was ready for a long, hot bath. I'm quite a big fan of hot baths, you'll have noticed. Being on my feet all day had taken its toll on my gippy legs as usual. Lavender is one of my favourite scents, so I splashed essential oil and bubble bath in the tub and soaked for half an hour before settling down on the sofa with Chris for snuggles and a good old-fashioned horror movie. Shibby came and sat near me, her little meow's gradually becoming more insistent.

I remembered the set of Reiki crystals I had bought at the fair and brought them out, putting them onto the cushion I've persuaded her to sit on for her treatments. As she clambered across for her Reiki, Shibby completely ignored the crystals. I activated my

Reiki flow and traced the symbols etched into the stones and instantly Shibby put her nose to the crystals and started patting them with her paws, rubbing her face against them. She pawed them into a pile, moving them around a few times, and sat down with her back legs right on top of them for the duration of her treatment. Honestly, that cat just loved Reiki!

Archery with Phoebe on Tuesday evening took me on a slow meander through our club woods, enjoying the fresh air, the summer warmth and the smell of trees, and I came across several long, speckled feathers, possibly partridge, that would be suitable for making a new smudging fan. Carla's meditation group a few days later was incredibly relaxing, though with no further epic visions of enraged Goddesses, and on another night, we had dinner with Jane, a friend I met through archery, to celebrate her new job.

Chris and I, somewhat reluctantly, decided it was time for a book clear-out. We are both book hoarders and the shelves are all two books deep with yet more perched on top of those, every shelf stuffed to bursting with books and more volumes scattered on virtually every available surface throughout the house. In retrospect, I would have preferred adding an extension to the house to be used exclusively as a library and reading room. After weighing up the merits of each book and reminiscing on the stories, lives, places and imaginings within the pages, the shelves were still overflowing, but we had a small number of books that would make their way to new homes, either by passing them onto friends or as donations to local charity shops. As a witch and pagan, non-fiction books are a valuable resource of knowledge and practical guidance, from the esoteric writings of Dion Fortune or Gerald Gardner, through to the academic and biographical research of Philip Heselton or Ronald Hutton, or the work of today's pioneers of witchcraft, Janet Farrar and Gavin Bone, Vivianne Crowley or Yvonne Aburrow.

The working week was broken up for me by a very tedious course and a meeting with one of the district councils to discuss the planning application process. In my ideal world, there is a home office in our garden, surrounded by brightly coloured flowers and filled to the rafters with book shelves, where I spend hours every day writing best-sellers, nestled in a comfy armchair, laptop on a rustic coffee table and a cat curled up by my feet, purring softly. The reality is that I need a steady and reliable income and I'm reluctant to give up the stability of my regular job.

A full moon at the weekend coincided with Phoebe's regular visit with her dad and gave Chris and I the chance to wander into the forest for a very simple but spine-tingling ritual of our own. There had been a few disagreements, times when we didn't see each other in the kindest light, and even after our weekend away in May at Cannock Chase, we hadn't fully come around to resolving everything between us. It can be hard to admit that things aren't right in a relationship, but we wanted to get everything out in the open, to reconnect and come back to a place of loving each other completely again. We both feel soothed and restored after spending time deep in a forest under the moonlight, so this would be a good time for reflection and honesty and peace with each other.

It's not often that we do this kind of thing with just the two of us, there never seems to be enough time for it, but when we do, it feels natural, unplanned and unhurried. We saunter round to find our quiet space among the ancient oak, yew, birch and rowan trees and sit quietly with each other, sensing the peace and calmness around us, opening ourselves up to the unique stillness of the forest that hides so much bustling activity of the animals, birds and insects hidden in the foliage. Looking up at the brightly shining orb of the full moon, I found myself thinking of all the other witches, men and women, across the globe who are looking upon it with me, opening their own hearts and minds to the wonders and magic of the natural world. I wonder what they wish for and hope that their dreams, as well as my own, will be fulfilled. I feel a calmness and serenity as Chris and I look fondly at each other, all recent conflict cast aside, at least for now, as we sit in silence together. It might sound as if I'm being idealistic, but those moments of coming together under the moon and really opening ourselves up to the sounds and sensations of the natural environment can genuinely help to make me feel better about our relationship. It's that joining, the sense of togetherness, sensing the same things at the same time in the same place, having an essence of the sacred come over me and knowing that he senses it too, that brings a feeling of healing and unity. It doesn't stop the arguments, resentments or disagreements, but it does bring a sense of togetherness and connection that keeps me going if things get rough.

On Saturday I paid a long-overdue visit to one of the very few witchy oriented shops in Nottingham. This place is a witch's haven filled to the rafters with packets of spices, herbs and incenses, silver and crystal jewellery, amulets, talisman pouches, tarot decks, altar tools, deity statuary, greetings cards, books and who-knows-what-else. A true witch's paradise. The rooms upstairs, which were available to hire for workshops, my ulterior motive for this visit, are beautifully decorated and filled with a serene atmosphere that fills me with a sense of ease and peace immediately on entering. There is something instantly calming that comes over me whenever I visit new-age gift shops and witchy supply stores where that same element of calmness, serenity and peace floats out like a wave.

What is it about places like this that makes us feel so good? I think it's a lot more to do with the people than the place itself. As customers, we have an expectation that a shop like this will have some noticeable atmosphere of calm, so we set ourselves up to feel that way before even we walk through the door. The staff who own and work in mystical shops go out of their way to make sure that this atmosphere is there. Using smudging herbs, cleansing aura sprays, deliberately filling the centre with Reiki and incense, adding their own magical charms and good wishes for the place – it all helps to build up a relaxed, pleasant state of mind. Not only that, many of the people drawn to this kind of shop tend to have some understanding or level of spiritual development themselves, and that emanates into the environment too. The ongoing use of these buildings for spiritual purposes, meditation, shamanic journeying, healing and chakra work, all adds to the atmosphere, along with the retail products themselves; incense, herbs, crystals, books, tarot sets and runes, continually emitting their fantastic vibrations. When this combination of factors is just right, it becomes something instantly recognisable as being good for the soul and spirit, deep inside, and so we feel happier, relaxed and serene as soon as we venture inside and smell that heady Nag Champa or sandalwood scent wafting around the room in drifts of hazy smoke.

I spent a while, a long while if I'm honest, browsing the shop, chatting to the staff, picking up crystals, ogling the jewellery, sniffing packets of incense and – I don't need to explain. If you were drawn to read a book like this one, it's likely that you already know it's like a kid being unleashed in a sweet shop. Before I knew it, an hour had gone by and after discussing potential classes, I made my goodbyes and promised to get in touch with a firm outline for a workshop I would run there later in the year.

School summer trips are looming and Phoebe and I went to a meeting at her school for an information evening on a week-long end-of-year trip to France. I was not convinced this was an entirely good idea: the previous years' away-trip to Perlethorpe in Nottinghamshire had resulted in a tearful phone call with Phoebe begging for me to bring her home mid-week. The assembly hall was full of equally nervous parents and although we were shown footage and photographs of previous trips to the same location and the teachers were as reassuring as they could be, I was still wary. I'd done a similar school holiday abroad when I'd been around her age and it wouldn't have been fair of me to hold her back. At least her two best friends would be there with her. Perhaps I shouldn't have thought of that – what on earth would they get up to between them?

One evening before the solstice weekend, Chris and I paid a visit to Tasha and Tony, a couple whose hand-fasting ceremony I had conducted the previous summer solstice. This was their first anniversary as a married couple and they looked every bit as happy as they had done a year ago. I presented them with a bottle of mead as a gift. It was the last of a batch I'd made years ago that didn't turn out too well. It was quite awful; I threw most of it away, but not before a few bottles had been stowed on my wine rack. Four or five years after that, Liz had persuaded me to try some her own home-brew mead and it was gorgeous. I remembered the few bottles of my own mead that had been collecting dust at the bottom of the wine rack. Not convinced that my mead would be as good as Liz's, even though it had been maturing for years, I opened a bottle. It wasn't as good as it could have been, but still rather nice and when the happy couple and I were planning their hand-fasting ceremony, I opened a bottle. Tony thought it was very drinkable and decided it would be a good addition to the ceremony.

They were delighted when I handed the last remaining bottle of the mead to them for their anniversary. Tasha also had a small gift for me, a necklace with a flying unicorn pendant. She had no idea that I had a growing collection of unicorns, so this was really fitting. I never intended to have a collection of unicorns – I bought one for myself a few years ago and called it Wilberforce. Since then I've been given around another ten or so from various friends and they are wildly entertained by the silly names I give them – Calliope, Cardigan, Cyclone Warrior, Queenie, Bruce, Angel, Thursday. The latest addition to the collection is Larry

'Harmonica' Underwood, a subtle nod to one of my favourite Stephen King novels.

To celebrate the solstice, we spent the weekend camping with friends, once again not far from Matlock in Derbyshire. The weather was terrifically hot and the long and winding stroll to Doll Tor for a ritual was rewarded with the cool shade of the trees in the forest where the stones are found. Chris and Paul went for a walk with Jack and Phoebe and the rest of us entered the circle of stones. We set up a sacred space among the grove of oaks and held hands in a circle, speaking out to the elements and giving thanks for glorious weather, the blossoming nature all around us, the height of summer.

We were approached by a couple of people walking along the path, dressed casually but looking alternative. They wished us a happy solstice and we talked with them for a few minutes. Our loosely formed ritual had two extra participants and we each called into the circle our thoughts on the season, our desires, our gratitude for the good things in our lives. The couple we'd met joined in with our drumming and chanting for a while before carrying on their way, leaving us to carry on our celebration with pagan songs and quiet time for personal meditations.

Joined once more by Chris, Phoebe, Jack and Paul for a long and lazy picnic, the afternoon passed pleasurably. The walk back to our base was quite long and the heat of the sun was relentless. Sarah and I both got thoroughly burned shoulders on the way, despite the sun screen we'd applied. It was a relief to get back to the campsite where we smoothed thick layers of soothing creams onto our bright red skin. In the evening, we sat by our little campfire and watched thousands of twinkling stars as they appeared in the sky.

Phoebe and I spent a few hours at the archery woods on Tuesday night, our Queen of Cats, Shibby, demanded as much fuss and Reiki as she could get, and I managed to squeeze in a couple of gym sessions in addition to working on my book and, of course, I was at work each day too. Every Thursday evening, a local spiritual development group meet at the community hall in one the nearby towns and several people had recommended it to me. The group is run by Abby, a gifted, spiritual woman, quietly spoken with a calming influence who exudes wisdom and knowledge. Chris and I were both interested in joining in this week, when the focus of the session was shamanic drumming. Although I owned a large frame drum, it didn't have a great sound, but we were assured there would be spare drums for us to use at the venue. The session started with a sociable meet and greet over a cup of coffee or tea and we recognised a few faces from other events, forest walks and pub moots.

Starting with a general warm up of drum banging with no discernible rhythm, we were then guided through quite a long pathworking as Abby and one or two others set up a monotonous, repetitive beat. Abby asked to us to imagine we were sat around a central fire with a shaman, chanting and drumming over the fire. I lost track of what she was talking about as my internal images started to take on a life of their own. A white horse, one of my spirit animal guides, appeared in the flames and told me I should take my blinkers off. Smoke from the fire was puffed into my face and I could hear chanting in the distance. The smoke from the fire stuck to my face in a thin grey layer and I pulled it off, a snake shedding its skin. Take my blinkers off? I didn't know what that meant but it seemed to tie in with the smoky paste I peeled off my face, a feeling of being hidden, vision obscured, not able to be free or to see clearly until this layer was removed. The drumming became louder and faster and Abby guided us back to the room and full awareness of our surroundings.

Next came a murmur of chatter as Abby turned to each of the group, asking for a relay of their experience. I am not a big fan of this part of open groups. People feel obliged to explain in detail what happened in their inner visions and I've seen people coerced into sharing their experiences when they clearly haven't wanted to. While it can be useful to share our visualisations, any interpretations and meanings given to us by other people are not always relevant, let alone accurate. Their interpretations of my journey would be based on their thoughts and beliefs, not mine. They have no idea what I may be going through at any given time, or how my journey relates to that. Nobody in that room would have known the significance of white horses for me or what obstacles in my life the blinkers might represent. I tend to analyse pathworking experiences myself or with people I work with closely and whose judgement and experience in the craft I know I can trust. I smiled and shook my head when it was my turn to speak and turned my head to the person next to me.

As a slight aside to this, remember that visualisation can take patience practise and not everyone possesses the ability to see internal mental pictures, so if this you, don't panic: you're not doing anything wrong. On rare occasions, due to a condition described as aphantasia, affecting only one to three percentage of the population, a person cannot see any mental images at all. Hyperphantasia, at the other end of the scale, is an extremely enhanced ability to see internal scenes, often including sensations of touch, scent, sound and even taste, along with the visuals. Most of us fall somewhere between these two states and practising visualisation techniques can often improve the level of detail and experience of your inner journeys.

After the pathworking, Abby set up a drumming session for healing, with four people sitting in the centre of the room while the rest of the group circled, drumming loudly to drive out negative vibrations and focus on spiritual healing. Tuneless banging and the occasional wail of a chant isn't my preferred medium for healing work, but those people on the receiving end looked happy enough. Abby handed each of us an animal oracle card to finish the session. I turned over Lizard and Chris's card was

Otter. We looked up the meaning for each card in the deck's accompanying guide book, but none of it seemed especially relevant.

I didn't record any dreams in my journal that night, though I do often have dreams that link to or expand on a pathworking exercise. A dream diary can be a useful aid, particularly if your dreams are vivid and memorable or stranger than normal. Reviewing dreams can shed a different light on situations and problems. Clues to dream interpretation are recurring archetypes, animals, signs, sigils, people, activities, or places encountered in dreams. A black horse in my dreams is a warning, indicating there is a challenge ahead of me and I'm following the wrong path; if the horse is galloping away, I need to review or step back from my current circumstances. When a black horse is jumping over a barrier or forcing its way through a hedge, it signifies that although I may be facing a difficult problem right now, if I persevere, things will work out well once this hurdle is out of my way. Other colours and a few specific breeds of horse have unique relevance to me as well.

It took a lot of patient pathworking and communication with Horse in the Other Realms to find out those meanings for me. Dream interpretation books are useful as a starting point, but if you continue to write down and study your own dreams, patterns will begin to emerge that are uniquely relevant to you. It takes time to develop a way of interpreting your dream symbols until you understand the answers to problems or worries.

Daily Meditation

Meditating is not a new-age fancy but has been practised by numerous religious traditions, with the earliest references being recorded in the ancient Indian texts, the Vedas, and it is also an important aspect of both Hinduism and Buddhism. Meditation techniques fall broadly into two categories: focused, concentrative meditation and open, or mindful, meditation. Focused methods include paying attention to the breath, a mantra or idea, and open meditation is mindfulness, awareness without concentration or thought. It is generally thought to be of most benefit when practised daily for between five and twenty minutes.

The positive benefits of regular meditation include stress reduction, relaxation, mental clarity, reduced anxiety and depression, increased levels of energy, pain management, emotional calmness, a sense of well-being and peace. Meditation can be done in silence, with back ground music, the use of mantras and chanting, drumming or singing bowls. Prayer beads or a set of mala beads can help you focus on a mantra or to count your breathing. Cleansing your room and your aura with a smudging stick or aura spray will help to create a peaceful atmosphere but none of this is essential.

Providing that you are comfortable and won't be disturbed, meditation can be practised virtually anywhere and at any time. Creating a time and place in your daily routine for meditation will help you establish the practise. This might be first thing in the morning before the family are up and about or when you have half an hour free in the afternoon or evening. If you find it hard to relax, stick to the habit of setting aside a few minutes for meditation every day and gradually, you should find yourself calmer, more relaxed and able to focus. You might meditate for five minutes or half an hour, but with regular practise, you will soon begin to notice the benefits of meditation in your mind, body and soul.

Sit comfortably and close your eyes. Breathe normally. Pay attention to each breath in, each breath out. Start breathing a little deeper if you can, breathe in, one two, breathe out, one two. Don't try to clear your mind at this stage, simply acknowledge each thought as it comes to you. Let your thought float away without paying any attention to it. Think the thought, let go of the thought. Bring your awareness back to your breathing. Breathe in, breathe out.

There is nothing else for you to do in this moment. Be still, be aware of your breath. Feel every part of you relaxing deeply.

When you are finished, become aware of your body and your surroundings, pay attention to the sounds and sensations all around you. Open your eyes. Stretch your arms and bring your awareness back to the here and now.

Spell for Relationship Harmony

To restore harmony in your relationships and clear up a negative atmosphere between you and your significant other, try this spell to soothe tempers and clear the way for peaceful resolutions. This spell works on two levels, first getting rid of underlying animosity, then working to create good wishes and harmony. This should come from a place of understanding and love, not blame or anger.

Cast this spell at on a Friday to add the energy of Venus, Roman Goddess of love and fertility, and at noon to bring the sun's warmth and vibrancy to your wishes for a happy and loving relationship. Adapt as necessary to make it personal and meaningful.

You will need:
Sage leaves or smudging bundle
Clear quartz
Black and red thread or ribbon
Paper & pen
Pink candle
Rose petals (dried or fresh)
The Lovers tarot card

Cleanse your aura with the sage. Place the pink candle and a clear quartz crystal on top of the Lovers tarot card. Sprinkle petals on the altar and light the candle.

Write down all the things you have been arguing about. Keep it brief and list only the issue itself, not your feelings towards your partner.

As the candle burns, roll up the paper and tie with black thread and burn in the candle flame.

Take a second piece of paper and write down this little charm:

Venus, Venus, Goddess of love, I ask of you this boon. Resolution of strife, an end to dispute, let only love and harmony remain. By the power of earth may we support each other, by the power air may our dreams be as one, by the power of fire may our passions be strong, by the power of water may our way be eased, by the power of spirit may our souls unite. Ancient Goddess, hear my call, let this spell work for the good of all...

Tie with red ribbon and keep with the quartz in a safe place.

Let the candle continue to burn as you reflect on the things that make your relationship worthwhile. Light the candle for a few minutes every day until it has burned down completely and sprinkle the rose petals around your front door.

July

A Song for the Season:
Whirl-Y-Reel, Afro-Celt Sound System.

A fragrant time of year, July is full of growth, activity and bounty. Fields of golden corn dress the countryside, and in forests, the overhead canopy of trees shine richly with the brightest of greens. In towns and cities the pavement cafes are flooded with people enjoying the sun and the season brings happiness and smiles, backyard barbecues and family gatherings and picnics, open air concerts and holidays are in full swing. The summer months are always a busy time of year and this July was to be no exception.

The weather was mostly beautiful, with long, light nights, good friends and interesting events to look forward to. With such a lovely start to the early summer in May and June, I was looking forward to some equally good times ahead this month.

July started with a visit Paul and Sarah's for a social evening. She and I talked about drums and their use in pathworking and she proudly showed off her new altar set up. She has an entire dressing table devoted to her tools and this includes an impressive array of crystals. Sarah found her witchy niche with crystals and John had been looking into spiritual mediumship, but Lisa asked if she had to decided which type of witch she would be.

'I don't like cooking, so I can't be a kitchen witch and I'm not green-fingered so that rules out being a hedge witch.'

The internet is a helpful resource and is often the place we turn to for answers, but there is so much conflicting information on the web about witchcraft and I don't think it always helps. Lisa, like dozens of newcomers to the craft, was overwhelmed by contradictory answers to her questions. Every witch has different talents, skills, interests, likes and dislikes. Being 'witch' or 'pagan' is enough for most of us. Celtic witch, green witch, crystal witch or fairy witch – I find these new labels restrictive, constrictive, and they can be demeaning. I felt quite cross recently on behalf of a good friend, a woman in her forties with adult children, was recently referred to as a 'baby witch' by a member of the pagan community who knew my friend was still on the first steps of her witch's journey.

'Are you sure,' I asked Lisa, 'that you want to be defined by only one aspect of your witchy life? A witch without a specialism is still a witch.'

I often visit the gym before or after work, it helps me keep my gippy hip mobile and regular exercise is vital for the mental health benefits it gives me. If I go any length of time without exercise, or without a long rambling walk through the countryside, I feel out of sorts and unsettled. Returning home one evening after a heavy work-out, I washed my hair and decided I had finally had enough of the speed at which my bright red hair-dye washes out. I picked up a packet of permanent dye in a dark burgundy colour and slapped it onto my locks. Goodbye fire-box red, hello dull and plain reddish-brown. I spent the rest of the week missing the bright colour so much that I had soon bleached it out and put on the fiery red again. Writing this book some time later, I have gone back to having dark-red or dark-purple hair, but I do miss that bright colour sometimes.

My friend Cathy and her husband, Rob, belong to their local amateur dramatic society and were involved in a trio of short plays showing at their community theatre this weekend and Cathy was performing in two of these. Chris and I had tickets for the Friday evening performance. The second two plays were short pieces filled with humour and dramatic family situations, but it was the first play which tugged at my heart strings. The characters in the play took the part of dogs in a rescue centre, dressed in doggy costumes and make up. The four dogs spent their days discussing their previous homes, finding new owners and what life might be like if they were adopted by the visitors who came to see them. It was a very sad and melancholy play and ended with one poor pooch's untimely demise, sadly lifeless, lonely and unloved on the concrete floor of his pen. I'm not ashamed to admit that my eyes were leaking.

The week-long school trip to France was looming and, being a teenager, Phoebe naturally wanted new clothes to take on holiday, along with something to wear for her Aunt's wedding, which was coming up not long after that. I love my daughter, I really do, but whenever we go shopping together it tends to end in arguments. I can pick out a plain white vest top and she will choose one which looks identical to me but I can guarantee that the one I have chosen only serves as further evidence, if any were needed, that I have no clue at all of what Phoebe thinks is cool and that my own dress-sense is down-right appalling. Neither of us was particularly looking forward to our shopping spree and after a lot of time in the changing rooms of five or six different clothing boutiques (let me point out here our closest shopping centre is Mansfield so 'boutique' might be stretching it a little), she finally decided on a navy blue dress for the wedding and a few sets of shorts and tops for the holiday.

I must admit I had huge reservations about her going off on this trip with school after the fiasco of the previous year's end-of-term escapade, when she was sharing a room with three girls she didn't know. None of her friends had booked on the trip and after I'd already paid the deposit, the school announced another holiday option, giving students the opportunity of a trip to Centre Parcs for a weekend. Phoebe's best friends all booked for Centre Parcs, but it was too late for us to change the holiday by this time. The week-long trip was interrupted with a tearful phone call half-way through the week with Phoebe begging me to collect her. The food was horrible, the room was horrible, the girls she was bunked in with were horribly unkind and she was worn out and hurting after an all-day cycle ride over rough terrain in the peak district. Phoebe assured me that her two closest friends would be bunking with her in France and I reluctantly agreed that she could go. I had no idea that I would come to regret that decision. She is not going on a school holiday next year!

After a few days at work and couple of days enjoying the sunshine in the garden at home, we went off to the archery competition we had been practising for, hosted by a club in Lincolnshire who always provide excellent catering. That saved me having to make a packed lunch before we set off. On an average archery shoot day, we tend to get up at around six in the morning, as most of the clubs are at least an hour's drive away and we need to check in by half past eight, so anything that means I get a bit of extra time in bed is good with me. We parked up in a bumpy field, scoffed the obligatory breakfast butties, paid our fee at the admin tent in exchange for score cards and set our bows up to begin the course. There was a good range of challenging targets catering for everyone from novice kids to experienced adults. Whenever I am rambling around woodlands, I cannot resist the urge to reach out and touch the trees around me. I don't know if the other archers notice or what they make of it, but frankly, I don't care. I like to make that connection with nature wherever I happen to be and often say out loud, hello Fern, hello Brother Oak, and I touch their leaves or lean upon their trunks. The whole day was good fun and we were put into a group with two members of our own club who had us laughing and joking all the way around. It was a bright, sunny day walking round the woods taking it in turns to shoot arrows at targets and at the end of the day we packed our equipment away and headed back to the admin tent to hear the scores being called out. Chris and I are only average archers, so we knew neither of us would have been placed but our two companions came first and second in their style categories and Phoebe got a second-place medal for her age and style group. Getting home at the end of a shoot at this time of year is much less hard work than in the winter, when it involves a lot of muddy boots, hot baths and drinks to warm up. This competition had been easy going and the weather was good, but after packing away all the bows and quivers and shuffling off heavy walking boots, I still needed a hot bath to ease my aching legs and hips after a long day of walking over rough ground. I added lavender and rosemary essential oils, Himalayan bath salts, and lit a couple of candles while I soaked in the tub. The lavender oil and candles both have relaxing, and soothing effects and the rosemary works to help get rid of muscular aches and tension as it has both anti-inflammatory and analgesic benefits.

Around this time, my friend Cayt got in touch and as we'd not seen each other for a while, we had a long overdue get together with coffee and cakes. After catching up on our latest news and gossip, Cayt revealed she had an ulterior motive for getting in touch. She has a small collection of dolls and takes an interest in the history and folklore of dolls too. After a particularly exciting bit of research, she decided this would make a great topic for a talk at Empyrean. I agreed – dolls, poppets and their spiritual and magical uses was a fascinating topic. However, I had to learn more of the history and legends I didn't already know, as Cayt was not intending to do this talk herself. She hadn't booked a speaker to do it either. No, that was my job, apparently. We set a date for the talk and I started forming my notes and researching the history of dolls.

Making dolls and poppets for rituals and spell casting was something I had been doing for decades, combining my craft skills with witchcraft and magic, so I had a good idea of what my own input would be, but I needed to research the history of dolls. My research led me to a magical world of mythology, folklore, legend, song and story; a world of hidden meanings, magic and fairy tales. A world where young people face up to incredible challenges with the help of a living doll imbued with energy, magic and agency. Not restricted to make-believe and play, dolls have been discovered in the earliest of human graves and have played a part in human development, teaching young children early caring skills, providing comfort in times of need and even as a teaching tool for valuable life-saving techniques. From paddle dolls, bisque dolls and corn dollies, to the rise of Barbie fashion dolls, ventriloquism dummies and eerie, life-like re-born dolls, there was a lot to go on. As the talk started to take shape, I faced the task of deciding which pieces of research to leave out; one hour is not enough to include everything and it would need considerable narrowing down to things of interest to a pagan-focused audience.

In the meantime, Lisa and I met up for another spiritual development class with a focus on shamanic drumming. Entering the hall, we were greeted warmly by our host and offered the use of aura sprays and smudging feathers to cleanse our auras before taking our seats. A range of percussion instruments, djembe and frame drums, rattles, bells, singing bowls, along with crystals and assorted decks of divination cards were arranged haphazardly in the centre of the room. Slowly, a heavy beat began to fill the room and Abby, leading the session, brought the drumming to a different beat and guided us through a pathworking exercise. Another time, another place, another state of being: pathworking can be highly detailed, precise and clear or – as it was this time – rather vague and seemingly unconnected and irrelevant to my circumstances.

The oracle cards passed around at the end of the evening were similarly disappointing, although Lisa was suitably pleased with the card she picked out – another lizard, very appropriate for her. The number of different oracle and tarot cards available today is staggering, though I prefer tarot to oracle cards. When I was fifteen, my sister gave me my first tarot set, the Tarot of the Cat People, designed and illustrated by Karen Kuykendall, and though I now have eight packs of tarot and several oracle cards, this remains one of my firm favourites. I hadn't used the Cat People deck for a few months and was disappointed when I took them out of their velvet pouch and unwrapped the cloth to find the cards had warped. I shuffled them and they were still useable, but for some reason they just did not feel right for me. I stored my cards carefully, away from any damp or cold, so I can only assume the powers that be are telling me it's time to move on. I selected one of my other sets, the Tarot of the Old Path, created by Sylvia Gainsford with contributions from some of today's leading authorities and teachers of witchcraft, and lay the cards out in the Celtic cross, a standard divination form, to see what the future might hold, writing notes on the reading in my tarot journal.

The final week of school rolled around – trip week. Phoebe and I had a very early start in the school car park and I nervously waved her off, best friends giggling with her, leaving with the other yawning parents who had braved a two o'clock start to the day. A week of peace and quiet – I was rather looking forward to it. I stumbled back to bed for a few hours before getting up again for work and later that afternoon I had a text from Phoebe.

Got sunburn very bad, it hurts so much, I hate France.

My heart raced; I was frantic. She had sun-tan lotion in her carry-on bag, why hadn't she put it on? Why hadn't the teachers been watching out for this? What were they doing about it? Typically, Phoebe was not answering her mobile. Another text:

Room horrible, sunburn soooo bad, it reeeally HURTS!

As a parent, you feel utterly lost and out of your depth when your child is suffering. I telephoned the school office, but they had no idea what was going on in France. There was nothing more I could do, and I felt completely helpless.

When I put it into context, you'll realise that I was not over-reacting. Well, maybe a little bit. A few weeks' previously Chris had told me about one of his work colleagues who had spent the day worried about his wife. She had been admitted to intensive care with third degree burns after sunbathing all day at home in Nottingham. Sunburn had given this poor lady such severe burns that she had been taken to the intensive care burns unit and faced the prospect of needing skin grafts on her shoulders – her face and her eyes had also been burned. In my head, claxons were blaring loudly: Phoebe needed urgent medical care and would be scarred for life. I left work early, upset and anxious, and the school had still not been in touch with the teachers who were looking after the students. I sat and fretted for hours. I may have found some unnecessary cleaning to keep myself busy until Chris came home.

It wasn't until late in the evening that Phoebe finally answered her phone. She was feeling slightly better after having a cool shower and putting cold cloths and flannels over her legs. With the weather lately being mostly warm, she had worn shorts and she and her two best friends, also pale-skinned with blonde hair, had sat on the outer deck of the ferry, completely exposed to the elements as they crossed the channel.

'You had sun tan lotion in your bag. Why on earth didn't you use it?'

'My friends both had jeans on, so they didn't use any and I just didn't think about it.'

'Send me a photo,' I insisted. 'I want to see how bad it is.'

'My battery is running low.' Phoebe told me, through her tears.

'What have the teachers said?'

'Keep it cool.' Great. Here I am hoping she won't need emergency treatment for burns and the teacher recommends keeping her legs cold. She hung up still in tears. I was in tears too. The next day I went off to work, tired from lack of sleep and worry. I had no more contact from Phoebe, despite my numerous texts to her throughout the day, until early evening.

'How are you feeling today?'

'Still hurts, but it's a bit better, and I've got jeans on now and long sleeves.'

'Keep it covered in cold cloths as often as you can.' I advised, knowing she probably wouldn't do, not if the initial stinging pain had eased off. Phoebe also stressed how horrible the food was but said that she and her friends were having a good time otherwise. I relaxed a bit. Only a bit. It was a long, long week with no further contact at all, but similarly no phone calls from hospitals or the school, and all I could do was wait it out. I was too upset to even think about helping Phoebe or myself with any witchy healing vibes.

Friday night came around and I drove up to the school at two in the morning to wait for the arrival of the coach. It was a long wait in the early hours of the morning before the coach arrived and sleepy-eyed teenagers clambered out, picking up their luggage and dashing off to waiting parents and guardians. I soon spotted the three blondies, grinning from ear to ear despite their tired faces; they shared big hugs as they said good night and then it was my turn. I swept Phoebe up into my arms, grabbed her bags and raced off home, full of tears and smiles in equal measure. I think she was as pleased to be home as I was to have her back, but it was very late, or early depending on your viewpoint, so we didn't have much of a catch up before bed. I did give her twenty questions on the state of her sunburn – her face and neck were reddened, though not worryingly so, and Phoebe assured me that her burned legs and arms were feeling much better. Reassured, I slept well for the first time all week.

The following morning, after she and I finally awoke and Chris had already left for work, I caught her coming out of the bathroom wrapped only in a towel and I was horrified at the sight of her bare legs. Her arms and shoulders weren't too bad, but her legs had turned a horrible dark purple-red colour and I slathered her in aloe vera. Fortunately, as the days wore on, the sunburn faded, but the event had left its mark, and even as I write this several years later, Phoebe still covers up her arms and legs at the merest hint of sunshine.

Dear daughter spent the next few days indoors, tucking herself away from the sun, while I applied aloe vera lotions to her skin every few hours like a deranged parent and she point-blank refused for me to give her any Reiki. I had a few days off work so that we could spend some time together at the beginning of the school summer holidays and when I finally managed to persuade her to come for a day out with me, she wore jeans and a long-sleeved blouse. We spent the day with Mum in Lincoln and took a long walk up Steep Hill to the Castle and Cathedral area. Lincoln Castle had recently been renovated and we explored the Magna Carta exhibition and scaled the heights of the castle walls. Looking down from the top of the castle walls made the castle quarter look very different, the steeply sloping rooftops jammed up against each other with timber frames and narrow, cobbled streets in every direction. The Magna Carta itself is now housed in a glass case and although the fading manuscript is hard to decipher, I still got a tingle down my spine as I gazed at this carefully preserved piece of important history.

Chris persuaded me to go the Thursday group where this time, the focus was meditations with angelic masters. He thought it would be good for me to get out of the house and focus on something other than Phoebe, sun burn and aloe vera. The word angel to describe spiritual beings does not sit easily with me. I'm not an angel worker, I'm a witch and pagan, and have always associated angels with organised religions and especially Christian beliefs. I was curious as to what exactly this experience would involve and knowing the group has such a well-intentioned facilitator with a genuine and peaceful spirituality about her in Abby, I thought I'd give it a go.

A large white cloth adorned with geometric, astrological and occult symbols was laid on the floor, scattered with shards of rose and clear quartz crystals, the lights were low, and an atmospheric CD of new-age music played softly in the background. We were guided into a state of relaxation and Abby started to speak to her unseen spirit guides, asking them to channel to us a being she described as an Ascended Master.

I closed my eyes, put aside my doubts, and focused on my breathing, making a conscious effort to relax. After a short time, I had the distinct impression of a tall, ethereal entity standing over us in the centre of the room. This being that I could sense but not see was green-hued, tall and wispy, with no distinct material shape. I felt a sensation or aura of calm and love spread through the room and a wave of energy emanated from the wispy light. We were invited to meditate for a while with this being watching over us, sharing its presence and higher vibration. The room was silent and still and eventually, Abby announced that our guest, the Ascended Master, was fading and asked each of us to offer our thanks and blessings to the entity. The sensation of this being faded slowly and I opened my eyes, coming back to the here and now. Instead of joining in with coffee and conversation with the other members of the group, I sat quietly, reflecting on my experience. I won't say that an angel or an ascended master visited us that night, as I'm not certain what this being was, but I do think there was a presence of some kind. Something beautiful and loving, outside of normal human awareness, had made itself known and given everybody there in that moment a sense of peace and comfort.

Whatever you want to call it, angel, spirit, elemental, Julian, it's not the name that was important, I think, but what we each experienced and that's good enough for me. I am still not comfortable with the word angel in relation to my own beliefs and when someone tells me they work with angels, I remind myself that they are referring to a spirit of light and goodness, and that gives me a frame of reference that I can relate to.

The end of July ran into the first weekend of August and the festival of Lughnasadh. I had booked tickets for a weekend pagan festival where I had been asked to run a workshop. Chris had to work on the Friday, but Phoebe and I arrived on the Thursday night to set up camp for the weekend. The checking-in procedure was a fiasco, as our names were not on their list of pre-booked campers and they were over booked so didn't have room for us. I politely told the person at the gate I wouldn't be able to run the workshop they had asked me to do and as I had my tickets with me, who could I approach for a refund? (Yes, you heard correctly: I had paid for tickets even though they had approached me with the invitation of giving a talk for free. I do wish organisers would treat all of their speakers with fairness and respect, not just those who are more well-known.)

The volunteers let me in with a half-hearted apology. We spent nearly half an hour looking for a pitch large enough to squeeze our tents into, luckily one lady from the local moots had saved us a small space, but the sheer volume of tents all jammed into the field meant it took that long to find her. I had to clear dog-mess out of the way before we could put the tent up. So far, I was not impressed. Our first night at the camp was spent with around twenty people I'd never met pitching their fire pit right outside our tent, as they vaguely knew the lady who had saved us a spot. This wasn't quite as bad as it sounds, because out of the blue a couple of old friends I'd not seen for years turned up to join in the fireside conversation and Phoebe seemed to get on well with two other teenagers who were there. The night got dark quickly and brought with it an onslaught of rain that was to last the entire weekend.

Circle Time

For a solitary circle when time is limited, try this crystal grid meditation and an instant crystal circle for protection. Crystal grids are a fast-spreading phenomenon among the spiritual community, though not necessarily among pagans or witches. An assortment of crystals are placed in a grid-like display, usually with a larger crystal as a centre point. There are thousands of websites and books you can browse to find out what crystals to use for different purposes, and whatever you come up with yourself will be fine too. There's no need to spend a fortune on crystals. I love using those tiny quartz needle-points that cost about ten pence each, this way I can get a whole handful for a few pounds. If in doubt about which crystal to use, clear quartz or rose quartz are always a good choice.

Start with a single crystal in the centre of your space and place three or four other pieces around it. Place one crystal in front of you, one to your left and one to your right. Sitting or standing in the centre of the crystal triangle, use your hands to draw a ring from each of these three crystals to the next, creating an instant circle around you. Connecting the crystals in this circle will form your sacred space to activate and enhance the frequencies emitting from the other stones. Hold your hands over the central crystal in the grid, your palms facing you to direct the energies and vibrations of the crystals into your aura.

The outer crystals will feed into the central one, like rivers feeding into the sea. Continue directing the energy to your aura, soaking up the beneficial vibes, and to finish, place your palms together to close the energy flow. Gather up the crystals and pop them into a cloth pouch on your bedside table or under the pillow overnight. After this, you can keep them on your altar until next time, where their constant vibrations will contribute to any spell workings or meditations you do.

Mojo Bags

Charm bags are an easy way of bringing magic into your everyday life. They can be hung around the home, stowed in the car's glove box, tucked into your bag, or worn on a leather thong as a pendant under your shirt. Although the word Mojo comes from Houdou practise, it is filled with power and mystery and colloquial use of the word suggests a type of personal power or vitality – I've lost my mojo, I've got my mojo back – that we cannot do without. Traditional mojo bags are made from red flannel and contain lucky roots, herbs, graveyard soil and small bones, depending on the goal.

Use herbs, rings, small coins and tiny toys to symbolise your desires, seeds, dried flowers, crystals, herbs and spices that align with your wishes. Put all of these into a small cloth pouch, consecrate and charge it on your altar and carry it with you as you go about your ordinary business, knowing that your mojo is working for you.

Try these examples to get your mojo started:

Confidence and Success Mojo Bag

To bring you confidence, success and good luck.

Orange or gold charm bag
Dried marigold or sunflower petals
Saffron
Cinnamon stick
Ginger
Amber or Citrine crystal
Slip of paper with your request written on it

Love and Passion Mojo Bag

To attract romantic love and spicy passion into your life.

Red charm bag
Rose quartz
Rose petals

Pink or red hearts cut from felt or card
A ring
A small phallic or lotus representation
Damiana oil (dab it onto a scrap of red cloth or paper)

Protection from the Evil Eye Mojo Bag

This may be a cliché, but I couldn't resist including a more traditional use for a mojo bag. To avoid thorns poking through this charm bag, a tough fabric or leather pouch may be necessary. Burn sandalwood incense while charging this protective amulet.

Blackthorn or hawthorn needles or rose thorns
Iron pyrite
Angelica root
Small mirror tile
Dried nettle leaves
Red pepper seeds
Hand of Fatima charm

August

A Song for the Season: It's a Beautiful Day, The Levellers

August brings warm days filled with excitement, late nights with friends around campfires, barbecues on the patio with a chiminea, live music, sunshine, clear views of the stars outdoors on long, warm nights, and the joy of pagan festivals. The fields all around the village are turning golden with rapeseed and corn, birds are fat-bellied and chattering all around, cats laze contentedly in the sunshine, stretching long limbs over bright grass to soak in the warmth. Brightly blooming flowers fill gardens and hedgerows with colour, the golden sun beams down to warm the earth and overhead the sky is blue and clear.

Summer camps are among my favourite ways to the pass time but the Lughnasadh gathering in Derbyshire isn't one I shall dwell on for long. My workshop on energy and elemental magic was scheduled for ten o'clock and I duly arrived at ten minutes early. I expected a few late comers, this was a pagan camp after all, but people were still walking into the marquee at half-past ten, one of whom asked me to re-cap from the beginning. I carried on, explaining that I didn't want to over-run my time-slot for the next speaker and, in any case, my session was already half-way through. I did get some unnecessary back-lash from that person, who stormed out of the marquee, shouting about what a terrible speaker I was, and didn't I understand that camps run on 'pagan-mean-time'?

Phoebe and I spent the rest of the day with two people we knew from the moots, as they had a large awning in which we took shelter from the hammering rain, keeping spirits up with frequents servings of coffee and hot chocolate along with good company and conversation. Chris joined us after he finished work and during the few shorts breaks in the rain, we managed to take part in a couple of craft workshops. Phoebe and I made flowered head-dresses and she had a go at smelting an iron pendant before spending some time with the small group of teenagers she'd met. The organisers had provided some entertainment for the final evening, though we struggled to listen to the music over the cacophony of screeching children, car speakers, and baying dogs.

We were glad to be packing up on Sunday morning, although it wasn't until this point that Chris and I met a nice seeming couple who were camped near us. They were also feeling let down by the camp and were leaving early to take part in Pagan Pride in Nottingham later that same afternoon. We had a friendly chat with them both, admiring their trailer tent, before we loaded the car and drove home.

I was disappointed and surprised that, with it being advertised specifically as a Lammas camp, there hadn't been a celebratory ritual for the Sabbat at the festival. Chris and I found a quiet spot in Sherwood Forest for our own rite to mark the turning of the wheel. Lughnasadh, or Lammas, is a celebration of the first harvest, the blossoming trees and flowers, the sun God, Lugh, and the altar is adorned with corn sheaves, flowers, berries and freshly baked bread. Sherwood Forest is a tourist trap in summer, full of families and ice-cream wrappers during the day, but at night, it is quiet and still. The branches of a large, old yew tree, surrounded by holly, hung low to create a small, hidden sanctuary, and here I laid a small cloth from my travelling altar kit on the ground. Our rite for the season was short and simple: breaking bread, toasting with mead, giving thanks.

After a mundane week at work and with Phoebe away with her dad, Chris and I were camping again. It would be our first time at The Artemis Gathering, organised by the Children of Artemis, and I was looking forward to it very much. The reviews were all complimentary and the programme had been announced far enough in advance for me to get excited about some the talks and workshops on the extensive schedule.

From the moment we arrived at the gate, it was evident that this festival was going to be a complete contrast to the previous one. The organisation was tight and the Dagda, who provide security and marshals for some of the large-scale pagan events across the country, were helpful, friendly, and polite. The entertainment was outstanding, with live music every evening and there were so many workshops put on that I had a tough time deciding which ones to choose. Once our tent was up, complete with bunting and solar lights around the canopy, we sat with a cuppa, enjoying the sunshine. Next to us, a young couple arrived with a handful of marshals in tow and proceeded to pitch up a small tent. Chris noticed our new neighbours both had white canes. Curious, we ventured over to say hello. Toby and Elaine, both completely blind, were on their first ever camping trip and after the introductions were out of the way, we asked them to call on us if they needed anything.

This was probably the best experience of the entire weekend; Elaine and I became friends and exchanged contact details to keep in touch. She linked her arm in mine to visit the toilet block, the Dagda kept in constant contact with the couple via walkie-talkie, and every time Elaine needed anything there was always somebody there to help her.

One afternoon I spread a picnic blanket on the ground between our tents and Toby, Elaine, and myself sat chatting in the warm sunshine, surrounded by the tweeting of birds and the occasional bumble bee. Toby talked to me about his deep love of music, the way it captures his soul. He plays drums, keyboard, piano and guitar and writes his own music, while Elaine is not quite as musical, playing only guitar, but she is powerful singer and song writer. Both of them feel the power of the words and the musical harmonies flowing in their souls and they described the sensation of sound in ways that I, as a sighted person, could not begin to understand. Elaine had another talent that I had noticed over the weekend and I asked her about it because I was overwhelmed by it.

'Every time you've needed to go somewhere, there is someone passing by who happens to be going that way.' I observed. 'And whatever you need, it's suddenly right in front of you, you seem to just know that everything will be there, as and when you need it.'

'I believe in the law of attraction,' she told me. 'I read 'The Secret' – I love audiobooks – and it made sense. It was backing up what I've always known. I believe the universe is a higher power that is there to support me and if I'm positive and optimistic, then things always work out the way that works best for me.'

'That's exactly it,' Toby confirmed, 'if Elaine needs to go somewhere, she asks out loud if anyone is there and there always is. And that person is always willing to help her. She's like a miracle worker, she's got utter faith in the universe.' He smiled a broad smile and turned his head to face the direction he knew she was seated in, and even though they couldn't physically 'see' each other, the love on Toby's face was unmistakable.

'I'm more comfortable away from home.' Elaine continued, 'I'm always worried about bumping into things or knocking things off shelves or tables at home, but outside, there's plenty space for me to move around. I have my stick and I go places I'm familiar with on my own or with Toby, but if I want to go somewhere else my carer takes me, or I just ask out loud once I shut the front door behind me and I know that I'll be taken care of. Someone is always there for me. We get exactly what we expect, and I expect to have people I can trust and who will be friendly and helpful, so that's what I get.'

We agreed to meet later by the main arena, where the market stalls were set up, for a shopping trip. Before that, I was determined to make time for a workshop with Kevin Groves on scrying and divination by the fire circle. Kevin is instantly likeable, and his magical principals are easy to grasp and interspersed with a healthy dose of common sense and logic. He follows a very unique pagan path with an Egyptian focus and through it all, he weaves threads of cyber magic, thought-forms, scrying, chaos magic. This blending of traditions and ideas is much in line with my own style of magic, which goes along the general principle of: if it works, keep doing it, if it doesn't work, try something else. Chaos magic and technology entered the conversation, along with off-the-wall ways of using everyday objects as tools for divination, including the spinning cycle of a washing machine and melting Neapolitan ice-cream. Kevin talked about more commonly used forms of natural divination too, watching a burning fire or observing the flight of birds. Kevin expressed his disappointment that the fire circle we were sitting around was not lit and told us about his practise of fire divination, which included him demonstrating something with a brick.

After Kevin's talk, I wandered back to the main arena and recognised one of the Nottingham pagan crowd, Ashley Mortimer. Ashely can be – let's say talkative – and at any given point at events he can normally be found deeply engrossed in conversations, accompanied by bursts of raucous laughter. He's probably grinning as he reads this – I'm confident this is a good sign, which is fortunate, as he agreed to publish Living Witchcraft with Fenix Flames. He was tending the stall for the Doreen Valiente Foundation and the Centre for Pagan Studies. Hmm, when say 'tending' the stall, I really mean that he was deeply engrossed in a hearty conversation with one of the speakers. He smiled and called out to me, so I ambled over say hello and the three of us talked, animatedly discussing one witchy topic or another, until I realised I had lost track of time. I was supposed to be meeting Elaine. I turned to look around the arena and spotted her with one of the Dagda marshals. I made my goodbyes and sprinted over to join her. The happy Dagda was being led around by Elaine, who was reaching out to touch and hold the various crystals, fossils and rocks that were laid out on a crystal stall. The stall holder was amused by her random questions as her quick, light touch led her to ask:

'What's this one? What about this one? This feels like a tree.'

'Spot on,' the gentleman told her. 'It's a piece of fossilised wood.'

'Oh!' she beamed. 'I was right. Ha! Wait till I tell Toby.' Her enthusiasm and general happiness were infectious. She handed the marshal, a friendly, dreadlocked man, another bag full of her purchases and took his elbow to move on to something else. While she and I decided to browse a bit longer, the marshal tagged happily along with us, nudging Elaine towards one thing or another that he thought she might like. The sunshine was brilliant and warm and enticing music was coming from the main marquee. Elaine and I went inside to hear it more clearly. I spotted a row of seats near the stage area and led Elaine to sit beside me so that we could share the experience of listening. I described what was going on to her – a beautiful and lithe young woman dancing to the music, and the musician's very unique didgeridoo. Around ten feet long, the bottom end billowed out into a wide funnel and it was handsomely carved. At his feet were several percussion instruments, which he sounded intermittently along with his skilful and continuous playing of the didgeridoo. It was just a glorious hour or so sitting with this peaceful woman, who seemed like a good friend after just one day together, with a slice of divine music. There were very few people in the marquee as talks and workshops were still taking place elsewhere and it felt as though the entire performance was put on just for those few of us who happened to be there at that one moment.

After Chris and I had been back to our base camp for dinner, we headed off again for a sound meditation. People were lying on the floor of a small scout hut, shuffling to get comfortable. As soon as Elaine and Toby walked in to join us, without anyone saying a word, enough space was made for them to lie down along with everyone else. Another incident to prove her firm belief in the power attraction in action.

'Hello Elaine, it's Moira, I'm right beside you.'

'Oh, I'm so happy to see you.' I had already learned that when Elaine is full of happiness, she cannot help but express it. 'Is there a dog in here?' She asked me. 'I'm sure there is.'

'Yes, a woman has brought her dog into the room, it's not that far away from you.'

How she had known this is beyond my ken, as neither dog nor owner had made any noise; the dog was not barking, sniffing, or even panting. Elaine's hearing must have been better than mine, perhaps the dog had made some tiny snuffling noise, or maybe she could pick up on its subtle, doggy odour. She has a deep affinity and love of animals and especially dogs. After the dog had its fuss from Elaine, the workshop began and everybody lay still and quiet as the didgeridoo played continually, with waves and vibrations of ethereal sound washing over us all. The acoustics of the hall made it haunting and ethereal at times. Toby told me later that he might well be tempted to add the didgeridoo to his list of favourite sounds.

Not all the speakers over the weekend were well-known, but they were all knowledgeable and well-versed in their chosen topics. Professor Ronald Hutton gave fascinating insights on the history and function of Labyrinths from a pagan point of view. He is always an eloquent and informative speaker and has a very pleasing voice, one which I could listen to all day, given the chance. I enjoyed the witch's question panel and wondered, briefly, how many questions I could get away with asking. I shuddered at the thought of being put 'on-the-spot' as part of a panel - little did I know that the following year, I would be on that very panel and hosting my own talks at both the Artemis Gathering and Witchfest.

Live music in the evening included Damh the Bard and The Dolmen and the marquee was now heaving with pagans, witches, druids, heathens and more. Chris and I thoroughly enjoyed it all. I knew I'd regret it later, when my hips reminded me that I shouldn't, but I did have a good dance to The Dolmen.

The following day I listened to talk on wicca, defined as Gardnerian and Alexandrian traditions, rather than progressive, independent or eclectic witchcraft. It was very informative and most of the people I met and chatted to over the weekend belonged to initiatory wiccan covens, although there were plenty of eclectic witches too, as well as those who were just starting to find their way on the path. The Children of Artemis team were altogether warm and welcoming and it felt like we belonged to something larger than us, something akin to family.

The highlight of the Saturday evening was the burning of a massive wicker sculpture and a good old-fashioned pagan sing-along, which I loved joining in with. I do sometimes wish pagan chants were done with a bit more enthusiasm, however. 'We all come from the Goddess' can sound more like a funeral dirge than a joyous celebration of the fact. We all come from the Goddess? Let's try to sound happy about it, then!

On the final morning of camp, we walked over to the main marquee with Elaine and Toby and found them seats where they could sit with breakfast from the Artemis Café while me and Chris strolled around, talking to people here and there at the various stalls and the healing tent. Kevin Groves was standing in an open area nearby, chatting to a few people and waved us over. He recognised me from his workshop the previous day.

'You'll like this, Moira.' Kevin stood back and gestured at the ground. Before us lay a large rope labyrinth. Well, I couldn't turn down the opportunity to walk a labyrinth after Ronald Hutton's talk, and it had been years since I'd had the chance to do so. This turned out to be a very interesting and, ultimately, inspiring experience.

The labyrinth can be used as a meditative walk, a journey to the centre seeking guidance, a time for quiet reflection, a chance to walk in with a question and receive answers on the way back out. When I finished, Kevin spent a few minutes quietly standing at each quarter of the labyrinth and then stood back, arms folded, a broad and cheeky grin plastered across his face. He gestured for me to walk the labyrinth again. I wound my way around the circular path and noticed subtle differences of energy in each of the places Kevin had stood. At the entrance to the labyrinth, this was particularly weird and noticeable. A slightly forceful feeling came over me, a pressure of some indiscernible kind. I couldn't quite identify whether this energy was welcoming me or try to push me out. When I returned to each of these energy fields on the way out of the labyrinth, I had a clear sense of being ushered on my way with a psychic wave of farewell.

'Tell me then.' Kevin said. I described my experience and he laughed. 'Yeah, they like people to enjoy it, but they are used to it only being me in there, so they like to make sure you do actually leave.' Unknown to me, he had invoked the four Egyptian Goddesses that he works with, one at each cardinal point around the perimeter. His primary deity was the one standing guard at the entrance.

After a few more conversations and time for a final workshop, we reluctantly went back to our tent. Packing up to leave that Sunday afternoon left me in a strange state of mind. Being with large numbers of pagan-oriented, witchy folk means a lot to me, especially when they are as welcoming and friendly as the people who go to and organise the Artemis Gathering. It touches something deep in my soul and makes me feel loved and at one with everybody. I couldn't help feeling sad that our weekend was over. Driving home after a festival is always an odd occasion and the first service station with its noise, chaos and demanding environment, is in complete contrast to the peace and friendship of a good festival. Adjustments are necessary.

Mundane Mondays are a let-down after such a great weekend, though this one was made brighter when I took a short walk with some of my colleagues at lunch time to the local supermarket, where I picked up almost nine pounds in weight of parsnips, at the bargain price of just seventy pence for the lot. They were still fresh and I spent a couple of hours at home that night chopping and boiling them, adding vast quantities of sugar, and then sorting the resulting liquid into sterilised demi johns with wine yeast and a cup of tea. This would be enough to make approximately twelve bottles of wine and it would be ready for bottling in time for the winter solstice. The cup of tea that I add to home-brew wine is full of tannin, which most wines need, but it's taken on more significance for me. If I have a guest in my home, I offer them food and drink and make them welcome. Giving the wine a cup of tea feels much the same to me, as if I'm making the wine feel welcome, giving it a kick-start to the fermentation process.

Chris's working pattern was a bit skewed with holidays and shift-swaps, so Phoebe and I spent a couple of days visiting my mum over in Lincoln while he was working. Mum's a lot like me, always making something. This time it was a crocheted quilt in brightly-coloured squares, which she was sewing together in diagonal stripes to form a rainbow pattern. I cooed over it for a while and remembered the quilt that I still have up in the box room, waiting to be finished. The merest thought of the darned thing is enough for me to renew my determination to leave it there, but at least the awkward sewing was done. I resolved to thrash out of the rest of the design and complete it over the coming winter months.

Another August weekend, another trip away. Cram the car boot full of tents, chairs and bedding and off we go, this time to sunny Cornwall. We had a couple of days on assorted Cornish beaches in the glorious sun and walked across the causeway from

Marazion to Saint Michael's Mount. The causeway to the island was still deep in water, but a few hardy souls were managing to walk over anyway. We followed, shoes in hand and trousers rolled up as high as they would go, but we still ended up getting wet, which Phoebe thought was hilarious. Next time, I'm waiting until the tide has gone right out. Saint Michael's Mount is a beautiful, sloping hill of ornamental gardens with a castle seated at the top. We had just come out of the building when a heavy rain shower came down and we ducked back inside until it stopped. I didn't have a problem with this, but it did eat into our time and we had to miss out on exploring the beautiful gardens surrounding the castle on the island.

We visited Newquay for lunch and strolled around the town where we found a tourist gift shop with a surprising array of witchy things on display toward the back of the shop, away from the castle-shaped buckets and sticks of rock. I found a delightful tarot set there, the Labyrinth deck by Luis Royo. The shop assistant refused to let me take off the cellophane wrapper in order to check if the pictures on the cards were good as the ones on the box. I took a risk and put them in my basket, dismissing the more commercial and well-known decks.

It doesn't seem that long ago that my sister gave me my first tarot set. The Tarot of the Cat People is a striking deck, especially back then, the year I turned fifteen, when there were only two or three popular decks to choose from and even those were hard to find in the sleepy small town where I had grown-up. Times have moved on and the shelf in this commercial sea-side tourist shop carried around twenty tarot decks and dozens of oracle cards. Themes of these decks included vampires, witches, black cats, pirates, fairies, and even a steam-punk tarot set. Fortunately, I get on well with the Labyrinth deck and the pictures on the cards are as beautiful as suggested by the outside of the box.

Phoebe loves beach combing, as does my dear husband, and while they rambled and clambered over rock pools I sat and read for a while, enjoying the warmth of the sun and the endless blue sky, dry golden sand between my toes.

One place we all wanted to visit was St. Nectan's Glen, a stunning waterfall situated roughly half-way between Tintagel and Boscastle. A peaceful, gently sloping walk leads to the glen, long and winding and full of beauty. A shallow, sparkling stream runs through a long, narrow woodland, where dips and shallows beneath the trees suggest the hidden places of the Fae and one can imagine easily the night-time creatures of the Other Worlds emerging from underground burrows and lairs, ready to play in the thick undergrowth. Walking down the mossy steps cut into the sheer, rocky face of the cliff from which the waterfall cascades, the vibrating noise of the water, a constant presence on that long journey, becomes strangely quiet as the steps reach the bottom and open into an area full of silence. The stream here is shallow, bounded on either side by dark, craggy rocks, and gnarled trees covered in moss; the silence is palpable. To the left, immediately beyond the rock wall into which the steps are hewn, a thin path curves out of sight.

The path leads to torrents of rushing water, droplets of spray gushing into the air in a bright array of sunlit rainbows and the roar, tremors, and gushing weight of the water falling from far above, rushes to meet the eardrums in a continual, thunderous hum.

Dozens of carefully balanced pebble structures are placed on larger stones that sit above the river and multi-coloured clooties hang on branches from every tree. There are pictures, drawings, poetry, photographs and epitaphs adorning crevices in the cliff and the trees sparkle and glisten with a myriad of crystals, coins, rings, pendants and other small offerings and effigies, left for the ancestors, the Fae, the Old Ones and the Beloved Dead.

We built our own small, stone cairns, took off shoes and socks to immerse our feet in the sparkling but incredibly cold water.

Glorious! Phoebe became engrossed in carefully placing stones on top of each other in a miniature cairn and Chris was happy in his own little world, thinking, I imagine, of inconsequential things. I moved away from them, following the edge of the cliff to a spot where I was hidden from view. I stood in front of the waterfall and was completely in its thrall. Nobody in the world could see me and nobody could hear me either, not over the thunderous roar of the water. It was a very blissful, private moment and I spent a while taking it in and then, looking at the offerings of trinkets, crystals, photographs and coins left here by others, I removed one of the crystal chip bracelets I habitually wear and placed it reverently into a small crevice in the rock face. A silent thanks to the Goddess for all the things I am grateful for.

As well as the breath-taking glen, we normally visit the Witchcraft Museum on our jaunts to Cornwall. If you haven't been to the museum, now called the Museum of Witchcraft and Magic, it's not to be missed if you're in the vicinity. There are displays, exhibits and information on virtually every aspect of witchcraft, from early medieval times right up to current events. There are examples of the devices used as torture in the early witch-hunts, posters of glamorous witches advertising everything from soap to chocolate, there are witches' ropes – tied three times for sailors to whistle up the wind - exhibitions of tools, photographs and grimoires of well-known modern witches. I bought a couple of souvenirs including a new besom and a witch pencil topper, now housed in my desk-tidy at work. The museum hadn't changed much since our last visit, but I could still have spent far longer there than anyone would consider reasonable and Chris reminded me of the time we visited with his sister and her daughter.

This was a few years previously, when Chris's niece was in her early teens and we were visiting the museum together. The displays included torture devices, chains, and a ducking stool, and it had left her quite anxious and upset, as pagan beliefs were something that she was starting to show an interest in, and this had spooked her. My sister-in-law asked if I'd mind going around the museum with them and discussing some of the exhibition pieces with her daughter, which I was happy to do. I tried to explain the difference between what used to be practised and how things have moved on today, putting things into context to help her understand things. Describing the more interesting and less frightening aspects of the museum pieces helped her to appreciate that this was a celebration of how things had changed and a respectful honouring of the past, as well as a reminder of the past. We moved on to other areas of the museum and by the time we made our way upstairs to a room of more modern displays, a few other people had gathered to listen and I realised I'd inadvertently become an impromptu tour guide. By the time we left, our niece had a better understanding of paganism and witchcraft and was taking a much brighter view of what she saw.

Time to say farewell to Cornwall as we took down our tent and loaded the car with camping gear and headed straight off for Glastonbury, where we had arranged to meet some friends for a long weekend before returning home. Remarkably, we had our tent set up and feeling like home away from home in time for dinner that evening. We lent a hand pitching up more tents as our friends arrived and before long, we were all sat around our new fire-pit, enjoying the sound of birds, children giggling on the playground, and our camping neighbours getting on with their evening. The campsite we stayed at is one that Chris and I visit often, just outside Glastonbury and very close the ancient oak trees named Gog and Magog. These magnificent trees, thought to be over two thousand years old and once making up part of the original avenue that led to the tor itself, are, like dozens of sacred locations honoured by pagans, were festooned with offerings of brightly coloured clooties, sparkling items of jewellery and trinkets, tiny dream catchers, twig-twisted pentagrams and photographs or poems, left by visitors as reminders and markers.

A lazy evening talking and swapping tarot readings, cooing over crystals and telling jokes by the campfire was followed by an early morning and the inevitable climb up Glastonbury tor. I had planned for this and brought my hiking poles with me so that I could manage the steep slope. I wasn't the only one struggling and everyone else took it in turns to carry Jack: he normally runs everywhere at a hundred miles an hour, but this climb had beaten even him. Neither Lisa or John had been to Glastonbury before and were awed by the magnificent views at the top, the perpetual, persistent wind, and the contrasting silence that cuts out that whistling wind as you enter the tower. The fabled Isle of Avalon spreads below the tor and when low lying mists sweep over the land, the mound of the tor rises high above it; disconnected and isolated, it sits apart from time and place.

Chalice Well Gardens, a short walk from the path leading up to the tor itself, is a delightful and sacred place; a rambling and well-tended garden with areas set aside for private contemplation, prayer or meditation. Sitting beneath an old apple tree at the top of the meadow with Chris, enjoying the beautiful sunshine, we were joined by robins and blackbirds while the rest of our group were getting their feet wet in the shallow healing pool of ice-cold spring water. Set into the shadiest area of the gardens, the small pool never seems to get above freezing point and the amount of iron-enriched water constantly flowing through makes the bottom of the pool treacherous underfoot. Phoebe, Lisa and John were splashing and giggling, and I took off my sandals and joined them, instantly wondering, as the freezing cold water hit my skin, what on earth had made me think it was a good idea. After a very short splash, I joined Sarah with Jack, who didn't want wet feet, on the nearby bench. A popular draw here, of course, is the spring water that gushes continually from a lion headed fountain, stained red by the iron-rich water. We filled our water bottles from the fountain before we left.

Another pleasant evening at the campfire, cooking a variety of goodies on portable barbecue grills, left us with full bellies and happy hearts and we were set for another night outdoors in warm weather gazing at the stars. The morning saw us all up early, thanks to the chorus of birds in the hedges, and after breakfast we paid a visit to Glastonbury town centre. Phoebe, who doesn't display any overt pagan tendencies, surprised me by displaying some very overt pagan tendencies, picking up virtually every crystal in every shop, smoothing them in her hands to decide which ones felt right. It reminded me of a conversation with a crystal supplier I knew some years ago. He was amused by the countless visitors to his shop, when he would casually observe customers laboriously assessing the healing or emotional properties of each stone, handling dozens of different crystals, before returning to the very first one they had picked up when they entered the shop. Phoebe was happy with a few large chunks of rose quartz and a short selenite wand.

Being both pagan and a book-worm, I was seduced by a book shop on the High Street and came away with a carrier bag full of volumes with a witchy, shamanic or pagan theme of some kind. A few of the books were novels, but most were non-fiction, to be used as study guides and learning aids. Even after decades of witchcraft practise, there will always be more to learn: from history and mythology, to practical applications of magic and the inner work of self-development.

Our weekend in Glastonbury came to an end and with it, the end of August. I knew that the following week would be a return to the familiar routines of work, school, laundry, archery on a Tuesday and more laundry, but packing away the camp this time didn't bring me that same sense of mild melancholy that I had felt on leaving the Artemis Gathering. There is a part of me that likes a return to familiar routines; it gives me a base on which to stand, a place to be centred and normal, even if I do miss the luxury of free time.

The summer months may have been drawing to an end, but there were still plenty of good times and sunny days ahead as the year slowly progressed towards early autumn.

A Craft for the Season: Aura Sprays

Wisps of incense can trigger asthma or allergies, and setting off a smoke alarms is always a risk. These aura sprays are useful for any environment where incense and smudging are off-limits.

Basic Necessities:

Spray bottle – glass or plastic, to be re-used
Water
Essential Oils
Herbs, flowers, tiny crystals
Vodka

Pour the water in a bottle or jug and leave on the windowsill for twenty-four hours to soak up the lunar and solar energy. Add crystals if you are using them.

Stir in ten drops of good quality essential oil and small amounts of relevant herbs or plants to infuse in the mixture.

Important tip: Make sure you strain this through fine muslin before use, as spray nozzles can get clogged with herbs.

Pour the finished aura spray into small bottles fitted with a spray or atomiser lid and add a small amount of vodka to act as a preservative.

Aura sprays can be consecrated and blessed in ritual and channelled with Reiki or magical energy to charge them up for added effect.

Label the spray with a list of ingredients so that each blend can be re-created easily when you run out. Experiment with different aromas, oils, herbs and crystals to best suit your purposes, but here's a rough outline of my favourites.

Deep aura cleansing – clary sage or white sage, pine oil, smoky quartz.

Revitalising aura spray – sweet orange oil, neroli oil, lemon balm leaves, citrine crystal.

Peace and meditation spray – lavender oil, rose oil, lavender flowers, amber crystal.

A Craft for the Season: Spirit Duster

Usually labelled as smudging fans or smudging feathers, these fans are often made with feathers from birds of prey or rare breed birds. The wooden handles are decorated with pyrography sigils, crystals and beads, but this attention to detail comes at a price. Making your own spirit duster (see September to find out where that name comes from) is easy and cheap, or even free.

Country parks, lakes and woodlands are good areas to spot a variety of feathers in different sizes and colours that appeal to you. You might gather a collection over a couple of months and choose the best ones, or perhaps you will find just two or three that immediately feel right.

You will also need a small, sturdy branch or a piece of sea or river driftwood – anything around four-to-six-inches in length should be fine.

Bring this all inside and put it on your altar along with wool, ribbon, cord or string to tie it together. With a little imagination and a few scraps of yarn, strips of leather or copper wire, and some crystals or beads, you can bind the feathers onto the shaft of the stick or branch and use your creative flair to make an attractive spirit duster with very little outlay. If you are not creative or prefer something plain, use some natural string or twine to tie the feathers to the branch – it will work just as well as something that has been elaborately designed with an ancient yew branch and golden eagle feathers. If you have any problems securing the feathers into place, don't hesitate to use a glue gun.

The glue will be transparent when it dries and you can cover any bumps or blobs with ribbons and threads.

To make the creation of your working tools a more magical process, you could set up a sacred space before you start and, once complete, bless and consecrate the finished product.

Use your new fan with aura sprays, incense and smudging bundles to cleanse your aura and brush away anything which does not belong there.

September

Leaves once aglow with glistening sheen,
Soon to lose their summer green,
As autumn brings its magic to bear,
To gift the trees with gold to wear.

Fledgling birds now fully grown,
Are pushed away to fend alone,
The time is now to feed and fill,
To fatten and grow against the chill.

A balance is struck, equinox returns,
To match the night to the day that burns,
Briefly though as the dark has won,
The long hours of light, its course is run.

The woodlands are aflame with auburn and brown,
As the land is enwrapped in its autumn gown,
All beings re-affirm the will to survive,
From deer in the glen to bees in the hive.

Time marches on to close the ring,
As everything knows what winter may bring:
Endless days of snow and hoar,
When all creatures shiver and bar their door.

(Neil Page)

September brings the autumn equinox, marking the change of the season and although the nights are starting to draw in, the weather is warm and the leaves have not quite started to change colour, from green to red, to gold, to brown, have not yet begun to fall; warm evenings are still be enjoyed, an abundance of berries ripen in the hedgerows, on farms and allotments, tall standing corn is ready for harvest, the change of the season is subtle, gentle, and slips by almost unnoticed.

August was a time of holiday and relaxation and now there's a rush of change and activity in the air that presses on me with a sense of urgency. I needed to prepare for a course of five sessions I was going to be running later this month. The community hall venue I'd hired would not allow candles or incense, so I used some of the chalice well water I'd brought back from Glastonbury to make some new aura sprays, leaving them on the windowledge for twenty-four hours to stand in the light of the full moon and absorb the power of the sun. I had several late evenings working to finalise my notes for the talk on dolls and poppets at Empyrean this month. I don't normally get nervous when I'm doing talks or workshops - I've been doing it for a long time now and usually know my subjects reasonably well, though I never profess to be an expert on anything. I enjoy talking to a rapt, attentive audience (at least I hope they are rapt and attentive) and I normally speak with confidence. This one, however, was not one of my chosen topics and I didn't feel particularly knowledgeable or familiar enough with the subject matter. The research was fascinating and engrossing and I had picked up a lot through sheer enthusiasm for the topic, nevertheless, my hands were somewhat shaky when Ian introduced me. Cayt gave me a thumbs up from her seat near the front.

The Empyrean crowd, which included a few familiar faces, gave me a polite round of applause before I had begun. This is slightly disconcerting as a speaker and I cannot help but send up a silent plea to the Goddess – *let me say the right things, dear Lady, let my words be worthy of that applause.* It helped that over the last eighteen or more years that I've been going, Empyrean has become a comfortable and homely environment for me. Once I started to talk, armed with lots of notes and a presentation of slides and photographs on my laptop, I soon found my feet. Some of the most fascinating snippets of research, for me at least, were the stories surrounding the sinister doll island in Mexico, and tales of dozens of so-called possessed and haunted dolls, some of which are said to be so dangerous they have to be kept in glass cases!

Perhaps the most widely known haunted doll, housed at the East Martello Museum in Key West, Florida, is Robert the doll. A plain boy doll dressed in sailor's white and a flat white cap, Robert the doll was originally owned by a boy named Robert Eugene Otto. The young boy gave the doll his own name of Robert, while he went by the moniker of Gene or Eugene. As he was growing up, Gene played with Robert to excess and often blamed bad behaviour on the doll. *It wasn't me, it was Robert!* The Otto house was sold after Gene's death in 1974 and a subsequent string of owners and tenants of the property have reported hearing strange noises coming from the rooms where the doll was stored. The alleged supernatural activity was specifically connected to the doll, rather than the property: wherever Robert went, the spooky happenings followed. In 1994, Robert the doll was donated to the care of the museum where he remains today, sitting on a rocking chair and kept firmly behind glass. He is still creating havoc and fraying nerves today, with museum staff experiencing strange noises and malfunctioning cameras and other electronics.

South of Mexico City, among the canals of the Xochimico region, is a small, uninhabited island, which has the reputation of being haunted not by ghosts, but by hundreds upon hundreds of dolls. Now known as Isla de las Munecas, Island of the Dolls, the story goes that many years ago, the island's caretaker, Don Julian

Santana Barrera, came across the body of a young girl who had apparently drowned, her lifeless body washed up on the shores of the island. His discovery left him wracked with guilt and sadness over the girl's death. Not long after this, a doll drifted ashore to the island, in the same place as he had found the girl's body. Don Barrera assumed this must have belonged to the poor drowned girl and he hung the doll up in one of the trees where it has remained ever since, joined now by hundreds, if not thousands, of other dolls. Don Barrera claimed that he was now being haunted by the spirit of the dead girl and he brought more dolls to display on the island in an attempt to make her happy. Over time, he found more dolls and doll parts, an arm-less doll, a doll's head, dismembered limbs, washed up on the canal banks of the island complex. These too were kept on the island, displayed in tree branches, peering out of shaded hollows and in the windows of abandoned huts – a somewhat macabre attempt to appease the girl's spirit. Although Don Barrera has now passed away – he was found drowned fifty years later under mysterious circumstances in the same location where he claimed to have found the dead girl – locals and tourists alike continue to bring doll offerings and hang them up all over the island. The dolls watch, it is said, as tourists roam the island to see the macabre collection for themselves.

The real focus of the evening, however, was the use of dolls and poppets in a magical and ritual context throughout history, including everything from ancient paddle-dolls to the wax images used in royal courts to instigate the downfall of Pharaohs and Kings. Magical dolls made of fabric, bone, wood, reeds, corn, leather, clay or wax can be filled with herbs and crystals, charged with energy for healing, pins pushed into specific points to activate the spells. I was asked a wealth of questions that I fudged my way through, and I must have done okay, because I had another round of applause when I finished. One member of the audience asked when my book on magical dolls would be coming out. No chance, was my answer, this was strictly a one-off. I would not write a book on the topic. Or so I thought. That off-hand question had gripped me, however, and the book I hadn't intended to write, The Folklore and Magic of Dolls, is now available, with many examples from that talk, complete with illustrations, photographs, history, legends, and a range of spells using poppets for benevolent magic. Thank you, Cayt!

Sticking with magical dollies for a moment, something I have wanted to do for a long time is to design my own pattern for a knitted Goddess poppet. My gran taught me most of my sewing skills, but it was from my mum that I learned how to knit. Gran was never very good at it and, in fact, I can only recall seeing her knitting once or twice in all my childhood. Mum, on the other hand, was nearly always knitting something, and I picked it up from her and have since graduated to creating some of my own patterns. The pattern for the Goddess poppet has been through several incarnations and this week, after the archery club committee meeting, I spent an hour or two refining the pattern while we watched my favourite detective show, the Murdoch Mysteries. I had the general shape of the doll's body looking about right but wasn't sure if I should add bobbles or shaping to her chest. The initial version of the pattern is at the end of this chapter for you to have a crack at if you'd like, and there are lots of online videos and tutorials if you want to learn how to knit. At some point in the future, I will get around to experimenting with a knitting pattern for the horned God.

Phoebe helped me print off and collate information hand-outs for the course I had planned and I duly headed out on Friday to meet the key-holder of the village hall. I set up a small table with a range of commonly used witchcraft tools, newly created aura sprays, feather fans, and all the other bits and bobs that make up a working altar, and welcomed my guests as they arrived.

This was the first of five sessions, beginning with introductions to the common beliefs and practises of witchcraft, with an emphasis on the links between the craft and nature and deity. It made a nice change that everyone had spiritual leanings or had made a start on their development in some way. Carla was one of my guests and took everything in, making studious notes every few seconds. I explained what the aura sprays and smudging fans were for and we all had a go at cleansing the space and each other.

'What are these called?' Carla asked, holding up the fan. 'I've got one at home. Are they just called sage fans?'

'Yes, or just smudging fans or feather fans.'

'Oh no, that's far too boring.' Her face lit up with a giggling excitement. 'I think it should be – ooh, I know what it is – it's a spirit duster!' She held it aloft, swishing it in the air.

'Oh yes, I like that Carla.' Pete said, taking it from her to 'dust' her spirit as a demonstration. 'That's exactly what it does.'

The term spirit duster came into being and I think of Carla every time I use mine.

The evening finished with a round of herbal teas, vegan cakes and animated conversation. I quite like herbal and fruity teas, but a glass of wine when I got home, grateful that the first session had been well received, was much more welcome.

September is still warm enough to camp and Chris and I had booked our places for a small local camp. This was for a single night at a private woodland, just off the main road near our village. Incidentally, this was the same woodland where I'd been blessed by such an awesome experience with Brother Oak many years ago. Organised by owner of the Nottingham's witchy shop, the autumn camp was just perfect. We arrived in the early afternoon and pitched up amongst tall oak trees and then set off to meet our hosts and the other guests. A large open fire was set up in a ritual circle and there was a simple ceremony which included everyone, leaving us feeling part of something special. We were invited to take a pinch of herbs to throw on the fire, with the symbolic intention of getting rid of things in our lives that we no longer needed. The fire crackled, the ritual gradually came to a close, and the small group of campers and organisers began to talk, to sing and dance and drum. My poor little frame drum didn't like the cold and the fire did little to warm it, so I didn't play it for long but enjoyed listening to the others. The drums and chanting in front of the fire, the warmth and flicker of the orange flames: it was hypnotic and my mind drifted back to Kevin Grove's scrying workshop at the Artemis Gathering. Completely tranced out and lost in my thoughts, I was surprised to look up and see that Chris had left the fire circle.

I rambled off through the dark but welcoming forest to find him sitting with a few others by our tent. Tony, Jane, Graham and Lucy were introduced, and we spent the next four or five hours together quite happily. As the conversation and food and wine got going, so did the giggling, most of which was coming from me and one of the other women. Julie and Pete headed off for the night and Graham tucked himself into a cosy hammock strung up in the trees for the night, leaving just a few of us still talking, as quietly as we could. We have kept in touch with Jane, Graham and a few others, seeing them sporadically at pagan moots and camps, or at Empyrean.

After a late night, interrupted only by the hooting of owls and the soft talking of our fellow pagans, we were treated to mild weather and not a hint of breeze or rain, perfect conditions for putting away the tent the next day. Before that, however, I was sitting on a rug outside the tent with my new tarot deck, getting used to the feel of the cards, when one of the other women, Jo, wandered over with an optional exercise for us to try. She held out a large mirror and sat behind it and handed me a piece of paper with questions to read out. Jo, hidden behind the mirror, replied with the answers, messages from the deep subconscious, from my reflection, it seemed. The dialogue was deep and meaningful, talking about the importance of forgiving ourselves, being honest and true to our own soul, feeling deep love and acceptance of the inner soul. I shared a thankful hug with Jo when we finished

A lazy morning was spent packing away and we exchanged details with several people, promising to keep in touch. I had another promise too. Graham's beloved cat companion, who normally travels everywhere with him, was not well, and I offered to send over some distance Reiki later that evening.

Several years ago, I won a stuffed teddy bear from a hook-a-duck stall at the Riverside Festival and knew straight away that this little bear needed a name and a purpose. He'd be my focus for distant Reiki sessions. No, I'm not crazy – not completely, anyway – a lot of Reiki healers use a substitute body for distance work. Little bear needed to be called Mister something. I couldn't think of what the 'something' might be, so he is now just known as Mister Something.

An unexpected bonus of camping close to home was being able to store everything neatly away by noon, leaving me with a free afternoon. A rare event, and I made the most of it, taking the quiet afternoon as an opportunity to organise an open pagan ritual for the autumn equinox in a few weeks' time, sending out invitations by text and email and compiling a rough outline of what to expect. I put together the bare bones of a ritual to flesh out another time. I made the house look tidy – easily achieved by hiding things in cupboards – and then lit some incense and cleansed the lounge thoroughly with sage, ready for the distance reiki session and a tarot client I was expecting in the evening.

I have a mantra that I repeat to myself before every tarot reading to help things go smoothly. I have never spoken my little mantra out loud because it works and I'm afraid I might jinx it, but it's something along the lines of:

> *Oh, Lord and Lady, give to me the right words, let me be guided to truth and clarity, guide me to say what needs to*

> be said, providing insights and help, as I do will, so mote it be.

The reading for my client went smoothly and we talked over the meanings of the cards, how they related to her situation, what areas of her life needed attention. She was confident that it made sense and fit with her current circumstances. Even after thirty years of reading cards, I feel relieved and pleased when I have positive feedback from clients.

After the tarot reading, I brought Mister Something downstairs and sat with him on my lap, ready to start channelling Reiki for Graham's cat. Shibby came over, meowing at me fiercely, trying to muscle her way in to sit with me. I pushed her gently aside a few times before she got the message and sat on the coffee table in a huff, turning her back on me and every few minutes shooting a jealous look in my general direction. I've done Reiki for people and animals plenty of times before and she's never minded, but this time, it was another cat who was getting the healing. I swear she was jealous. Cat Reiki was only for Shibby, in her opinion. As soon as I had finished and put Mister Something back in his customary place, Shibby ran straight over, jumped onto my lap and rolled over, waving her paws insistently in the air, meowing at me loudly:

> *Come on human, my turn now. Did you forget who the number one cat is around here?*

I had some sad news on Monday. My friend Sheila had passed away and her funeral was going to be held in a few days' time. She'd slipped into a coma from which she didn't recover. Sheila was a bright spirit, always positive, always caring. The pagan community lost a dearly treasured Priestess and friend with Sheila's death. I cried at work that day and I cried again later when I told Phoebe. Chris didn't really know Sheila, having only met her on a handful of occasions, but Phoebe and I had been to her rituals and celebrations countless times in the past and had been friends with her. She had been a huge part of the

Nottingham pagan community and it was heart-breaking to know she was gone, that we would never spend time with her again. Never hear her voice invoking the Old Ones, never have her cleanse our auras before ritual, never listen again to her laughing at innuendos about staffs and wands.

The deepness of my grief surprised me, because apart from the time I went over to see her at the hospice a few months ago, I hadn't seen much of Sheila for a long while. I wept for her. She was only a few years younger than me and had been full of life before her illness. She left behind her family, her husband, and a wide circle of friends who miss her.

I was pleased to be among the trees and woods the next night for archery practise. I held back from the group a little, touching trees for comfort every now and then along the path, and it did a little bit of something to restore my soul.

The next day I had some better news. The publisher to whom I'd sent The Witch's Journey had replied to say they liked it very much and wanted to offer me a contract. When I climbed down from the buzzing high this gave me, I opened the rest of the day's post. A letter, finally, from the hospital with a date for a consultation for my hips. Phoebe was not feeling very well this week and on Wednesday, we all had an early night. I felt like I needed it. I was not looking forward to the next day. Sheila's funeral.

Chris and I took Phoebe to school in the morning and pottered around the house before making ourselves respectable for the funeral in the afternoon. Fortunately, this was one of Chris's off-shift days and I took a compassionate leave day. Sheila had known her condition was terminal and had spoken at length with those in her close circle to arrange her funeral. She had chosen some of her closest pagan friends to receive her ritual tools and designated another member of her working group to take on the role of Priestess after her death.

The crematorium was busy, with dozens of people waiting to enter for the service. Despite the sadness of the occasion, everyone was wearing bright colours at Sheila's request, including myself and Chris. As we stood outside the building, what I can only describe as a crowd began to form, all of them gathered to see her off. There was a lot of crying taking place as we all waited, a lot of laughter too. Then the thundering roar of motorbikes as Sheila's biker husband and his friends arrived, complete with a wicker coffin transported in a smart black sidecar. We watched silently, over a hundred of us, as the coffin was reverently carried inside.

The service was the most touching and heart-breaking that I have ever been to. I hope one day that all funerals will be like Sheila's: full of love and joy and gratitude, as well as a deep sense of loss and grief. Her family were not pagan, so the funeral was partly done by Sheila's chosen Priestess and partly by a Minister of her family's faith. The two worked so well together that things felt seamless and perfectly balanced. Members of Sheila's family and few of her closest friends read eulogies and shared their memories of her.

Finally, it was time to leave. The curtains around the wicker work coffin were drawn to a close and one of Sheila's favourite songs saw her off on her journey to the Summer Lands.

I cried with some of my dearest friends, Donna, Ian, Margret, Cayt; hugging one another with sorrow and tearful kisses before we left. Phoebe hadn't come to the funeral, but her dad was there as he'd been part of Sheila's group years ago when we had both known her very well, and we spent a few minutes together, sharing memories. I went to say goodbye to the rest of my friends in the gathering and talked for a few minutes with Sheila's husband. He told me she had already come back to him in spirit, returning to him as a Goddess.

She chose to spend some of her time with us, and for this we are thankful.

Blessed Be. Blessed Be. Blessed Be.

The weekend was going to be a busy one and I had to set this all aside, book news and sad news both, as I focused on leading the next session of the witchcraft development group. I had two themes for this class, divination work followed by an introduction to healing disciplines. One thing I'm often asked when I read tarot for someone is where all the information comes from. There are several schools of thought on this; some of them make sense and sound reasonable, others not so much. My own theory, for the moment, is that it comes from several potential sources. My connection on a psychic level with the querent can spark a two-way conversation of subtle energy and thoughts, visions and ideas which pass between us. I don't know how that would explain the predictive element of a reading, unless I subconsciously work out the most likely result of any given situation. Another part of me wonders if some force of power outside of me, a divine force, you might say, can see the broader picture and gives me that information to share. Part of me wonders if I tap into the information stored in the Akashic records, picking out pieces that are relevant to the client. In all honesty, I really have no idea. And that's all right with me. I am more concerned that divination does work than with how it works. I tried to explain my thoughts on this to the group and then went through some of the tools of the trade. Pendulums, tarot cards, dowsing rods, my little-used rune set, Ogham staves and a couple of hefty books for bibliomancy, were tried out with more enthusiasm than success.

After a quick refreshment break, filled with cakes and some of Carla's dubiously green and bitter tasting herbal concoctions, we moved on to healing. The group took it in turns to channel energy for each other, in pairs at first and then in larger groups, using crystals and wands to direct and focus healing vibrations.

The evening sessions were three hours duration, but the time passed very quickly, and I packed up my divining rods and Reiki stones before going home.

I had an early start in the morning with final preparations for an archery competition on Sunday. I sometimes wonder how on earth I manage to get myself so fully booked up. I swear it happens without me realising it, my diary is empty in January and by the middle of spring, every page is full, right through until December.

Chris was a big help to me over that weekend as I had a nasty migraine and the headache persisted with thundering peals and a few episodes of confusion and blurred, brightly-speckled lights that danced like holograms and filled my vision. I channelled some Reiki and dosed up with pain killers and, thankfully, it didn't get any worse; once my vision returned to normal, I was left with a wretched headache that lasted two days, but it was far better than a full-blown migraine.

All in all, it was a mixed week and I was keen to see it come to an end. The funeral was still fresh in my mind, as was the offer of a publishing contract, as I climbed into bed at the end of that long Sunday, my head pounding. Although I still had a ritual to finalise for the equinox gathering that I was organising, I was too tired and wrung out to do anything other than sleep soundly until the first rays of morning sun brought fresh light and a new dawn to light the way ahead.

My good intentions of going the gym for an hour before work didn't work out as I woke up and realised I hadn't set my alarm. Consequently, it was much later than usual when I got in from work, having done my work-out on the way home, and I realised that the Sherwood Oak development circle was supposed to be meeting tonight. I had nothing planned and the lingering headache meant that I wasn't thinking straight. I had known well in advance that this was coming up as I regularly check the schedule in my diary, but with everything that had been going on, I genuinely hadn't had time to think about what we might do this evening.

Healing circles are easy to set up, so when the group had settled in after a gossip to catch up with each other, I opened my gran's old bureau and started pulling out all my crystals, heaping them up in a big pile on the chest that serves as our coffee table. With the addition of a sack-full of crystals that Sarah carries with her almost everywhere, we soon had a large crystal grid laid out, with a small opalite skull glowing at the centre. We cast our sacred space around the room and wrote a few words in my healing book for anyone who needed any healing, building up a picture of exactly what we wanted to achieve.

Vibrations from the assorted gemstones radiated out in all directions, filling the room with a heady blend of buzzing energies that seemed to emanate heat, light and a tangible electric charge of some sort. Scientists and magicians alike have experimented with crystals to analyse exactly what goes on – all I can say for sure is that every one of us in that room was feeling the effects of the crystal grid. Paul, Chris and John were overly hot and bothered, with each of them getting headaches at some point, while Lisa, Sarah and myself felt calm, content, peaceful and full of loving feelings. Was this due to an excess of crystals? We played about with different grid layouts, choosing different crystals, reducing the number and changing their order in the grids. This was not scientific, of course, but it was interesting to sense that the atmosphere and mood of the group was altered with each shift of the crystal grid.

I keep a large chunk of smoky quartz on my desk at work, it sits beneath the computer monitor and gets moved occasionally by our cleaner, much to my amusement, as it's right beside one of my little witch figurines that she never touches. I sometimes only notice that the crystal has moved when I realise I'm starting to feel odd and develop a slight headache. When I put the crystal back under the monitor, I usually feel better within half an hour or so. Our cleaner is a star and I appreciate how much she does for us, often without recognition, so a big thank you to her.

After we had sent out a wealth of healing and settled down, we took down our circle and I briefed the group on what to expect if they were able to make it at the weekend for the equinox ritual. When the last person left it was very late at night and it took me ages to store the myriad crystals away in the bureau.

I really could have done with giving archery practise a miss on Tuesday night; I was exhausted after a long weekend and a difficult week, with mixed emotions of grief over Sheila's passing, stress of helping to organise an upcoming archery competition on top of the open ritual, and elation over the new publishing contract. If I didn't take Phoebe to the woods for our regular session though, I wouldn't hear the last of it, so I drove her there as soon as I came in from work. She dashed straight off before even stringing her bow to see if her friend had arrived. I'm still only a very average archer and some days I don't even class myself as that; as for Phoebe and her mate – well, let's just say that his dad and I both wonder if their aim will improve when they are old enough to pay for their own new arrows to replace all the lost and broken ones. When we completed the course and got back to the car, it was still beautifully warm and light. The fresh air must have done me some good because I was feeling much brighter, full of enthusiasm and energy.

'Come on,' I said to Phoebe. 'We're picking blackberries.' There were literally thousands of them, large and juicy, dotted on thorny bramble stems throughout the woods and we returned with enough fruit for two demijohns of blackberry wine and plenty left over to use in apple pies.

I finished writing the equinox ritual, making sure to include time for reflection, a focus on gratitude and thanks-giving, with a fuddle afterwards (for those of you who are wondering, fuddle means much the same as buffet, originally meaning 'to be befuddled or confused as a result of inebriation') and I had a perfect spot in mind for the equinox ceremony. Sherwood Forest is serene and gorgeous, filled with beech, yew, oak and hazel, but also with tourists, dog-walkers and a disappointing amount of dog-mess and litter. Half a mile or so along the main road, away from the village, is another part of the forest, more of a heathland than a wooded forest, where a large herd of horned cattle often graze. The noble creatures roaming gently around are enough to deter all but the hardiest of dog-walkers and I have often used this area for open rituals.

As a slight aside to this, I had a great afternoon with a friend one day in the same location not that long ago. We had taken a lazy, sunny afternoon walk together one weekend and settled down among some trees to sit for a while, talking quietly about this or that, absorbing the calmness and peace of the trees on the heath. We lit some incense and were siting peacefully on a tartan travel rug, soaking in the quiet aura of the trees, when, a little way off, a run-down flat bedded van pulled to a halt in a large, clear area. We watched, safely tucked out of sight in the trees, as two men climbed out of the cab. One of them, complete with a long beard, scraggy features and worn denim dungarees, started pulling buckets, spades and heavy-looking sacks off the back of the van. He dumped them on the ground, just out of our sight, but it looked as if he was struggling with them. He kept kneeling down with his spade and doing something with these sacks, just out of our line of sight. The second chap got back into the van and drove a short distance before stopping again. The first man started shouting unintelligibly again, waving his arms about. It was disconcerting and I'm not ashamed to say that I was concerned. It's at times like this that I curse my love of horror novels and films. The monkeys in my brain were screaming: he's burying a body! A few minutes of shouting and arm waving later, we finally saw the situation for what it was.

Thud-thud-thudding, a noise like thunder came pounding through the woods, the earth beneath us trembling with every booming noise. Along came those fantastic long-horned cattle: calves, horned bulls and hefty mothers. The van pulled slowly away and the cows followed as one of the men grabbed another bucket of feed to spread out for the cows. We felt like a pair of idiots, but were relieved it wasn't anything sinister in those heavy sacks.

Slightly off the beaten track from here is a wooded area that I use regularly for private rituals and meditations. Sometimes I go there to sit. Just sit. The trees listen, the birds answer, the ground supports me, and I feel at one with everything, tucked away in peaceful contemplation.

I'd chosen a location near to my regular spot for the ritual. With everyone gathered at the meeting point by the main road, we headed through the sparse trees to spread out picnic blankets, put out jars for tea-lights, lit bundles of incense and made our sacred space. There were nearly thirty people in total, a good sized group for a small and cosy ritual. I had several copies of the ritual and I'd arranged a few volunteers in advance to call in the elemental quarters. The ritual went smoothly, with everyone in the group having the chance to say what they had received, what they had given, or how they had developed over the year. Had we achieved the goals we set for ourselves at Imbolc? What do we want to give thanks for? We can be grateful for anything, it doesn't have to be material things, and giving thanks is a way of getting our expectations for positive shifts in our lives into the universe, inviting more good things to come to us.

> *I give thanks for the friends and family who have supported me this year. I give thanks for my friend getting the all-clear on cancer. I give thanks for the growth I have seen in my new business. I give thanks for a stable home life. Whatever we are thankful for, blessed be.*

The circle was surrounded by trees, mostly silver birch and pine, and the ground was strewn with leaves of gold, bronze, red, yellow, fallen pine cones, twigs and branches. Rugs were spread over the ground and bags opened to reveal packages of food and drink to share, always a good way to finish a ritual. Pete had brought foil-wrapped baked potatoes, kept hot in a food thermos, there were home-made biscuits and cakes, Jane had brought herby potato wedges, Carla provided a cous-cous dish, and there were flasks of hot water for tea and coffee. It was a pleasant afternoon of conversations on pagan topics, swapping the stories of our lives over the last year. Times like this really do contribute to a sense of community, not just in pagan society, but with people from all walks of life.

As I'm writing this book some time later, I have struck up a friendship with a Christian Pioneer Minister, incidentally the same gentleman whose forest church my work colleague had invited me to some time ago, and we talked about this at some length one time, agreeing that ritual could serve as a base for forming a meaningful community. No matter what spirituality one follows, ritual serves to bring people together – strangers or friends. There are elements of ritual and the simple act of sharing food afterwards that have a tangible effect on those taking part. Even when in ritual with people I've never met before, as our eyes meet around the circle, it creates a connection and a sense of shared experience, though smaller groups are, naturally, more conducive to this. In this moment, right here and right now, we are together, unified in purpose.

The combination of good food, ritual, laughter and nice weather left me satisfied and content. As with any ritual, at home or away, I had my accoutrements to put away. I sometimes wonder if the people who attend open rituals realise it can take anywhere up to an hour or more to pack up all the tools I bring along. The set of deer antlers I use to cast the circle, the glass lanterns and tea-light holders that need wrapping up to protect them from breakages, the incense containers, spirit dusters, sage bundles, chalice, plates, cakes and mead for the offerings, a cauldron, sometimes a fire pit complete with ashes to dispose of, not forgetting my picnic blanket and hamper. And that's aside from the time it takes plan and write the ritual itself and the emails or phone calls back and forth as people want to check directions or times. Can I bring the dog? Yes, and you'd already know that if you read the details I sent you last week! Don't get me wrong, I love doing this and I get such a lot out of these open celebrations, but it's time-consuming.

On Friday it was time for the weekly witchcraft development course and for this session, our focus was learning to create rituals with specific goals. Everyone was receptive to the ideas I put forward and we covered some of the common reasons for doing rituals with purpose, not just on a magical level, but with respect to self-development too.

Witchcraft is more than sacred incantations and spell casting. Pathworking is a valuable tool for witchcraft and spiritual development too and I took the group through a pathworking exercise. Pathworking is not the same as meditation, though the two terms are often used interchangeably. Meditation is striving for the stillness of the mind; pathworking is focused and detailed.

Pathworkings are a way of connecting to the subconscious mind, bringing emotions to the surface to be healed; they are a dream-like journey to meet the archetypal Goddess and God, seeking answers or guidance. Pathworking can act as a gateway to releasing the blockages we put in our own way, a gateway to emotional growth. Seen as a way of walking in altered states of consciousness, pathworking is normally led by one person setting the scene, followed by time spent in silence so that each person can have a unique experience. I find it a very valuable technique to use and despair that it isn't more widely used or becomes a light-hearted jaunt through pretty woodlands, instead of the deep, inner work that can be so beneficial for self-development.

However, one must start somewhere, and to begin this session, I read out a pathworking I'd prepared in advance with vivid imagery, designed to give my class a firm understanding of what was involved and what to expect. I had made gluten free vegan cookies to share and after a break for refreshments and general chatter on the subject, we forged ahead with a longer, more individual pathworking, bringing the session to a close, at Carla's suggestion, with a spiral dance and chanting.

After the evening was over, I returned home and lit a few candles on my altar in the lounge. I sprinkled incense and herbs on a charcoal block in one of my cauldrons, with left over cake and wine to bless and leave outside as an offering. I opened the back door and stepped into the garden, gazing at the stars and the moon and listened to the call of an owl in the fields across the road.

Goddess Poppet Knitting Pattern

Suitable even for beginners, this pattern can be worked on any gauge needle with any yarn. Gauge is not important, providing that yarn thickness is proportionate to needle size, e.g., 4mm needles with double-knit yarn.

The pattern is knit backwards and forwards on two needles, with two identical pieces sewn together for the front and back, and another section folded lengthways to form the arms in a complete arc over the poppet's head.

Abbreviations

RS – right side of work WS – wrong side of work
M1 – make one – pick up and knit into the back of the loop between stitches
K2tog – knit two together
PSSO – knit one, slip one, pass slipped stitch over
ST/ST – stocking stitch – alternate rows of knit and purl

Body and Head (make two)

Cast on 3 sts.
1st and every alternate row: Purl
2nd row: K1, M1, K1, M1, K1
4th row: K1, M1, K to last st, M1, K1
Increase as set to (15sts).
Work 9 rows of st/st.
Shape Waist
Continue working st/st while decreasing at each of next two RS rows as follows:
PSSO, knit to last two sts, K2tog. (11sts)
Next row: Purl
Next row (RS): K1, M1, k to last two sts, M1, K1 (13sts)
Work 7 rows st/st
Shape Head
With RS facing, decrease for shoulders by repeating decrease row * twice until 9sts remain
Next row: K2tog twice, K1, K2tog twice
Next row: Purl
Next row: Knit into front and back of every stitch (10sts)
Next row: Purl
Next row: K1, M1, knit to last st, M1, K1
Work 7 rows st/st
Next row with RS facing: K2tog six times
Draw yarn through remaining 6 sts, pull tight and fasten off
Arms (make one)
C/O 38 sts
Work 10 rows st/st
Cast off

To Make Up

Sew body pieces together stuffing* lightly, stuff head and draw thread around the outside of the neck to pull in. Secure ends. Sew arms together across the long edge, stuff lightly, sew arm openings to shoulders of the body.

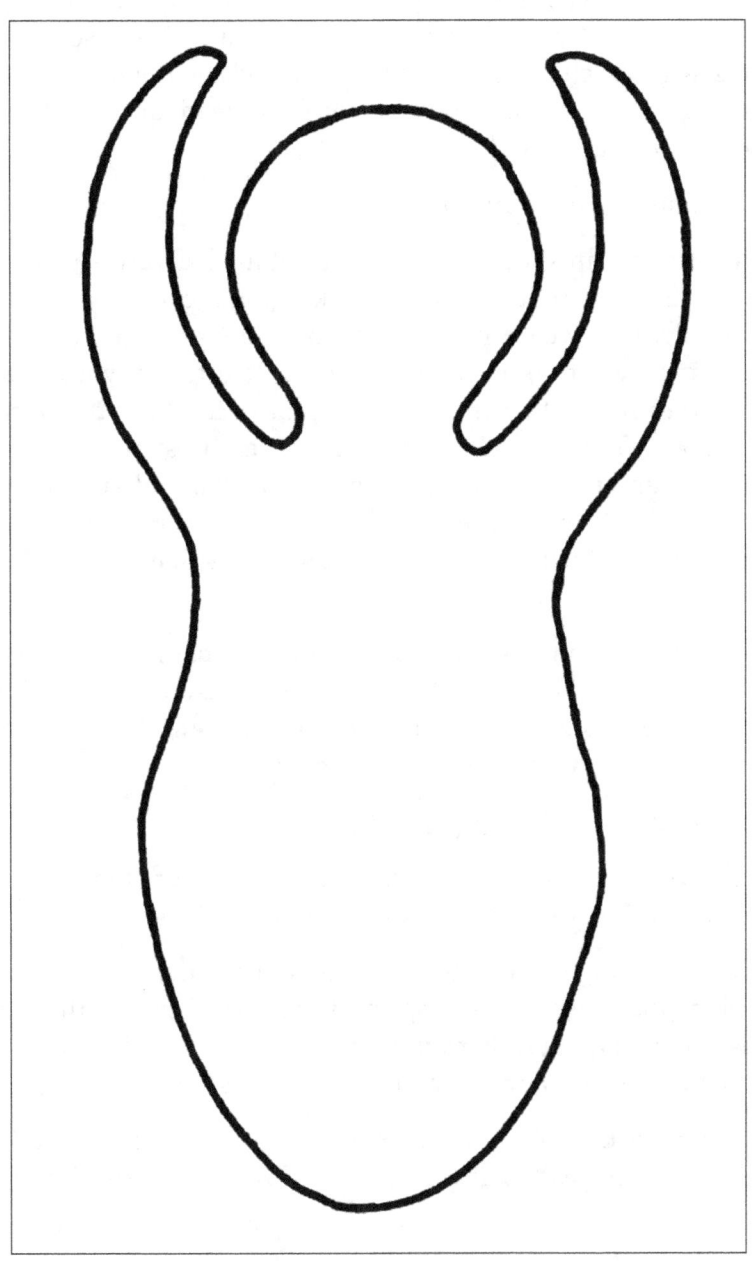

Poppet Sewing Template

Trace the template from the page in this book onto pattern paper or newspaper. Cut two pattern pieces from your chosen fabric and sew by machine or hand around the edges, leaving a gap for stuffing* at the bottom. Lightly stuff the head, arms and body and sew the gap closed.

Personalise Your Poppet

Whether the finished doll will be used as decorative piece on your altar or as part of a spell working, you can adorn it with embroidered flowers and vines, glue on beads or crystals, and use your imagination to personalise and tailor it to suit your needs. Fill it with herbs, flowers or crystals, make it a little dress from your favourite coloured fabrics, tie tiny feathers into strands of woollen hair or sew a hand-written spell or chant into the body of the doll. With every spell or charm you cast, remember that personalising it will give you far better results than doing it half-heartedly or by rote.

*You could use an old pillow or cushion and cut it open to tease out the stuffing. Gran used to use old socks, tights and stockings, cut up into small pieces as filling for her toys and I love the idea of recycling old things into something new!

<u>Jane's Herby Potato Wedges</u>

Cut two or three large, well-scrubbed potatoes into long wedges, leaving on the skins, and put into a large bowl.

Drizzle with vegetable or olive oil and add rosemary, sea-salt and black pepper to season and sprinkle with paprika. Mix the potatoes and seasoning well, transfer to a large baking sheet in a hot oven and bake for approximately 25 minutes.

Serve with a salsa or onion and garlic mayonnaise. These wedges are a relatively healthy alternative to chips and go well with pizza and a green salad.

October

A Song for the Season: Wytches, Inkubus Sukkubus.

The season of pumpkins, dark red and orange leaves falling to the ground, fields bare after the autumnal harvest. October is true witch season with dark evenings and warm robes, wind and rain to create atmospheric ceremonies outside in the woods, owls hooting overhead. Symbols of witchcraft and magic abound in shops, in the streets, in the windows of houses. Cobwebs and spiders, cauldrons and black cats – what's not to love?

In addition to the course in the village, I was scheduled to run an all-day workshop at the witchy shop in Nottingham. The workshop, Elements of Magic, would include work around the meanings and uses of each element, a short pathworking, and examples of spell casting ideas using the four elements of witchcraft. I packed the car with bags and boxes full of ribbons, yarn, twigs, bottles of water, balloons, bubbles and all kinds of other craft materials, as well as the usual and expected array of crystals, altar tools and tarot cards. I hadn't planned too heavily for the elements of magic day, as I have done this workshop dozens of times before, and had a fair idea of what I wanted to do. A page or two of notes would suffice as a reminder.

As with everything else on this path, I usually get more from events like this by going along with the flow to some extent, listening and responding to what people are saying in the classes, being guided by my intuition and inspirations, adapting what I'm doing as people reveal what aspects of the subject they are most interested in.

The room was laid out with a large table and I set up an altar in the centre, arranging some of my tools neatly, with the rest of my things shoved underneath the table, out of sight until later. I laid out a crystal grid, small statues of the Lord and Lady, my athame, my deer antlers and wand, a piece of wood for earth, a feather and aura spray for air, a chalice for water, and a small candle for fire. I sat down and listened the meditation track I had playing in the background, barely audible over the noise of the boiling kettle. My thoughts turned inward, I felt completely relaxed, drawing energy up from the earth below and the sky above, pulling it into the core of my being for strength and confidence for the day ahead.

I greeted people with an optional hug as they entered and sat around the large table, cooing over the crystal grid and altar display. After coffees and introductions were over, I began to explain the associations and meanings for each of the elements used in witchcraft, along with ideas on how they can be harnessed for spell craft and rituals. Encouraging people to express their own thoughts and ideas on the elements, I kept the conversation up while handing out scissors, balls of wool, and lengths of thin dowel. I showed the group how to make Mexican God's Eyes, pouring intention into every twist of yarn and selecting colours appropriate to their individual goals. One member of the group made an incredibly elaborate and beautiful example and completely showed up my own paltry efforts. He claimed innocently that he'd never done any textile related crafts before but I'm not so sure, it was a truly brilliant piece and he clearly enjoyed doing it very much.

'I've got a logical background in science and maths, so this is a rare event for me. I love this wool.' Simon was using an organic yarn, dyed in variegated terracotta, browns and greens, creating a multi-coloured pattern on his stick frame.

'Take the rest of that ball home with you, if you like.' I said, impressed with his happy enthusiasm. 'You can make another one when you're not rushed in a workshop and take more time over it.'

We discussed different ways to channel and tap into elemental energy using everyday objects and I brought out small bottles of bubbles, blowing our intentions into the air with every round of bubbles. The sun suddenly started to stream brightly through the picture window, illuminating the room. With eleven people blowing bubbles into the centre, it looked gorgeous as the sunlight created a bright rainbow amid the gently moving bubbles that filled room. I made a mental note to go around with a cloth later to clean any marks left from where the soapy bubbles had landed. When the bubble blowing was over, the sun returned to a softer glow. We took a break for lunch after we'd carried out some simple blessings on the God's eyes we'd made.

Each element has a place in ritual: air is our inspiration and dreams; fire is our passion, drive and motivation; water is the flow of emotions that must be balanced for magic to work; earth is the manifestation of goals, the solidity of achievement. Our own associations and connections to the elements are more important, however, than anything you see written in a book, for it is our intuition and instinct that brings the magic to life.

I gave the group examples of how to connect with elements in the physical world, how the elements can be used to help us to let go of past traumas that are holding us back in life. I led a short pathworking exercise, watching out for the inevitable tears. There is nearly always one member of any group like this who finds it emotional, especially the first time. Sure enough, as I brought everyone back to the here and now, one woman, Sally, was silently crying. I asked if she was okay.

'Oh yes, I'm happy, honestly.' Sally sniffed, a neatly manicured hand going up to her face to blot the tears away before they could smudge her perfectly applied mascara. 'I just can't believe I've never done anything like this before. I don't even know why I'm crying.'

'We're both really new to all this stuff.' Her friend Lynne patted her on the shoulder. She also had a hint of water around her eyes. I handed out tissues.

'It can be powerful.' I said. 'When we first set foot on this path, a lot of old emotions can bob up to the surface when we least expect it.'

'I'm okay, honestly.' Sally was managing to compose herself a little now. 'I can't thank you enough for this whole day, I feel like my eyes have been opened, but I've got so much to learn, haven't I?'

'You're not wrong there.' I assured her. 'I'm still learning and everything I learn opens up a whole new world that I haven't explored yet. The more I know, the more I realise how much I don't know.'

We went through the rest of the activities and exercises I had lined up for the class, including some things that had I made up over the years which seem to work, even if they are unconventional. We blew up balloons and released the energy and intention stored in them with a loud pop, shouting out key words for our intentions. I drew Reiki symbols and love hearts on the bottom of glasses of water to charge it before drinking. We tied strips of ribbon and brightly dyed feathers and horse-shoe symbols into a charm bag for good luck, chanting out words connected to our goal and sending energy out for our future selves to pick up on over the course of the next week.

I talked about how to direct and focus anger with fire before going ahead with any magical work, making sure we are standing in a place of peace instead of flying off the handle. Using our finger as a laser pointer, we can focus all our rage, hatred, blame and anger over a situation, blasting it out into the universe. A laser gives out an intense, narrow beam of light that doesn't diffuse – they are always focused and sharp. And a laser never stops once you set it in motion, until it reaches its target, it keeps on going and going, right into outer space and beyond. If we channel our negative energy, beaming out into the sky as a laser finger-pointer, then our anger and aggression will keep on going far, far away from us.

'I don't believe it.' Simon spoke up again. 'I've spent decades trying to explain to my university students how lasers do that, and you summed it up in two minutes. I'd love to see you doing a talk at Eton.'

I wasn't sure that was what I had done at all and pulled a face. 'Yeah, right,' I replied, 'I'd fall flat on my face.'

'I'm serious, the way you talk about energy as part of this web of wyrd, how magic flows along it, they'd love it.'

'Eton are not going to ask me to do a talk on lasers and energy, however, I will be at the Mansfield Show, so perhaps I'll see you there.'

Time passed quickly and after taking final questions and giving advice and answers, I wound things up. There were hugs all round, especially from Sally and Lynne, as I packed up my witchy belongings.

Simon and Graham had struck up a friendship early in the day and were now giggling together in a corner, nodding to each other and whispering in conspiracy.

'Yes, she is.' Simon said, arms folded across his chest, big grin spreading out from beneath his significant moustache.

'Okay, spill the beans.'

'How do you describe yourself?' he asked me.

I had to think about this for a moment. 'Hmm, a witch, I suppose.'

'No, you're not just a witch.' Graham said, 'You're a jazz witch.'

This was unexpected. I didn't see a connection, especially as I don't like jazz.

'You are, honestly,' Simon agreed. 'You take a bit of this, a bit of that, mix it all together, throw in a bit of improvisation and then you stand back to see what happens, and, guess what? It works and it's brilliant.'

Well, that was me told. I couldn't argue with this description of my own, unique brand of witchcraft. Jazz Witch, eh? I love it!

As I unpacked my bags and put away my altar tools at home that evening, I smiled and started to laugh out loud.

'What's up with you this time?' Chris asked, coming to join me in the lounge.

'According to Graham and another gentleman in my class today, which went brilliantly, by the way, I am officially a Jazz Witch.'

'O-kay.' He kissed me on the forehead, puzzled expression on his face. 'What does a Jazz Witch do then?'

'Anything she likes.' I replied. 'Because there are no rules in jazz magic.'

'Of course.' He didn't have a clue what I was talking about, of course, but after I explained, he agreed wholeheartedly with Simon and Graham.

We had pizza for dinner and played games with Phoebe in the evening. I wonder why some people see regular, daily family occasions like this as something separate and apart from their pagan path. My family and friends and my deep connection to them are what makes magic and ritual worth doing.

On Sunday Chris was working, so it was time for a pyjama day with Phoebe. We did some baking and my fingers nearly got sore from the number of texts I swapped with a couple of friends over the course of the day. I sent an email to the Nottingham venue to thank them for hosting the workshop. They would be very happy to have me back, as everyone who'd attended had been telling the staff how much they'd enjoyed it.

The week went by quickly with work, cooking, stirring things clockwise with good intentions, a few sessions at the gym, and one night I went over to Jane's for a while and talked about trivial things over a glass of wine. Phoebe had now been taking vitamin D tablets for six months and needed a follow up appointment and blood test, while I finally had an appointment for an MRI scan in a few weeks' time.

On Friday night I went to the village hall for the last session of the witchcraft course and spent a lot of time answering questions and discussing the various topics that came up in conversation. By now, the format for rituals was set in and nobody said 'um' once during their invocations. There are worse things than being part of a ritual where the people calling in the quarters say something along the lines of: we invoke the element of earth in the – um – north, element of um, um, welcome earth; but if you genuinely can't speak from the heart about the elementals of earth, then it could be time for you to think about reviewing and renewing your relationship with them or trying to learn a short invocation as a starting point.

One of the questions that came up was around the subject of covens and where to go from here. Covens are only one way of practicing witchcraft, certainly not the most common in my experience, and it can be difficult to find one. Covens tend to be close-knit circles of friends, they are magical working groups and build up strong bonds over time and can seem reluctant to welcome newcomers and disrupt that closeness or they simply don't have space for more members, meeting as most witches do in our own homes.

Being a solitary witch doesn't have to mean that you miss out on the social side of things and it can be a very rewarding way of practicing. There are so many events, rituals, workshops, moots, pagan picnics, regional conferences, festivals and social gatherings going on across the country, that one need never follow a lonely path, especially with the emergence of internet forums and video calls. I handed out a final round of typed up notes for everyone to take away and promised to keep them up to date with details of any events I had coming up for the rest of the year.

The Sherwood Oak circle came around on Monday night after we'd all finished our respective jobs for the day and I planned to do some path working, meditation or journey work with everyone, but Sarah and Paul brought Jack along, so it was another round of kid's entertainment. I tried to steer the conversation towards pagan topics, but it was short-lived, with constant interruptions from Jack, spilled coffee to clean up and half an hour of trauma when Sarah tried to force Jack into his coat for the three-foot walk from our front door to the car in the driveway. We agreed that our next gathering would be at Sarah and Paul's house, with the intention that by the time everybody arrived at eight in the evening, Jack would be tucked up asleep in bed. Once the house was empty and quiet, I tidied up and lit a few candles and incense cones, spending a while just sitting in that beautiful relaxed silence before retiring for the night.

The next day I emailed the people from the development course, inviting them over at the weekend for a social gathering. The final session had ended with one or two questions left unanswered through lack of time and I thought it would be nice to see everyone again in more relaxed circumstances. I walked to the village hall on Wednesday for Carla's meditation class and it was nice to be able take part in something, rather than having to organise, plan, scheme, and pander to everyone else's needs for a change. I've always enjoyed Carla's vibrant energy and her tonal chanting, which soothes the soul with cleansing vibrations. Sometimes she uses Buddhist chanting, other times she'll play a pagan chanting CD, and there can be up to half an hour or longer of singing out with each other before starting a long pathworking or meditation that varies with each session. I felt restored spiritually and emotionally after feeling ragged and rushed lately. I love all the different activities that I do, but it does seem such a pity that working full-time gets in the way of my real life. It does just about pay the bills, so I can't complain too much, and I am thankful to have a relatively stable job.

Coming up next was another event, this time an introductory talk on witchcraft at what is probably the largest event of its kind in the area. The Mansfield Mind, Body, Spirit Show at the beginning of October is well-loved by everyone in the area and after my talk at the Galleries of Justice in summer had been so well-attended, organiser Erick figured it would go down well at this event too. After work one day, I opened the bureau in the lounge, knowing I needed some motivation to start planning, and picked out some pieces of citrine and blood stone, shoving them into my pocket. I carried on the rest of the early evening with the usual things, talking to Phoebe, going through homework with her, making dinner.

Later, after watching a film and saying goodnight to my ever-growing teen, I pulled the gemstones out of my pocket and sat for a few minutes with them in my hands, quietly letting their gentle vibrations soak into me. I visualised myself sitting with my laptop, fingers plinking away at the keys, and then holding up my finished notes, neatly typed on a crisp white sheet of A4 paper, complete with a little doodle of an oak leaf in the bottom corner.

I think even this visualisation was another form of procrastination, however, so I forced myself up and pulled out my laptop. Ah ha! It had worked after all, I now had ideas flowing freely from my brain to the page on the screen. I am so glad I learned touch-typing when I was in my late teens, it makes writing much easier and far quicker than using a pen, though I'm never far away from a note book and a trusty biro. It only took an hour or so to produce a comprehensive outline for my talk. I printed it off, did a little doodle of an oak leaf in one corner, and said a happy little thank you to the moon and stars before turning in for the night.

The rest of October was sedate as we moved through the routines of work and school without any major mishaps. Phoebe was still suffering from occasional lethargy and general aches and pains in her arms and legs, a feeling of exhaustion and slight nausea. Although her most recent blood test showed her level of vitamin D was now within the expected range, it would still be another few months or more before her symptoms cleared up completely.

I went with Chris to the regular drumming circle on Thursday, another opportunity for me to just be myself in a spiritual setting, no need to put on my public persona of calm and efficiency, no pressure to perform. Again, this was just what I needed for a bit of rejuvenation. The drumming sessions with this group are energetic and always good fun, with several opportunities to either do the drumming or to lie down while the drums are played over you for healing and emotional clearing. We had picked up Lisa en route from the village and she was happily banging away loudly but did confess that she had her eye on a larger frame drum for future events, as soon as she could afford it. There was a huge peal of laughter from the opposite side of the room as the head of somebody's drum beater flew off and landed on the floor, and Abby handed out animal oracle cards at the end of the evening. I turned mine over to see that it was beaver, which is the animal totem for my birth month of May on the medicine wheel, Chris had a hawk and Lisa's card, relevant to her once again, was a snake.

Phoebe was due to spend the weekend in Nottingham with her dad and I drove over there with her earlier in the day as I had a tarot client later. My daughter is a very good passenger and companion for long car journeys and we talked about her school work, her friendships and other miscellaneous things that concern teenage girls in the duration of the drive. By the time I returned home, it was already dark – how quickly the nights draw in once the equinox is over – and Chris had arrived home from work. He made himself scarce, reading a book for an hour upstairs after a quick hello to my client, who arrived promptly for his reading.

Once the kettle had boiled for coffee, always an essential part of any tarot reading, I think, I muttered my tarot mantra under my breath and began to lay out the cards. We discussed the selected cards in detail, and I pointed out how some of the major arcana cards were facing each other, indicating positive communication with a close companion. I had to explain that one card everybody loves to hate: Death, the often un-named thirteenth card of the major arcana, is not quite the omen of death it's reputed to be. Instead, Death usually represents a sudden and complete change of circumstances, the end of one situation and the start of another. The tarot is only an indication of how things could turn out and nothing is written in stone. My new cards were easy to read now that I had got used to them, and my client was very satisfied with what I told him. After he left, Chris and I talked for a while about our respective days and I told him about my self-imposed writing challenge.

Every November an international novel writing competition takes place and millions of ambitious authors worldwide get involved. Nano, or sometimes Nano Wrimo, (short for National Novel Writing Month) is an annual challenge with each participant aiming to complete a full novel from start to finish in just one month. The minimum word-length to count as a novel is set at fifty-thousand words and it's up to individual participants to decide if their work is finished at this stage or if they will carry on into December to write the remainder of the book. Fifty-thousand words is not very long in terms of novel writing and would be a thin book rather than a chunky paperback, but it's still a very sizable amount of writing to finish in just four weeks, especially when you work full time and have a host of witchy events, archery competitions and who-knows-what-else to contend with.

I've tried writing a Nano novel several times before and never managed to finish because I ran out of either time, ideas or energy for it. I was determined to see it through this year and signed up on-line, pledging that I would not be beaten. You see, this year, I had a cunning plan.

Writing websites and blogs often feature articles by well-known authors with words of encouragement and handy writing tips and I'd been reading a lot about the virtues of plotting. I plan my witchy articles and non-fiction writing quite carefully, but tend to have only very sketchy plans or vague ideas when it comes to writing novels and stories. When I write fiction, I normally start with a basic premise and leap into writing straight away, developing the plot and characters as I go along, but with a tight deadline and my great talent for procrastination, I would not get very far without a clear outline. I took few hints and tips from some of my favourite authors and decided on what exactly I would write. A paranormal romance with a feisty female werewolf and a centuries old vampire as the two main protagonists. I'd read a lot of paranormal romance, so felt confident that I could come up with a decent outline as a starting point. Once I'd nailed the basic plot, I could fill in the gaps and flesh it out until I had a full synopsis, which, I hoped, would make it much easier to write an entire novel in only four short weeks. This pre-planning is allowed within the rules of the Nano challenge.

The next evening after work, I made a batch of cookies and the folk from my witchcraft development group came around for a few hours. I introduced everyone to Chris and our three cats spent the entire night purring loudly as they strolled from one person to the next for a fuss. We put on a small spread of nibbles to eat and conversation revolved almost entirely around mystical themes, only occasionally going off-topic. I was quite content and felt satisfied that I was able to answer those few lingering questions people had been left with, and offered advice on what to do next, giving out information on moots and gatherings across the county. A few of the group would be going to the Mansfield show in the morning and I promised to look out for them and say hello while I was there.

My talk was not scheduled until the afternoon, though Chris and I arrived early enough to go to a few talks ourselves. I had checked in with Erick and was distracted by shiny pagan merchandise on the numerous stalls and was further led astray when I saw Simon and his wife. He started fishing around in his man-bag and pulled out a linen-wrapped parcel, handing it to me with grace. Curious, I carefully unwrapped this unexpected gift to find a beautiful and carefully crafted Mexican eye amulet, made with the variegated wool I'd given to Simon, nestled carefully in the linen. It was decorated with dried camellia pods that shone with a hint of golden glitter. I was touched, this was such a lovely thing to do for me, and a gracious way of thanking me for the course he had enjoyed so much.

Chris was in awe of it too and while we were talking, Graham arrived, complete with his pet-safe back-pack and his feline companion, Luna. Luna was still not very well and unfortunately deteriorating, so Graham didn't stay long, but did manage to see a couple of his friends.

I wasn't sure which room my talk was scheduled for and every time I tried seeking out Erick to clarify this, I was dragged into another round of hugs and hellos with somebody else I knew. The spiritual and pagan community had come out in force and I was torn from one person to the next while poor old Chris stood patiently and quietly by my side. Although I would be happy at these events on my own, he insists on joining me. He deserves a medal, truly.

Now, where was I supposed to be giving my talk? Oh, yes, the biggest of the auditoriums. I barely made it through the door in one piece, as a gaggle of pagans were crammed outside in a very long queue. When I realised all these people were waiting to hear me speaking, a few little butterflies in my stomach made themselves known. Crickey, I hadn't expected this amazing turn out for little old me. The hall was crammed and Erick, grinning at me from the doorway, gave me a confident thumb's-up. He was right, I'd be fine. I had a microphone, I had my notes, I had my inner strength and I had, according to Graham and Simon, all that jazz.

I stepped up to the front, thanking everyone for coming, and started to waffle on as I do, explaining some of the fundamental things that make witchcraft a viable and valuable way of life. Forty-five minutes later, a round of applause rang out in the hall and when I opened the floor for questions from the audience, there were plenty. There were still people waiting to speak with me when I had to leave to free up the room for the next speaker. Stepping away from the little podium, I was swamped by a queue of folk all wanting a few minutes with me in private. Erick is always well prepared and promptly ushered me into side room, where I spent another hour answering questions, giving advice, and signing copies of my first book, The Witching Path.

Although it had been a fun packed day, I was very glad to be heading home at the end of it. Spending all day on my feet had left my hips and legs in a painful state and I leaned heavily on my walking stick, hobbling across the car park. Carla was one of the shiny, happy people I'd seen at the show, and we offered her a lift home, she and I talking excitedly about the event all the way back to the village. I slunk onto the sofa the moment I arrived home and didn't move much for the rest of the night. I was thoroughly exhausted and I think Chris must have been too. He gets up shortly after five in the morning on his working days and doesn't return until at least seven in the evenings, so normally spends his first day off-shift catching up with some sleep and I knew he'd missed that today because of the show. We both slept soundly that night.

No rest for the wicked as this was another week packed with work, school, routines of mundane house-hold chores and another of the Thursday classes, this one focusing on healing and meditation. Another evening was spent with one of my good friends and we read tarot cards for each other, lighting sage wands to cleanse our auras, sharing the peace and magic of a simple ritual.

Each October the archery club held a have-a-go archery range at the annual Robin Hood Country fair at the Newark showground and we packed up our camping gear and headed off to join the rest of the club members on Friday evening. Pitching up our tent in the dark, cold October evening was not much fun at all, but the weekend made up for it. The stream of punters wanting to have a go at archery didn't let up all day and I spent most of it organising the brief sign-up procedures and handing out equipment. I had a great time with other ladies manning the admin stand, laughing and joking with each other, sharing sandwiches and flasks of hot coffee, handing out certificates and sweeties to a myriad of children, a reward for their sterling bow and arrow work. Some of the youngsters were only knee-high and, with Mum and Dad or big brother coaxing them on and a little assistance and encouragement, every one of them came away shouting proudly that they shot a bear or a bison.

One of Phoebe's friends came to the show on the second day with her family and Phoebe showed off her own archery skills before setting her friend up with equipment and demonstrating how to hold the bow correctly and aim. A well-earned break on Sunday afternoon gave us time to wander through the showground; Chris spent at least half an hour trying on hats and I found a hippy clothing stall, quite out of place and unexpected, among the rows of traditional country traders selling wellingtons, wax jackets and shot-gun pellets. The indoor arena had been turned into a food hall for the weekend and the smells were tantalising. Chris rarely drinks, but when he does, he chooses good quality ciders, so we sampled a few locally produced brews, bought a supply to take home and snaffled down a few samples from the assorted delicacies of food being handed around on platters.

Back home once more to an ordinary week of routine family life. Shibby cat demanded her regular Reiki treatments every evening, meowing loudly until she had me under her control. If cats had opposable thumbs, we would be in a world of trouble! I tried out a recipe for gluten-free carrot cake, which I wanted to bake for a friend next time I visit her. A dental appointment for his routine check-up had poor Chris shaking and quaking. He's terrified of the dentist and needs to psyche himself up for it. I suggested he do some meditation or pathworking around this, but even that would send shivers down his spine.

At the weekend, we had an archery day with a difference, for one thing Phoebe, would not be coming with us as she was with her dad for a few days. This was a good job, because the other major difference at this event were the targets themselves, which were all based on a theme that Phoebe would not have been pleased with. A club in Yorkshire had set up a zombie themed event for the first time. We teamed up with Neil, whose superb poems having been summing up the seasons so well in this book. Zombie targets, fancy-dress zombies and victims, dozens of archers dressed as doctors, (un)armed response units and a zombie response vehicle were stationed all around the woodlands. Despite struggling up and down the steep slopes of the valley that made my legs ache with every step, I had a thoroughly brilliant time. The first surprise of the day came early in the morning as I paid a visit to the ladies' room. Just before I pushed the door open, I noticed Neil and Chris standing nearby with one of the home-club crew, all three of them grinning, arms folded like they were waiting for a show. I didn't think much of it until I pushed the door open and had to duck swiftly to avoid a decapitated zombie head that swung towards me, dislodged from the inside and aiming for my head. I was given a zombie survival guide and my score cards, extra points for a head-shot, all ready for a day of zombie-slaying. The hunting ground was a woodland valley with zombies at almost every turn and over every steep rise. One of the undead must have been getting hungry in Smurf Glade over the last few days, because every one of the 3D Smurf targets, a regular feature at this club, was now a zombified Smurf. Over a stream and then up to the top of a steep valley, we shot several zombie deer and a gorilla-wolf hybrid creature that had been zombified. Although the terrain was rough and hilly, it was thoroughly enjoyable and if we go again, gore-spattered costumes are definitely on the agenda!

Friday October 31st, Samhain, our great celebration in honour of the Beloved Dead. With so much going on, I had neither time nor energy left over to lead a ritual with the circle or an open celebration, but it would be such a shame to miss the night altogether. My altar is on top of my gran's old bureau; the front panel folds down to reveal the compartments where all my witchy tools are kept so this would make an ideal base for a solitary Samhain rite. A photograph of Gran, a photograph of Sheila, a few cat treats in honour of Luna, and lots of candles to light up the darkness. Even though I was alone for this short ceremony, I put on my ritual dress and crown as a mark of respect and solemnity for the ancestors, and laid out something to eat and drink.

Casting the circle and calling invocations to the elements and the Lord and Lady, I sat quietly for a time, thinking about my Gran, about Sheila, and sparing a thought for a friend at work who had recently lost her father. I read a poem, not one of mine as my own poetry is not very good, but a piece suitable for a celebration of ongoing life in the Summer Lands. I gave silent thanks to the ancestors, not only those who are linked to me by the ties of friendship and family, but all those people who have in some way contributed to my life. My gran had taught me her tailoring skills, but who had taught her? Her mother, a teacher, or a neighbour perhaps? The people responsible for writing the books and essays on witchcraft that I love so much are part of my heritage too, just as much as my flesh and blood kin, and I honour them all. Death is not something we look forward to, but it is the start of a new chapter in our development, a separation from the living world to the realms of the Summer Lands, where we begin our journey anew. What fresh wonders await us there are not for us to know, not yet.

I picked up my tarot cards and spread out my casting cloth; a silk handkerchief with purple and pink patterns on it and the initial 'M' in silver on each corner. I love this cloth, made for me years ago by one of my closest friends. Shuffling the deck, I picked out three cards at random, placing them face up on the cloth. I don't often read cards for myself; they either tell me things I already know or prove to be completely irrelevant. This time was no exception.

Samhain is a time of remembrance, of farewell to our Beloved Dead, a time of letting go of all those things in our lives that no longer serve us. I took up a pen and paper and wrote a letter to the Cailleach, listing all those things I no longer need in my life.

Take this from me, I don't need it any more.

Take this from me, transform it into something new and bright and hopeful.

I burned the paper, letting the ash crumble and fall into my cauldron. I touched each photograph one last time and threw the cat biscuits from Luna's place at the altar onto the garden for the birds and hedgehogs, along with a small amount of wine and cake.

<u>Divination</u>

Samhain is traditionally a time of divination and lots of the Hallowe'en customs practised today are adaptations of divination. Apples etched with the initials of eligible bachelors are thrown into a large tub and fished out with the teeth by ladies eager to see which young man might court them. Another simple form of divination using apples is still done today by young children. Carefully cutting the peel off an apple in one long strip and throwing it over your left shoulder is supposed to reveal the initial letter of your future spouse's name. Two hazelnuts in a fire hearth to represent a couple will indicate the stability of a relationship – as the hazelnuts heat up they either jump together or apart from each other, signifying the couple will do likewise.

Brushing your hair in the mirror at midnight on Samhain eve, especially if the moon is also reflected in the mirror, will conjure up a reflection of your true love peering over your shoulder. Beware, however, for if you turn around to look behind you, or so it is said, the image will disappear, and your true love shall never come for you.

Popular divination methods today include tarot and other oracle cards, runes, ogham and palmistry, but it can take a long time to become proficient. An easier and more intuitive way of fortune telling is readily available: a collection of plain, smooth pebbles or wooden discs, engraved or painted with unique symbols to signify relevant concepts, unique to you and therefore, far easier to interpret.

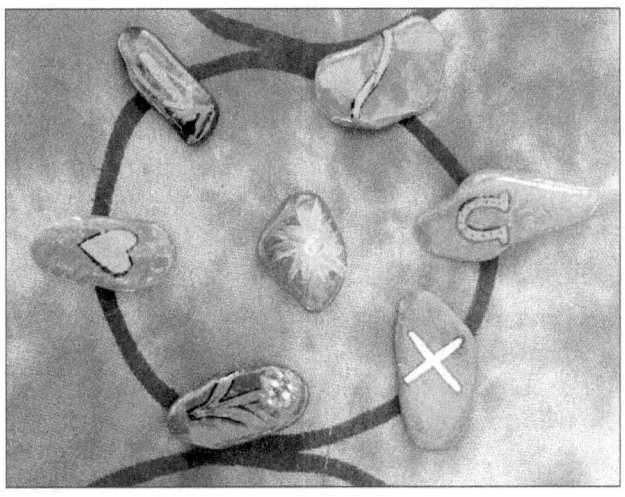

A love heart for relationships, a horse or a car for travel, a key for success, an arrow or a sword for arguments. There are hundreds of possibilities you can explore to make a very personal and highly effective tool for divination. A short walk by a stream, a woodland path or beach should provide you with plenty of small pebbles or shells to use, and some deep meditation work is a nice way of coming up with your own symbols. A square or circular casting cloth, marked in fabric pens with different areas for relationships, health, career, family and so on, can be tied around the stones as a pouch.

Rowan Protection Charm

Remember how beautiful the bright orange and scarlet berries looked on the rowan trees in September? There is often a plentiful supply, even this late in the year. Rowan trees, sometimes known as mountain ash, have been associated with witches for centuries and are said to ward off evil and offer protect against curses.

Pick the berries and use a long needle to pierce each berry, threading them onto a long strand of red embroidery silk or thin ribbon. Complete the charm with twenty-seven berries and tie the ends of the thread together. Hang up to dry for a few weeks inside an airing cupboard or in the windowsill.

The finished charm doesn't need any additions to make it look nice as the red berries will retain most of their colour, turning slightly darker as they dry. Place by the front door to protect the home or in the bedroom to ward off unpleasant dreams. Rowan will protect you and your home against evil spirits and curses as well as from anyone who wishes you ill.

> *Rowan berries give to me*
> *The protection of your sacred tree*
> *By all the power of three times three times three*
> *As I do will, so mote it be.*

November

A Song for the Season: Stag Lord, The Dolmen.

Samhain is perhaps the most emotional festival of the year, when our thoughts return to the Beloved Dead. The pagan altar is dressed with witchy accoutrements alongside photographs, prayers, petitions and offerings left for our Beloved Dead. We honour our ancestors by remembering them, talking to them and wishing them well in the next world. The trees of the woodlands are bare, fields barren; the weather is getting colder and nights draw in earlier each evening, leaving us craving daylight and sunshine. And yet, the cold darkness of winter is not seen as the end of the year, but as the gateway towards the next one.

The last weekend of October and the first of November merged together. Time for dressing up at the annual Whitby Goth Weekend and a trip to stay with Chris's Mum in nearby Middlesbrough. I wore ridiculously long hairpieces and plastered on three weeks' worth of black eyeliner and my favourite dark red lippy. I was disappointed that Phoebe wasn't spending the weekend with us, but she is now of an age where she might not have enjoyed it anyway. Whitby Goth Weekend is quite the fashion show and we could barely take more than a few steps through the old town without being asked to pose for photographs. The abbey was our first stop early in the day and it was breath-taking, if a little windy. Climbing the one hundred and ninety-nine steps to the abbey was hard work, I must say, so I was happy to find a gorgeous little tea room in the town for coffee and cake. Chris and I both enjoyed the hilarious Brenda and Effie novels of Paul Magyrs. His protagonists are two feisty older women who live in Whitby, running a small bed and breakfast and a run-down antique shop, all the while secretly saving

Whitby residents from the shocking supernatural shenanigans that plague the town. In the books, Brenda and Effie often take tea in the Walrus and Carpenter café, and this is where we had found ourselves, sitting at a small corner table on plush velvet chairs.

'You'll never guess what?' Chris asked me, after placing our order with one of the waiting staff at the counter.

'If I won't guess, there's no point in me trying to. You'd just better tell me.'

'That seat you're in right now is where the author used to sit when he was in here writing the books!'

I could pretend that I felt linked to Paul Magyrs, or that I'd known all along because the creative vibes were strong in this place, but although I did think this was indeed a pretty cool fact, it was after all, just a comfortable chair in a nice café that served good cakes.

Steam punks, Victorian goths, neo-goths, cyber-goths, emos, punks, cos-players, hippies and a general collection of odd-balls in weird, wonderful and outrageous costumes, crowded every part of the town and markets, where they posed for the dozens of photographers who turn up every year to photograph the event. I do love an opportunity to dress up and wore a beautiful gothic dress with corset lacing and voluminous skirts, my hair piled precariously high on my head, tendrils of the long hair pieces trailing down. I felt quite pleased with some of the lovely comments people said about my dress, particularly as it is one that I had made myself. I absolutely loved all the sensational outfits, especially the long and substantial skirts of the Victorian goths.

We stayed overnight with my mother-in-law and we exchanged news and set the world to rights with her before Chris and I made our way home in the morning.

The start of November marks the first day of the Nano challenge and I made a good start on my werewolf novel, now titled Blue Moon, soon getting into the flow of the story. Before long, the characters came to life in my mind, speaking in their own voices, and I pictured it all in vivid detail. Having a clear outline to refer to was incredibly useful and is something I now endeavour to do with all my novels. Only another forty-seven thousand words to go by the end of the month.

I missed the companionship of a close-knit coven for Samhain, so I set aside a time and date with a few other pagans nearby for a labyrinth walk in Sherwood Forest. I didn't have time, with my self-imposed writing deadline, to write a ritual and as normal nobody else was offering to organise anything locally. A simple labyrinth walk with drums and a winter picnic would have to do. It would good to bring people together in the woods and fresh air for a while, if nothing else.

The week flew by, with lots of writing late into the evenings, the words flowing out of my little head and spilling onto the page quite easily. Phoebe's birthday was coming up this week. I did feel sorry for her having her birthday on a school day and I was disappointed that she'd be spending the weekend with her dad, so I made a big fuss of her on the day. Her celebration involved pizza, gifts, and a DVD marathon of her favourite programme at the time, the Vampire Diaries. Every year she is more mature, articulate and sophisticated, and as she grows up with endless possibilities ahead of her, I just see more grey hair and lines on the face that returns my gaze in the mirror and I wonder where on earth the time has disappeared to.

On the Mansfield social media grapevine I'd heard about a meditation night in the town centre that took place on alternate Friday nights and decided to give it a try. Another conventional hall was turned into a sacred space, with chairs placed in a circle, a large crystal skull in the centre with myriads of crystals, fairylights and pretty wands all around. We started with tea and coffee and introductions before our hosts began the evening's session, playing a CD of beautiful, ethereal and soul-touching music. Other than the music and the occasional shuffling noise, there was silence. Blissful, sweet silence.

We sat in this peaceful state for some time before our hosts gently brought us back to the present moment to have a short break followed by a spoken pathworking, a single frame drum beating softly in the background. As one person guided the group along the path, another gradually moved around the group with the drum, changing sound and direction as he circled. The soft vibrations could be felt as a wave through my whole body, healing and energising. There was a positive, calming energy in this meditation session and I wish I could make it every time; unfortunately, with all the other things I do, it isn't possible.

The labyrinth walk on Sunday afternoon was well attended, with twenty or so people joining me with their assorted drums and rattles and cakes to share. I had chosen a spot right in the heart of the main forest, within sight of the Major Oak. An English oak of significant size and history, the tree is named after antiquarian Major Hayman Rooke, who described the oak in his informative book "Remarkable Oaks in the park of Welbeck in the county of Nottingham" (1790). The Major Oak is an average of 337cm in diameter, 10m around the trunk and is 16m tall with a canopy spread of 28m. Allegedly Robin Hood's former hiding place, the centuries-old tree is now supported by scaffolding and held together with metal straps and bands, the deep crevices in its bark filled with resin or steel plates to prevent further damage. When I was very young, we frequently visited Sherwood Forest and the surrounding country parks on day trips with my grandparents and I grew up loving this ancient, majestic, magical tree. Today the Major Oak is enclosed within a wooden fence to prevent people from trampling the compacted earth around its giant trunk and at first glance, you would be forgiven for thinking the tree looks quite sad, dead and decaying. Despite its shabby appearance, however, this old oak hasn't reached the end of its life just yet and bursts with fresh green leaves and new acorns every year.

I laid out the ropes of my portable labyrinth, clearing a few large branches and twigs out of the way. Some of the group had been at my equinox ritual and others had come for the first time, so there were greetings as we introduced ourselves. One couple, Lucy and Pete, who we had met at the local September camp, had travelled some distance to be here with their two young children, both blue eyed and blonde. Lucy brought the eldest, her five-year-old daughter, over to say hello.

'So good to see you again.' Lucy said, 'This is Evie, and she's very excited to be here because I've told her all about you.'

'Hello Evie, I'm Moira.' I bent down to her level and she immediately leaned forward and spoke to me softly.

'Are you the witch?' she whispered, nervously toying with her hair.

'Yes.' I whispered back, making sure I was smiling.

'I've never met a witch before.' she told me. Her bright, round eyes were wide with curiosity and wonder.

'Has Mummy told you about the labyrinth?' I asked. She nodded, tucking a little finger into her mouth. 'Would you like me to show it to you now? Is that okay with Mummy?'

Mummy said of course it was okay with her and I led the little girl over to the labyrinth. 'If you like, you can be the first one to walk round it. We need to make it feel special first though.'

I called the gathering into a circle around the labyrinth and lit a large bundle of sage, walking round with my spirit duster and letting the heady scent of the burning herbs wash over everybody. There was nothing else to do, so after a quick introduction to the concept of the entering the labyrinth as an act of walking with intention or as a tool for reflection, prayer or meditation, I invited people to walk the path. Djembe drums and rattles rang out in the clearing and it began to rain heavily. Carla yelped with excitement.

'Ooh, that's so cleansing.' she said, embracing her wild side. 'I love rain.' After that, I could barely hear what she was saying because the sky decided to drop the entire ocean on our heads. The torrential rain kept up for at least half an hour though fortunately it was not cold. Huddling under trees for shelter and holding our coats over our heads, we must have been a sorry looking bunch of pagans, but we couldn't get away with hiding from the rain for long. As soon as it became clear that the rain was not going ease up for some time, I had a 'stuff-it' moment and walked around the labyrinth anyway, wet hair hanging over my face. I was soon followed by some of the others. Carla, with her invincible, innocent spirit, took off her shoes and socks to leap and run about in the rain-soaked grass. Our enthusiastic drummers, tucked up against the trunk of an oak to shelter from the downpour, picked up a beat and eventually the rain began to slow.

The children, excluding Phoebe who is far too mature for that sort of thing, joined in. They practically raced round the labyrinth path, squealing with laughter and jumping about, showing us adults that while it's all very well being serious and meditative, sometimes it is absolutely essential to have fun, to be delighted by simple things and to run and dance and sing and laugh in the rain. Dancing and paddling in the soggy ground with a bunch of happy pagans, moss and grass squishing between my toes, I had thoroughly good fun. At last, the rain came to a halt and the sun braved its way to us through the bare branches of the oak trees above us. Nobody had brought chairs or rugs to sit on, so we stood in a rough huddle together, sharing food and drink, taking photographs of muddy, bare feet joined in the centre of the labyrinth.

It seemed a shame to put my shoes and socks back on and the fact that my feet were drenched through didn't make it any more joyful. Barefoot walking is something that Carla does regularly and she is sure that her general health is better as a result of the skin-to-earth connection she has with every step. There are several routes through the forest that she assures me are soft underfoot and far enough off the beaten track to be undisturbed by nosey tourists. The area around the Major Oak is usually very busy, even on a wintry Sunday, but today the rain had kept everybody at bay, all except for a few of us hardy pagans.

It was a great afternoon, spent with some of the nicest people, all barefoot dancing and singing in the rain in the heart of an ancient forest. One or two people had texted earlier in the day to apologise for not coming along, the weather having put them off. I get wet regularly, and although being out in the rain is not always my favourite activity, every single time, I have been able to get dry and warm afterwards. Snuggling up with my husband and daughter on the sofa under a blanket with hot drinks afterwards makes it worthwhile.

The once-white ropes of the labyrinth had turned a muddy brown colour and I puzzled for some time over how to get them washed and dried without spending three hours untangling them. In the end, I zipped them into a net laundry bag to go in the washing machine and then hung the ropes over the banister to dry. Alas, this reminded me that I had yet to tackle the rest of the laundry mountain, including the ironing. If only, I lamented once more, real magic worked the way that it does in fiction. Despite the fresh air and dancing, I didn't sleep well at all that night and stayed up writing about vampires and werewolves until the small hours.

I telephoned Elaine one evening, thinking it would be nice to have a quick catch up while Chris was still at work and Phoebe was in her room, busy with an ongoing art project for school. It was a long phone call, talking about healing therapies, her theories on the law of attraction in action, our respective childhoods, and most of the time, we were laughing like maniacs. When I eventually hung up the phone, Chris had arrived home and was busy making dinner. I sat down to write, picking up the story where I'd left off until Phoebe emerged from her room to spend some time with us. She proudly showed off her art project, a three-dimensional dragon head. She has always enjoyed drawing, painting and crafts and can spend hours sketching or painting. She has a genuine artistic flair and I'm always in awe of her talent, which obviously she gets from my mother and my sister, not from me.

The MRI appointment for my hips and lower back finally came around and I duly turned up to the mobile unit at the hospital in Mansfield. The MRI unit is extremely brightly lit, incredibly noisy, and the tube of the scanner encloses you completely. Almost shroud-like, the tunnel is only seven-inches or so above your face and I was glad that I hadn't inherited my mother's claustrophobia. The noise of the MRI scanner is like an industrial metal working factory, combined with alien-like clicks and whistles, bangs and clattering sounds that vibrate in your ears. I'd had another MRI for something else a few years ago, so I knew what to expect and put a flannel over my eyes to shut out the bright lights. I handed the machine operators a CD of meditation music to play for me through the headphones. All I had to do now was keep still.

It was the first time in a long while that I had nothing other to do than lie quietly on my own, knowing I wouldn't be disturbed. In fact, it was essential that the only thing I did now was to lie still and try to relax. I shut out the noises by using some meditation techniques and focusing on the music, and I took myself off on a pathworking exercise, becoming more deeply relaxed with every breath. I know a lot of people find the scanner too noisy and claustrophobic, but for me, having had such little sleep and rest lately, it was bliss. Forty-five minutes later, the noises and clattering bangs and vibrations stopped and I was pulled out of the tunnel. I hoped the resulting scan would show something useful and I booked an appointment with the consultant for the results.

Since writing this book, I've had major operation to fix the problems with my hip and I cannot praise the staff of the NHS highly enough for looking after me.

I went over to visit Lisa one evening, giving her some healing energy with Reiki to help her recover from a mild chest infection. Graham telephoned to ask if I would send more Reiki treatments to his cat and each time I did so, Shibby turned her back on me, casting a steely-eyed glare in my general direction. The spiritual development meeting in Rainworth was focusing on crystal grids this week and my own crystals, gathered from their assorted places in the house, came with me in a wooden box to charge up on the altar. I had an afternoon off work to take Phoebe shopping with her birthday gift tokens and before I knew it, she was away again, staying with her dad for a long weekend, while I was excited to be heading off to London for Witchfest. Chris insisted it would be easier and quicker to drive there than to take the train and, as he was prepared to do the driving himself, I packed a good book to read and off we went, checking in at a nearby hotel.

Witchfest is organised by the Children of Artemis. A day full of witchy talks and workshops, pagan themed music in the evenings and a witch's market for all your pagan shopping needs. Several of the workshops I fancied clashed with each other and it was hard to choose between them, though I wasn't disappointed with the ones I picked out. The day started with an opening blessing, where over five-hundred witches, druids and pagans gathered together in the main hall. Perhaps there was incense burning nearby: my eyes leaked when the speaker, this year the highly respected witch and author, Tylluan Penry, called out:

'Blessed be, blessed be, blessed be!'

So many witches in the same place and time, all of us there to learn, to enjoy, to connect, to meet old friends and new. As one, the audience intoned the words along with her and it sent a warm feeling of belonging, family and unity shooting along every strand of my hair, every vein in my body: my soul was bursting. It felt like being at home with an extended family of relatives who I hadn't had the chance to meet yet. Chris reached over without saying a word and squeezed my hand. He knows.

Kevin Groves kindly signed my copy of A Path Laid Bare, his first book, which I had ordered after going to his workshop at the summer gathering. He had an impish grin on his face as he opened the front cover and jotted down a couple of lines. It was a busy day and I was keen to browse the market stalls before the next talk, so I wasn't quite paying attention. It wasn't until much later that I had time to open the book and read what Kevin had written. No wonder he'd been grinning like a fiend as he signed it – it was written in Egyptian and I had no idea what the translation might be. Thanks, Kevin! Cheeky thing, I wasn't letting him get away with that! I duly hurried onto the internet to find out what it meant. Kevin is thoroughly knowledgeable with a wealth of experience to draw on and he is a highly entertaining, patient and informative teacher. If you ever have the chance to attend one of his workshops or talks, you won't be disappointed. As a slight aside, Kevin is very good at writing up his notes and information on his website and his excellent books on magical practises are packed full of ideas and research, so do find time to look him up if you can.

Over lunch, we sauntered around the market stalls once again, and a few choice witchy items followed me out of the main hall. I'm not a fan of over-priced, mass-produced goods, but I so rarely get a chance to do witchy shopping that it seemed a shame not to treat myself to a new tunic-dress, purple of course, with a flying witch motif on the front. I bought several new books and a handful of back issues of Witchcraft and Wicca magazine. Several people I knew from the Nottingham pagan crowd were dotted around the venue, including our good friends Cayt and Tim. Cayt and I enthused over the talks we had attended so far and read our programmes again for the afternoon sessions we would each like to go to.

I listened to the witches' question and answer panel, Kevin's talk on cyber magic, and a session with another well-known witch on bringing wicca into the family and community. The last formal session, on initiators and initiates in Wicca, was given by Alexandrian High Priestess, Mary Rands. She spoke with a vibrant passion and love for her subject; it was an interesting and informative talk that went too fast for me to take it all in. I made a bee-line for her, along with a few others, to ask questions and say thank you afterwards. Fortunately, there was no further talks and Mary was more than happy to chat with us all for another hour. She very kindly gave me her details and extracted a promise from me keep in touch with her. While I gossiped away and greedily ate up every snippet of information, Chris made small talk with one of the people standing near us and by the time I had finished my chat with Mary and a couple of other wiccans, he was deep in conversation with another person. It was my turn to wait for him for a change.

With the workshops and talks over for the day, we took a breath of fresh air outside and found somewhere to get a bite to eat before heading back in time for musical magic. Damh the Bard and the Dolmen were just brilliant, and, despite my aching hips, I did enjoy flinging myself about with a dance at the front of the stage. It was a long day and a late night but worth it, even though I was in a lot of pain the next day. The hotel was superb, Witchfest had thoroughly lived up to and exceeded my expectations, and when we made our way home on Sunday morning, I read one of my new witchy books from the assorted volumes I'd bought, while Chris did the driving.

Returning to daily life after witchy events feels disappointing; back to work on Monday, archery on Tuesday, and a workout at the gym, all combined with frantic writing every night. Blue Moon, the paranormal romance, was coming on nicely, and having an outline to work towards was proving to be more valuable than I ever thought it would be. On top of this, I had promised Graham that we'd go along to the pagan moot in Nottingham on Wednesday evening, and I was glad I decided to stick to that, instead of writing. I had been talking to Cayt and Sarah and the rest of the crowd for over an hour when the door opened, and Graham came in. My skin went cold and clammy as soon as my eyes met his.

Graham's face was ashen white and I knew. I squeezed through the tightly crowded snug in the pub to reach him, but I had no words that would express how sorry I was. Standing in the middle of the crowded tables felt awkward and clumsy, nevertheless, I gave him a long hug and cried with him for his beloved Luna. When we managed to find somewhere to sit together, Chris in his quiet and understanding way, joined us. Luna had died in Graham's arms that morning. Our mutual friend, Simon, had been the only person Graham had been able to get hold of at short notice to be with him for support when Luna had been put to sleep. I was so sorry I'd not known how much he'd needed a friend that day and hoped that us being there now was helping in some small way. Luna was a truly unique cat, gentle, unshakeable, a hardy character who was well loved. I know Graham will miss Luna dearly for a very long time yet to come. Rest in peace, dear, sweet Luna.

After a few weeks of restless nights, I started to suffer a severe case of insomnia around this time; every night I was writing until at least midnight and even then, the creative monkeys in my brain would not switch off. I was determined to finish my novel by the end of the month and had become so engrossed and excited by the characters in my paranormal novel that, despite how tired I felt, I spent long, long hours lying awake at night. A few pages of whatever novel I'm currently reading usually sends me to the Land of Nod. If that doesn't work, I have a stand-by lavender pouch to soothe me into dream-land. Meditation or using the soothing rainbow countdown visualisation sometimes helps on nights when sleep eludes me. No such luck this time.

Night after night, I was wide awake, often getting only two-or-three hours sleep, if that. This had started to become a real problem over the last the couple of weeks and there were several long, tedious nights without any sleep at all. When I went about my normal routines the next day, I felt ill. Physically and mentally shattered, sleep deprivation is not fun. Standing by the photocopier at work one day, I jolted myself awake as I began to fall asleep and fall over, tipping forward on my feet. It was embarrassing. Not only that, it was giving me headaches. My limbs began to ache, I couldn't concentrate or think clearly and my vision started to blur.

A rare Saturday with nothing planned was bliss, yet although I managed to sleep in the early hours of the morning, it hadn't made me feel any better and I was noticeably irritable and tetchy. I could do with something to cheer me up and get rid of the stress that was starting to take its toll.

Chris was busy at work for the day, so I decided to pack our archery gear in the car and headed off with Phoebe to the club woods to enjoy the greenery and fresh air. Several cars were parked along the track beside the cabin, but there was no sign of anyone nearby. Phoebe checked the chalk-board outside to see who had turned up.

'John, Paul, Tony, and a few others. Oh, Neil and Rob are here too.' she called over.

We strung our bows, slung quivers full of arrows over our shoulders and began our trek round the course to catch up with them. A few minutes later, we heard the distinctive sound of arrows piercing the 3D resin targets. Phoebe called ahead and Rob and Neil waited patiently for us to catch up. They are both very good archers, rarely missing the zone we call the inner kill, and they put me to shame, my light wooden arrows zooming in for the kill and only managing a wounding score. Field archery is good fun and our companions soon settled into their usual routine of jesting and teasing with Phoebe.

Walking through pines and birch, I hummed a tune and said hello out loud to the trees and the birds. I reached up to touch an oak apple, hanging from a high branch, and Neil caught me red-handed.

'What's the pagan significance of oak trees, then?' he asked, plucking another oak apple from a branch and handing it to me. I smoothed it between my fingers, enjoying the sensation of the woody outside layer on my skin, soaking up the sturdy strength of oak.

'Where should I start?' I took a moment to gather my thoughts on this. 'The oak tree is one of the twenty trees on the old Ogham alphabet. Its symbol, Duir, represents stability, wisdom. It's the old tree of the druids, but it's more than that. Oak is a symbol of strength and longevity; a very protective tree too. Think of all those thousands of creatures who make their home in an oak, using its bark and branches as protection from the elements, squirrels and birds who hide and nest in the tree itself.'

We talked for a few minutes about our respective connections to trees and nature before our conversation was cut short by the noise of other archers making their own way through the woods. I followed Neil and the rest of our small group along the track towards the cabin and one chap thrust out a hand to help me clamber over a tree trunk that lay across the path.

'Should have brought your broomstick,' he said. 'You could have flown over that.'

'It's in for repair, otherwise I would have done.'

The last target of the course was a six-foot tall faux deer and I managed to miss it completely. I was starting to struggle a bit with the pain in my hip and hung back to make my own way at a slower pace. I needed a new beater for my frame drum and after my initial shock at how staggeringly expensive they can be to buy, I had been wondering how to make one of my own. How hard could it be? A sturdy wooden stick with some padding and leather over one end. I kept an eye out for a piece of windfall wood I could use, but the ground was damp after some rain overnight, and every suitable sized stick I found was soggy. I wasn't entirely sure how to dry them out without cracking the wood. I would have to keep my eyes peeled over the next few weeks on my walks.

Taking down my bow and stowing it in the car boot, I looked down and right in front of me, hidden slightly in the grass verge of the track, was a perfectly dry, stout looking stick. I assumed it would be rotten or damp underneath, but something in the back of my mind told me to go ahead and pick it up. Approximately thirty centimetres long, the stick was only slightly damp in places and it didn't bend or develop any cracks when I tried to flex it. This was exactly what I'd been looking for. I still had some thick wadding left over from when I had made my beast of a quilt and that, with some sturdy fabric over the top, should provide enough padding for the head of the beater. I put away the archery gear and my new find in the car boot and headed back home with Phoebe.

We had steaming mugs of hot chocolate and a plate of hot buttered toast to warm us up when we settled back at home.

Phoebe made a start on some of her never-ending home-work and I picked up my laptop and carried on with my novel, letting the story come out in its own way, writing solidly for the rest of the day and into the evening. I was making good progress with the novel and, much to my surprise and delight, had managed to reach my target of fifty-thousand words by the end of the month, though it looked like the novel itself might take slightly longer than that to finish.

November had been a good month and now the winter solstice was fast approaching. It would be nice to hold another open ritual in the woods, I had yule gifts to buy or make, and it seemed far too long since the last meeting with the witchcraft development circle. With Witchfest, work, meditation groups, pub moots and writing, I was starting to feel overwhelmed and my sleeping pattern wasn't showing any signs of improvement.

 I tried one last time to have a good night's rest, lighting white candles and boiling some of the sleepy herbs Carla had given me for a cup of tea. The vile tasting brew was as bitter as I'd been expecting, but I remain grateful that such a kind soul had offered some help. I could only hope that December might turn out to be more sedate. Who was I kidding? You've seen how that kind of thinking worked out for me so far this year!

Fun with Labyrinths

My portable labyrinth is made with two lengths of thick white sisal rope, approximately forty-nine feet long (fifteen metres) each, making a labyrinth with a finished diameter of roughly ten feet (three meters). The rope came from a DIY store and cost twenty-five pounds, a worthwhile outlay for a labyrinth I can use again and again.

To create your own portable labyrinth, use the diagram provided below as a guide, laying out one rope in a large loop, starting from the centre. The second rope goes over the top of the first to form rest of the labyrinth. Sweep the area with the besom and, if outdoors, remove any sharp branches or obvious trip hazards.

I tend to smudge around the perimeter of the labyrinth and set up crystals, photographs, statues, altar pieces or positive affirmations around the path, either in random places or at the cardinal points.

If you don't have the room, time or energy to use a full-sized labyrinth, you can trace the template with your fingers, slowly circling inward while meditating. Kevin Groves has some great ideas on how to make the labyrinth more dramatic. Spreading the design on a beach at night, ropes dowsed in glow-in-the-dark neon paint, is one of his suggestions, and I'm sure that by now he's come up with plenty more.

Ropes are only one way of creating the path. Large stones can be laid to mark the design, footprints in the sand at the beach, or if you have a large garden, create a labyrinth out of shrubs and planters, a small seating area in the centre. The labyrinth can be painted onto a large sheet of canvas or thick cotton to be spread over the floor. A painted cloth would also allow you to use different colours in each quarter for the elements and paint symbols and sigils around the edge of the labyrinth or at different points along the path.

The labyrinth has always been associated with journeys, spiritual or otherwise, often a quest or a journey of discovery, leading adventurous types to receive a prize, recover the missing piece of a puzzle or complete a challenge, while others might receive a sense of peace, comfort or enlightenment.

Use the labyrinth as you will: a walk of solitary reflection can be just as beneficial, even more so, than a shared experience. Pacing barefoot in the rain or warming sunshine, grass and shoots tickling the toes, by oneself or hand-in-hand with others, a walk round the labyrinth can be a liberating, transforming experience.

These are the chants I've created so far to accompany a labyrinth walk, the first of which is one that Carla and myself came up with that afternoon as we danced in the rain and the sun, ad-libbing, calling out the words in time with each other or in a round.

I feel the Earth

(After each line of this chant the drum beat rang out and we repeated the line with humming instead of singing.)

> *I feel the earth beneath my feet,*
> *I feel the rain upon my face,*
> *I breathe the air within my lungs,*
> *I feel the fire within my soul,*
> *I feel the call of the goddess of old.*
> *I feel the call of the goddess of old.*

Walk the Earth

> *I walk the earth, the ancient path,*
> *The Old Ones calling me on,*
> *The Old Ones calling me on.*
> *I place my feet on the witch's path,*
> *I feel it in my soul,*
> *I feel it in my soul.*
> *I journey to the land of the ancestors,*
> *My spirit living free,*
> *My spirit living free.*

I walk my path, my head held high,
In love and joy and truth,
In love and joy and truth.
I live with the love of the Old Ones,
Deep within my soul,
Deep within my soul.

December

Endless days of snow and hoar,
All creatures shiver and bar their door,
Against the cold and forever night,
When all is dim in a dearth of light.

Predator and prey must brave the chill,
To seek their food with tooth and bill,
To ensure survival with a will of steel,
With a threat of death present and real.

Winter trials fill every hour,
As the cold white blanket holds the power,
To cover the tracks and trails that lead,
Living things to their drink and feed.

The battle is tough and fraught with strife,
Hope and instinct ensure the life.
Solstice day is nearly done,
Bringing shorter nights and warmer sun.

(Neil Page)

The year's end – time to let go, time to rest. Rain, wind, snow and low temperatures are promised, the chill in the air is tangible and night falls early. Trees have lost their final leaves, birds are quiet, fields are bare; winter is well and truly underway. Brightly coloured decorations in windows and hanging from lamp-posts around the cities cheer up the cold, grey days and children burst with excitement as their visits from Santa approach. Robins and holly berries add a flicker of colour to the natural world.

December took me by surprise, how had an entire year managed to pass by so quickly?

I managed to make it to Empyrean on the first Wednesday of the month. The talk was interesting: *Eating like Our Ancestors*. Our guest speaker, a counsellor and hypnotherapist who helps clients with a range of dietary and weight issues, explained how we can improve our health and well-being by modifying our diet to include seasonal, native foods, at the same time avoiding processed sugars and carbohydrates.

An advocate of this diet herself, she suggested that high-fat and low-carb content in our diets is one way ahead for healthy eating. She was certainly an inspiration, as she looked amazing with her glossy hair, beautiful skin, and a slender and healthy physique. Several years ago I studied NLP, neuro-linguistic programming. Another student on this course was an advocate of a raw food diet and, although this wasn't quite the same, some of the principals and results were remarkably similar. Both women were incredibly healthy looking, slim without looking gaunt, skin virtually glowing with energy and vibrancy. This talk, right before the festive end of year celebrations, always so full of rich foods and drink, was a timely reminder to at least try and eat more healthily.

I continued to work on my paranormal fantasy novel late into the night. I was so close to the end that I couldn't bear to be at work every day, frustrated that I had to spend time working on dull highway applications. Things for my werewolf characters were getting tense, building up to a violent finale and it felt like reading the final scene of book you just can't put down. The main character had resolved most of her problems, but suddenly found herself kidnapped by the rival werewolf pack, her dashing saviour nowhere in sight. When I wrote the last chapter, the last sentence, and finally the words *the end*, my heart skipped and leapt about in my chest. I'd done it. An entire novel in only thirty-five days and with a total word-count of just over sixty-five thousand words.

You might think, after the last few months, that I would now have a chance to sit around in my pyjamas watching television all day, but I couldn't spare the time. Television was the last thing on my mind. I had Yule gifts to organise and a ritual to plan for the solstice. I found a few spaces in my diary to squeeze everything in and thought about what sort of gifts I could make this year. At this time of year, my kitchen is normally home to a range of baked goods and brightly coloured liquids fermenting or clearing in glass demi-johns. I pulled the air lock out of a demi-john full of deep red liquid and tried it. Hmm, this blackberry wine would be a bit of a disappointment as a gift, I'd have to keep that myself, such a hardship, but the parsnip wine had turned into a crystal-clear golden liquor that warmed my throat. Wine-making isn't too time consuming, but with the brewing process finished, I needed to sterilise a dozen bottles and syphon the wine. Chris whizzed up some professional looking labels for me to put on the bottles and hey presto, I now had twelve bottles of tasty country wine that would make lovely gifts.

I planned to join in with the drumming group one week this month and made a start on my new drum beater. Our box room is full of craft materials, including a stash of fabric remnants, and I rummaged through boxes and bags until I found what I needed. I cut the wadding left over from the beastly quilt into a strip roughly one inch wide by about twelve inches long and wound this round one end of the stick, using my trusty glue gun to secure it. I had a large patch of purple camouflage material in my fabric stash, left over from one craft project or another. Chopped into a rough circle, I wrapped it over the wadding, held it in place tightly and bound it with purple embroidery silk. I gathered the fabric around the wadding and the stick and stitched it up, adding more glue to be on the safe side. I had no idea if this was how beaters are supposed to be made, but it looked like fair facsimile of a drum beater to me. It didn't fall apart when I used it and it made a suitable sound so that was good enough for me. If I'd had more time, and if I was more of a perfectionist than I am, perhaps the addition of a few beads or feathers would have made it look more professional, but who needs perfection anyway?

I had booked a small and cosy room at a newly opened venue in Hucknall for an evening of tarot readings at the weekend. I had one client straight after another, five in total over the course of the evening. It was exhausting, but I was pleased that information came to me easily and my clients all went away happy. This isn't always the case, sometimes clients are difficult to read for, though usually I manage to get some relevant information coming through for them, even if it doesn't make much sense to me. Every now and then, however, a client will sit with one leg crossed over the other, arms folded, an expression of indifference, or even defiance, plastered across their face. I can't help but feel as though I am being tested when this happens. The aura some people give off is one of pure negativity. They are saying very clearly with their attitude and body language, *come on then, prove it*, and expecting that I will give them a disappointing reading full of meaningless drivel that any Tom, Dick or Helen could make up.

To give you an example of this, here's a genuine reading that I had trouble with some time ago. My lady client shuffled the cards and immediately crossed her arms in front of her – a clear blocking gesture if ever there was one. I turned the cards over and started to talk to her about the impressions I was getting. I felt my hands starting to drift in front of me gently, to and fro, to and fro, like a wave. The image of a car popped into my head and the motion of my hands, wave-like and buoyant, felt tied into this vision of the car. I suggested there was an issue to do with a car and water or the sea.

'No,' she replied. 'I don't have a car right now.'

'Okay.' I said, taking her at her word. The more I talked, the more the forces that be kept swishing my hands around in front of me, as if they were being guided by the swell of the ocean. The image of the same car came to me again.

'Really,' I asked this lady, 'do you not have a car? There's something here about the sea and your car.'

'I told you, I haven't got a car.' She seemed rather put out at me asking her again, a stony expression fixed firmly on her face. Fair enough, I thought, even though I couldn't rid myself of that feeling of waves and the car. The rest of the reading was a struggle if I'm honest: I could not shake the sea-car connection and my lady client was putting out very negative vibes, pulling faces and tapping her fingers on the table. Had she only come here to waste her money and my time?

I muttered something about her planning to travel and that was when the penny dropped.

'Ah, well,' she said, confessing at last, 'I have got a car. But it's in Germany. I'm trying to organise bringing it over here on the ferry.'

Honestly, I don't know why I bother sometimes.

When the tarot readings I was doing this month went well for my clients, it felt good to be able to help them, even if the little money it brought in didn't go far enough to swell the bank account by very much.

Announcing my book deal to everyone, once I'd signed the contract for The Witch's Journey, was a big deal for me. One of the things I find challenging, as you know by now, is the over-used and annoying question: 'how's the writing going?' My family were all thrilled and looking forward, I'm sure, to the glitzy launch party with buckets of champagne, sparkling dresses, red carpets and the camera flashes set off by hordes of adoring journalists as I step up to the podium to receive the Booker Prize. I should be so lucky! However, I was still incredibly proud of myself and my work. It had been over a year since my last published piece, a Samhain feature in Soul and Spirit magazine, so I was over the moon that I would soon see my writing out in public again.

When one book finds a home, another one starts to bubble away in the back of my mind. With my non-fiction finding a home and my Nano novel finished, I wanted to put myself back into writing mode. I had a few thoughts on what I wanted to work on next and would need to plan a concise outline and a well-constructed proposal for another non-fiction. Blue Moon, the paranormal romance novel, could do with a bit editing to make it ready for submission too. My typing fingers were going to be busier than ever before.

An appointment from the hospital became available, offering me a steroid injection for my hip disorder. These injections are not pleasant at all. I've had several over the years and they have not helped at all so I was reluctant, even though the consultant who had arranged the MRI scan thought they would be able to give me at least a few months of pain relief. When you have spent years in constant pain, you are willing to try anything. This time, the injection would be guided by ultra-sound into the base of my spine as well the hip, so there was that to look forward to.

A selection of Yule gifts needed making, and in addition to that, I wanted to go through my stash of green and brown wools to make some appliqued leaves and vines that would eventually be sewn onto the quilt. I selected fabrics, ribbons, sequins and buttons and put myself to work on a range of small sewing projects to give away to family and friends.

Me and Phoebe were looking forward to spending a weekend with Jules at the beginning of the month. Our two daughters have been best friends since they were babies and the four of us always have a fantastic time together. Jules is one of my top female role models; composed, refined, elegant and intelligent, this remarkable woman dedicates herself whole-heartedly to everything she does. She has been a good friend of mine for over twenty years and she is an inspiration, not only because of her amazing pumpkin quilt. With a case full of yule-tide gifts at the ready, we arrived early on Friday evening for a weekend of fun.

Jules and I are both big advocates of charity shops and as her locality is an affluent area, I looked forward to finding a few good quality items. I snared a couple of bargains, including a long black velvet skirt – I always think a witch can't go wrong with a long black velvet skirt, it's a staple item in my wardrobe – and a dark red lacy top. We took the girls ten-pin bowling, indulged ourselves with chocolate brioche for breakfast, and scared our teenagers, or possibly bored them, with a good old classic vampire film, The Lost Boys.

I had been thinking hard over the week of the different writing projects I wanted to get underway and was tying myself in knots over it. I knew that if anyone would be able to help me pin down exactly what to write about next, it would be Jules. We went through my ideas and mulled them over late into the night, sipping Prosecco and snaffling chocolate truffles like they were going out of fashion. One potential book would focus on doll and poppet magic, based on the research I'd done for my talk earlier in the year. We agreed that this would be a well-received book, but Jules thought that my idea of a year in the life of witch would appeal to a wider audience. After thrashing it out for a while, it became clear that both books deserved to be written. The book on magical dolls could include history, folklore and spell craft, while Living Witchcraft, which Jules encouraged me to start straight away, would be a nice way of giving a reasonably comprehensive answer to one of the questions I get asked most often at talks and workshops: *What do witches actually do?*

Our weekend away was over all too quickly and once more came the unwanted alarm call of Monday morning as the working week beckoned to me with its cold and bony fingers. Combined with more crafty projects to make as solstice gifts and a trip to the gym before work one morning, it was a busy week, but a good one. I had slept well during my visit with Jules and finally started to sleep a little better overall, getting three to four hours most nights.

The steroid injections for my hip were scheduled this week and I was not looking forward it one little bit though, as I knew from prior experience exactly what to expect. Painful is not the word I would use to describe the injections. Lying uncomfortably on my side, trousers round my knees, tunic dress pulled up out of the way, scratchy blue paper towel tucked around my undergarments. It was neither dignified nor pleasant. Ultrasound jelly is cold and slimy and the injection itself was preceded by the consultant rattling off a list of potential side-effects he thought I ought to be aware of. These included infections, damage to the tendons in my leg, worsening of current symptoms and let's not forget the possibility of temporary paralysis if the needle hit any of the nerves around the joint of my hip or my spine. The needle was long enough to reach the bone. Half way into the muscle, the consultant stopped to make sure I was still able to wiggle my toes before plunging the needle slowly right down to the bone. I won't describe the intense pain, or the sense of pressure building inside my hip as the steroid was squeezed into it. Two injections in my hip and three spinal injections, all without anaesthetic.

One lady I know from local pagan gatherings, who shall remain nameless, had recommended that I take along a piece of rose quartz to hold during the procedure. She assured me that this would take away the pain virtually instantly. While I do use some complimentary therapies, I marvel at some people's complete lack of understanding and grasp of the severity of chronically painful or debilitating conditions. Surely people cannot really believe a that holding piece of rose quartz is going to be of any use in a case of chronic-acute pain that has been ongoing for over a decade? Trust me, it doesn't help, and neither does their advice, however well-intentioned it may be.

A nursing assistant wheeled me back to the waiting room with strict instructions to stay put for the next thirty minutes to make sure I didn't have any problems walking. It was very weird to walk after this resting period; my left leg was completely numb and the rest of my hip, pelvis and thighs across both legs, and my lower back were all excruciatingly painful. I hobbled around like a zombie, groaning and clutching at Chris's arm as he arrived to support me. After a caramel cappuccino and a bite to eat in the hospital café, I was still feeling dreadful and in so much pain I wanted to cry. I was scheduled to hold another tarot reading session at the Hucknall venue in just over an hour.

There was no way I would be able to sit still all afternoon and focus on other people when all I wanted to do was go home, curl up in a blanket while crying to myself with a big box of chocolates and a decent horror movie, not to mention taking a whole bunch of very strong pain killers. I didn't want to let everyone down at such short notice though, and I had arranged this session long before I knew the treatment date. I have never cancelled an event to date and had no intention of doing so now if I could help it. Chris had to take me there, as I was not allowed to drive for another forty-eight hours and my legs wouldn't have been capable anyway. I stumbled in through the door and to my relief, a registered massage therapist was working in the shop to offer free taster sessions for the afternoon.

The second I hobbled in, she ushered me into her treatment chair and worked on me gently with her warm, healing hands until the first of my tarot clients arrived. The pain was still there and absolutely screaming at me, but I felt better mentally and emotionally, and managed to give four positive readings, with results that left each client feeling satisfied. When the last reading finished and I was able to focus on myself again, the pain came back and hit me with a shock. I felt like someone had flicked a switch on to release the floodgates of pain.

Chris left me alone that evening, on a well-deserved night out at Rock City with his mates to see New Model Army, and Phoebe was away with her dad, so I had to console myself with Reiki, comfortable blankets and an average rated horror movie that didn't do much to cheer me up. I was wallowing in agony and feeling truly sorry for myself when the telephone rang. I was in one of those moods when I really didn't want to talk to anyone. I answered anyway and was thrilled to hear Elaine's voice on the other end. I was instantly cheered up.

She has an infectious laugh, a soft and soothing voice, and she is full of small gems of insight and wisdom. Elaine is an enthusiastic listener and always keen to talk about any subject you care to mention. She asked me what it was like to be a mother and showed a great interest in my relationship with Phoebe, as she adores children. Our chatter reminded her of her own childhood and one time when she knelt on the floor in front of the sofa and felt around her to 'see' what was there. Nothing. A great expanse of space. She thinks she would have been around five years old and even at that age, due to her blindness, she had a sense of safety drilled into her. Knowing there was nothing in her way, she clambered back up to the sofa, jumping around on the cushions like any small child would do, then took a flying leap into the air, landing on the floor with a big thud. She did it again and again, loving the freedom of flight for those few precious seconds that she was airborne.

Her sense of adventure is still apparent, as seen by her determination to go camping unassisted with Toby, against the advice of their care workers and friends who claimed they wouldn't be able to manage. We talked for a long time about inconsequential things before finally hanging up. I picked up Mister Something, my raggedy treatment bear, and spent half an hour sending Reiki over to Elaine. My gammy legs and hips were still very painful, but it didn't seem to matter quite so much and Elaine was playing her part in this by sending her own special magical thoughts my way.

Nevertheless, I spent most of the next day feeling sore and sorry for myself. Chris did his best to cheer me up with zombie and vampire horror films. He made me laugh, ran me a scorching hot bath with bubbles and rosemary oil, and by the end of the day, I vaguely resembled my usual self.

In the evenings of the next week or two, I thrashed out a rough outline for the new book I planned to write and made final arrangements for a winter solstice ritual on the outskirts of the forest. I made another assorted range of craft gifts for friends and family, transforming our dining table into a messy heap of craft materials and wrapping paper in the process. I selected different items from my textile collection to knit or sew arm warmers, hats, goddess poppets, herb-filled sleep pouches and wheat bags, tarot bags and woolly socks. Aura sprays would make a nice present for some of my pagan friends, and I made batches of cookies, mint fondants, butter tablet and mince pies for others.

The last weeks of December are always busy. The archery club laid on a Christmas party, I went to another evening dinner with the club committee, Christmas lunch with my work colleagues, and the Sherwood Oak development group convened at our house one evening for a pagan gathering. I laid out a small supply of sugary and savoury treats in the kitchen before everyone arrived. It seemed a long time since we had last seen each other and we spent a while reconnecting before setting up our sacred space. At one of our meetings, Sarah had asked about planetary magic and after some discussion she and Graham arranged to investigate further. They each come across different source materials and texts and the key aspects surmised in their notes was almost identical for each planet across the board. We held a healing circle too, offering energy to friends who had asked for it, before swapping solstice gifts and tucking into biscuits, cakes and mince pies. Mulled wine is another favourite treat at this time of year, one that always goes down well.

The last week at work in the run up to the holiday was a rather jolly affair with chocolates and mince pies on our cake shelf and Andy organising trivia quizzes in between taking phone calls and doing a bit of paperwork. We had a fuddle one day with a few other teams in our building and an over-load of nibbles, although posh bottles of pop had to take the place of alcohol; we were at work, after all. Finally, we broke up for a few days off before the big event itself.

The Yule celebration in the forest was lovely, around thirty-five people coming from across the county to join in. I collected up the ritual tools I would need and lugged everything to the car. Phoebe complained under her breath – did she really have to come with me? I insisted that she did and, by the end of the day, she grudgingly admitted that she had enjoyed it. The weather was quite pleasant for the time of year, slightly chilly but with barely a breeze and not a hint of rain. The sun was shining brightly as Chris helped me lay out the labyrinth ropes, clearing a few large branches off the forest floor. The ritual circle was set up slightly apart from the labyrinth, surrounded by tea-lights in jam jars and with a large bowl of gold-foil chocolate coins in the centre.

I knew most of the people who came along; Empyrean regulars, the Sherwood Oak Circle, moot goers and more. It was quite a gathering and I was treated to warm hugs and well-wishes as everyone put their assorted bags, drums and picnic chairs around the circle. I had already picked out and briefed a few volunteers to invoke the elements, while John and Paul would be the Oak and Holly Kings. Finally, we were ready to start.

The ritual provided at the end of this month is similar to the one that took place on this lovely afternoon, but one thing we did in addition was a staged fight between the Oak King and the Holly

King, battling for the right to rule over the coming year. John's exuberance made him the perfect victor and he thoroughly enjoyed taking the title from Paul in their play-fight as they acted out the battle of the two Kings, vying for victory. The calls and applause during the staged fight were hilarious and as Priestess, I took the crown from the fallen Holly King. Paul hammed up his acting and just as I was about to snatch up the crown, he gave a few more wailing moans and clutched his chest, gave his legs a final shake and flopped back down to play dead. I placed the crown on John's head, the Oak King, and he paraded proudly, mighty staff held high.

> *Hail to the Oak King! Hail to the Oak King! Welcome, Lord of the new year!*

Chocolate coins were offered to all and the labyrinth was declared officially open. Carla, as I should have guessed, immediately took off her foot wear and went off to walk the winding path. She was soon followed by others, but only a few brave souls bared their feet this time. Sitting comfortably, wrapped in blankets all around the trees, our pagan community celebrated, chatting and laughing to the sound of drums, sharing food and drink and good company. Phoebe climbed trees, Wendy and Luke did some dowsing, and Paul explained what we were doing when a solitary and curious dog-walker happened to pass by. I missed that conversation, but as we didn't get lynched, I assume the gentleman was satisfied with the answers to his questions.

After putting away my ritual tools and the left-over food and putting a bag of assorted litter in the bin at home, there may have been a glass or two of hot mulled wine to warm me up in the evening.

I tend to spend a lot of time over the winter festival visiting friends and family and for the last six years, have travelled away from home and stayed with different family members for a few days around the twenty-fifth. As much as I enjoy visiting family, it was starting to feel like a chore every year; packing clothes and gifts to take with us, the long drive there and back, and I find it hard to relax and sleep well away from home. This year, Phoebe was spending Christmas at home with us and would be with her dad and his family for the rest of the school holiday. I was determined to stay at home and have people visit us for a change. I had had enough of travelling away, year upon year, this time, Mum came to stay with us for a couple of days and we had a very relaxed and chilled out time together.

I'm often asked how I celebrate Christmas as a pagan with a child in the family, especially if I 'let' her believe in Father Christmas. When she was very young, I explained to Phoebe that Father Christmas, or Santa Claus, is lovely story, but nothing more than that. She once insisted, aged around five or six years old, on laying a trail of glittering reindeer food for Rudolph so that he could guide the sleigh to our house. I asked her if she thought it would work and told her again, as gently as I could, that it was just a nice story. She shrugged her shoulders as if to say, nothing ventured, nothing gained. Besides, I knew her friends were all putting oats in their gardens on Christmas Eve and it wouldn't be fair for her to miss out. The glitter was still there in the morning but most of the oats had been nibbled by garden birds. Perhaps a hedgehog had come through the garden overnight and joined in with the feast. I suggested this explanation to Phoebe and she was so excited at the prospect of a hedgehog in the garden that it overshadowed Santa completely.

'I knew it was just a story,' she had told me, 'but can we put some more food out? For the hedgehog?'

Phoebe's paternal grandma used to give her a single present 'from Santa' every year and Phoebe knew that the jolly man in the red suit is just a cosy, happy story, so she was quite pleased that, as a pagan child, she managed to con an extra present out of her Nana! Another of my thoughts around the myth of Santa is my firm belief that it's horrible to lie to your children about something that matters so much to them.

My sister is two years older than I, my brother three years younger. When she was nine and I was seven, she whispered to me loudly one day in the run up to Christmas:

'There's no such thing as Father Christmas! It's just Mum and Dad!'

I wasn't terribly upset at this revelation, having already started to figure out the big secret for myself. Off we went to tell our brother. He was only four years old and I am so sorry we told him. He was completely heart-broken. His face crumpled with tears, devastated. I swore then that if I ever had children of my own, I would never put them through this same disappointment. Over forty years later, I'm still haunted by my brother's sad little face. Even though Phoebe knew the truth about Santa, she was careful not to reveal it to her school friends and played along with it whenever she was with them. While writing this piece, I asked Phoebe what she thought of the Father Christmas legend and how I had dealt with it when she was little. She didn't feel that she had missed out at all and had been happy to go along with at school it for the sake of her friends. She has always been a very thoughtful person, taking the feelings of others into consideration; as a parent, I can't ask for much more than that.

The twenty-fifth saw us loafing around in pyjamas and slippers for a lazy breakfast of chocolate croissants, brioche rolls, coffee and juice, exchanging a few gifts and playing games in the afternoon. I cooked a massive amount of food and though Mum offered to give me a hand, I had been looking forward to doing the festive dinner myself for years, so I kept plying her with drinks to keep her out of the kitchen (she didn't object). It was an enjoyable experience to serve the seasonal feast for a change and didn't take much time, as I had done some of the preparations the night before. One of the things I missed most through not being at home for Yule in the past was having left-over food to pick at over the next few days. Soups, sandwiches, salads, casseroles, cakes and biscuits – when you spend every year dining with family away from home, there are no left-overs in the fridge. Now that I was the one doing all the cooking, I made sure to over compensate and there would be plenty to use up over the next few days.

Good food, a comedy film in the evening and a few glasses of something nice to drink with my family left me happy and content. I made time to bless an offering at the altar, giving thanks to the Old Ones, and sprinkled a little food and drink outside. I know the hedgehogs and visiting birds will appreciate it, even if the flying reindeer are imaginary.

Now the year is almost done and after saying goodbye to Mum and driving Phoebe over to stay with her dad to enjoy the new year, Chris and I had a few of days of freedom to enjoy before either of us had to go back to work and they were glorious days spent simply enjoying one another's company with no set plans or commitments.

The weather was chilly but not too cold for a walk, and we strolled through the forest, coming to one of my favourite spots. Where three pathways merge together, forming a V-shaped wedge of hedgerow and forest, there are several bird feeding stations among the trees. We listened to their chatter, admiring the birds as they squabbled over the choicest delicacies left for them by a woman we had seen feeding the birds a few minutes earlier. She had very long white hair and carried a rucksack over one shoulder, heavy looking bags in each hand, a distinctive figure.

A small brown dog bounded towards us from one of the paths, momentarily halting to sniff first one thing and then another. A moment later, another dog appeared and so did the dogs' owner. Carla, deep in a world of reverie, no doubt talking silently to every tree she passed on the way. We talked for a time, indulging her dogs with tummy tickles. I briefly mentioned that my sleeping pattern still wasn't quite back to normal, and she delved deeply into her satchel, pulling out small packets of different roots, herbs and barks. She gave me directions to make some of them into another sleep tea.

In the distance, the white-haired lady was making her way slowly along the path, scattering bird seed.

'Ooh, I can't believe she's still doing that.' Carla said. 'That lady has been coming here every week in the winter for years to feed the birds. She brings nuts and seeds and grains by the bag full and walks all around the forest putting it out for the birds. All those bags she carries are full of bird food.'

'Every week?' We hadn't seen her before, but it's a large forest.

'Yes,' Carla said. 'She comes on the bus all the way from Nottingham.'

That's one dedicated wild-life lover!

I walked home with Chris, glancing back over my shoulder for a final view of the forest with its mighty oaks, hidden wildlife, secrets and dreams.

I had come full circle, ending the year in much the same way as I had started it. A peaceful walk in the ancient forest that I love so much, just minutes away from my home.

It was an amazing and beautiful year.

Thank you to everyone who shared it with me.

Crafts for the Solstice Tree

Try making your own ornaments to decorate the solstice tree with a pagan theme. Younger children will enjoy making and painting salt-dough shapes and older children and grown-ups can make felt hanging decorations, as suggested below.

Salt Dough Decorations

2 cups plain flour
1 cup salt
1 cup water to mix (approx.)
Cookie cutters
Assorted paints to decorate
Varnish (optional) to finish
Paper clips

Providing you stick to the 2:1 ratio, the mixture can be made in any quantity, large or small. Mix salt and flour together in a large bowl, gradually add water to mix into a firm dough. Add a little more flour or water, if needed, until the dough is stiff enough to roll out.

Knead on a lightly floured surface for five to ten minutes - this helps the dough to roll smoothly.

Roll out the dough and cut out shapes using biscuit cutters, roll into balls or pat into shape with your hands.

The thickness of the dough is not essential but bear in mind that very thick dough, more than a few centimetres, will take longer to dry and very tiny or thin pieces of might crack a little or break off. You can create a template out of card and cut around this to make your own shapes. Try adding small beads of dough or form small holly leaf shapes to put onto a larger piece, using a little water to fix them into place.

Use a skewer to pierce a small hole to hang up the decoration or push a paper clip into the back of the dough.

Place on baking paper on flat trays in the oven at its lowest setting for between three to five hours. This slow bake allows the dough to dry out without bubbling or browning. Allow to cool before painting. If you prefer, the salt dough can be left to dry naturally, but this will take two to three days.

Acrylics, gold and silver aerosol sprays, poster paints, felt-tips or gel pens can be used to decorate. Try toadstool shapes in bright red and white. Plain circles can be painted with pentagrams, the Awen, Thor's hammer, rune symbols, the Goddess of the moon and Horned God shapes.

Add glitter, glue on tiny beads or sequins, coat your beautiful salt dough creations with an optional layer of varnish for a glossy, shiny finish.

Finally, thread embroidery silk or ribbon through the hole or paperclip to hang in the tree.

An easy craft for all ages and, if you wrap a few decorations in pretty tissue paper or delicate fabrics, they could make a lovely hand-crafted gift.

One year I made toadstools, painted with bright red and white spots and a touch of silver glitter, tied up with a glittery thread and nestled in a gift box as a set of three. This makes a unique gift and they can be proudly displayed on the Yule tree year after year.

Felt Decorations

You will need several felt squares in your chosen colours, needle and cotton, small amount of stuffing, assorted sequins, beads, feathers, charms and embroidery silks to decorate.

Create cardboard templates or find something you like on the internet to copy. Stars, crescent moons, small toadstools, tiny Goddess and Horned God shapes or plain circles can be used, decorated with a sigil, rune or pentagram.

Trace the shape on the felt, two of each design. Using embroidery silks, sequins and beads, carefully decorate one side of each shape by sewing on runes, spirals, beads or sequins. Remember that a trusty glue-gun is the crafty witch's best friend!

Place two of these shapes together with the right sides showing. Use a needle and thread to sew around the edges, fill lightly with stuffing. Blanket stitch makes an effective and pretty edging, especially in a contrasting colour, but you can use an easy running stitch if you prefer.

Feathers, beads, acorns or dried red berries (try hawthorn, holly or rowan) can be hung from the bottom. A short length of embroidery silk at the top will be your hanging loop.

Hang on your tree, stand back and admire your handiwork.

A Yule Ritual

This ritual is suitable for any number of people, though you will need seven to take the part of the elements and the Lord and Lady. Ask for volunteers ahead of time who can speak confidently, and encourage the rest of the group to join in with calls of blessed be or hail and welcome.

Preparation:

Place a dish of gold foil chocolate coins on the altar, with seasonal food and drink, a box or bag of pre-written blessings*, ceremonial robes and head dresses for the Horned God, an athame for circle casting, and incense or sage sticks for purifying the circle.

The focus of this rite is the Sun King, who is crowned by the Goddess and parades around the circle, improvising a chant and calling out for the returning sun to shine. A simple crown can be made easily out of card, covered in gold spray paint with a star or sun motif on the front, if you don't have anything else to use, and try to find a red or orange robe or at least have your Sun King dressed in bright, sunshine colours.

*Blessings on pieces of card or paper should be placed in a cauldron or bowl and each participant takes one at random. Come up with your own ideas or use the ones below and encourage the group to join with calling out 'blessed be' after each one is read out as part of the ritual.

> *May the light of the solar return bring light into your life and the lives of those who you love. Blessed be, blessed be.*
>
> *May you spread peace and happiness wherever you go as you support those who work to support us all. Blessed be, blessed be.*
>
> *Let all who are alone, sad, grieving, upset or hurt be filled instead with pleasure and delight. Blessed be, blessed be.*
>
> *The world has shown benevolence to many this year, long may it continue. Blessed be, blessed be.*
>
> *Let those who have been through tragedy and disaster be healed. Blessed be, blessed be.*
>
> *I give thanks for all the positive things that I have gone through or received this year. Blessed be, blessed be.*

The Ritual

Goddess opens the circle, walking deosil with sage and spirit duster to cleanse participants.

Earth: Welcome earth in the north, bring stability and comfort to our circle, give us a place to stand in kinship and unity against the darkest nights. Hail and welcome, earth.

Air: Welcome air in the east, bring inspiration and peaceful communications to our circle. Bring us winds of benevolent change. Hail and welcome, air.

Fire: Welcome fire in the south, bring transformation of harmful influences to positive change, light our way and bring warmth to our souls. Hail and welcome, fire.

Water: Welcome water in the west, heal our emotions and let unity come to us on gentle waves. Hail and welcome, water.

Spirit: Welcome spirit in our centre, bring harmony, connection and friendship to our circle. Hail and welcome, spirit.

God: Welcome All Father, Odin, Thor, Pan, Cernunnos – you who are father of us all, hunted and hunter, Lord of the forest and guardian of all. Hail and welcome, Horned One.

Goddess: Triple Goddess of the moon, Diana, Selene, Ceres, Cerridwen – you who are sister and mother to us all, maiden, mother and laughing crone, Lady of the silver moon. Hail and welcome, Queen of Winter.

Goddess: Winter has come and with it, darkness. The King of the dark half of the year has seen his last day and must give his crown over the New Lord of the growing year. He will not give us his warmth just yet, for he needs time to grow. Until then, the world is cold. An icy stillness covers the land.

Water: Our emotions have been tested, grief has been long lasting, and we feel caught in its grip.

Air: Cold air fills our lungs, hail and rain, snow and wind beat at us, but we will not let despair grip our hearts.

God: Even if we have suffered and lost, out of the greatest darkness comes the greatest light. The wheel turns, the tides change and light returns. The solstice is here, the point of returning brightness and joy.

Goddess: Behold, Sun King, Lord of the returning light! *(She places the crown on his head.)*

(He now parades with antlers or golden crown, banging a staff on the ground, chanting and calling out for the return of the sun.)

All: The light returns, the light returns, the light returns!

Fire: With this great returning light, our land and lives re-awaken. Remember the friendships and the sounds of laughter that rang clearly, even when we lived in fear or grief.

Earth: Remember our kin, our times of happiness. We stand in unity with our brothers and sisters, all of us with a single focus.

Spirit: We shrug off doubt, worry and fear look forward to joy and happiness ahead. We choose to live with honour and integrity.

Goddess: Hold in your hearts a sense of beauty and peace, cherish those moments that light up your lives and warm your hearts.

God: We step forwards to the light half of the year with harmony and peace in our hearts, in honesty and unity with others. Blessed be, the returning light.

All: Blessed be, blessed be, blessed be!

Goddess: We ask for our blessings and wishes to be granted. Please take a blessing slip and give thanks for what we can give as well as what we may receive.

(Everyone takes a blessing slip from the box on the altar to read out, repeating blessed be with a clap. If anyone doesn't want to call their blessing out loud, they shouldn't be pressed into doing so.)

Goddess: As we look out into the dark world, we know that in the deep night, the Sun King is reborn. Child of hope and promise, he is nature's King, the light renewed. We honour the new-born Sun and the Great Mother who gave him birth. Hail and welcome to the returning sun!

All: Hail and welcome! Hail and welcome! Hail and welcome!

God: At the winter solstice, we are blessed with returning light and life and we give thanks for this gift by offering a gift of our own. Will you offer the gift of weeding for a neighbour, babysitting for a friend or the gift of companionship? Take a moment now to reflect on what you have been fortunate enough to receive and what gifts you can offer to others.

(Leave a few minutes of peace and silence for this contemplation, people can call out if they wish.)

Goddess: Take your coin and pass it to someone who you don't already know, and they must give theirs to yet another person, not back to you.

(Coins are shared, each person, including any children, taking one from the central pot and offering it someone else and any remaining coins can be given to the children.)

God and Goddess: We bless this food and drink in the spirit of charity, love and friendship, may you never hunger, may you never thirst.

(Pass plate and chalice around the circle.)

God: We give our thanks to you, Odin, Thor, Pan, Cernunnos, you who are father of us all, hunted and hunter, Lord of the forest and guardian of all. We bid you hail and farewell.

Goddess: We give thanks to the triple Goddess of the moon, Diana, Selene, Ceres, Cerridwen. Sister and mother to us all, maiden, mother and laughing crone, Lady of the silver moon. Queen of Winter, we bid you hail and farewell.

Earth: We thank you, spirit of earth, in your caves and mountains and forests. Return now to your sacred dwelling, leaving us with your blessings. Hail and farewell, earth.

Air: We thank you, spirits of air, seen in the wind and heard in the rustling trees. Return now to your sacred dwelling, leaving your blessings with us. Hail and farewell, air.

Water: We thank you, spirits of water, in crystalline lakes and flowing streams. Return now to your sacred dwelling, leaving your blessings with us. Hail and farewell, water.

Fire: We thank you, spirits of fire, blazing desert heat and warm hearth fires. Return now to your sacred dwelling, leaving us with your blessings. Hail and farewell, fire.

Spirit: We thank you, beloved spirit who connects us and guides us all. Return now to your sacred dwelling, leaving your blessings with us. Hail and farewell, spirit.

The circle is closed.

May the circle be open, yet unbroken,
May the peace of the Goddess be forever in our hearts.
Merry meet, merry part
and merry meet again

Afterword

The wheel turns...

And we reflect on what we have achieved, how we have developed and grown over the year, and we begin to look ahead, to dream and make plans. We set goals and ideas into motion, having learned, hopefully, from our past mistakes to avoid repeating them. We walk into the new year with a light step, thinking of the endless possibilities ahead, wondering how we can bring them into our lives, how we can repeat those things that went well and discard or change what didn't work.

I began the year with no particular plans or goals in mind, other than to devote more time to my writing and to be as kind and helpful to others as I could be.

My writing is going well, with four non-fiction witchcraft books now in print. I'm delighted that my writing dreams are coming to life, with three of my novels now on the shelves, including pagan fiction, paranormal fantasy and a magical mystery novel for young readers.

Opportunities continue to present themselves to me, and if that's the Goddess's way of prodding me further along the witching path, I will keep on taking them and forging my way ahead. I believe we should grab the good things while we have the chance, strike while the iron is hot, and plenty of other metaphors about living life to the full.

Whatever you do to celebrate the wheel of the year and all the times in between, keep on doing what makes you happy and be kind to others.

Acknowledgements

My sincere thanks to my friends, my family, and to those acquaintances, sometimes fleeting, who have all contributed in some way to making my pagan path, and my life, full of love, joy and happiness.

Chris Hodgkinson, Phoebe Stirland, Chris Brinded, Hilda & John Dolan, Nadine Angela, Liam Brinded, Philip Heselton, Jo Anderson, Daithi O'Gannon, Nancy Wilson, A-M, Tim Stimson, Grevel Lindop, Alison M, Cayt Hewitt, Tim Hewitt, Jessica Karalus, Lissadell Breinholt, Donna Towsey, Corinna Bruce, Ian Overton, Ro Anderson, Heinz Fromman, Isi Dixon, Pia Morgan, Jan Beech, Nicola Harrison, Helen Ryder, Cheryl Wild, Karen Green, Soroya Cordery, Jo Cousins, Rani, Sam Langford, Matt Arnold, Angela Barker, May Borroff, Eleanor and Tim, Les Willmore, Jess Padley, Ashley Mortimer, Sarah-Louise Kay, Julia Atkins, 'Naked' Richard LC, Morgan Dale, Lisa Barnard, Claudine West, Jenny Cartledge, Susan Baker, Kell Chapman, Patricia Crowther, Camille Fox, Mary Rands, Vivianne Crowley, Kevin Groves, Elric Sullivan, Jane Burton, Dave Mercer, Cathbodva Clarity, Diane Narraway, Tylluan Penry, Margret Vince, Pete Jennings, Alison Rouse, Neil Page, Angela Gripton, Wayne Goundry, Jeannie Thompson, Glennie Kindred, 'Telescope' Richard, Angie Milbourne, Big 'Viking' Dave Smith, Erick Henderson and Eric Henderson, Mick Lawlor, Yvonne, Jenny and Ryan, Graham Ciborski, Sheila Boughey, Steve Davis, Monica, David, Damh the Bard, Jennifer Kendall, Melanie Mosse, and all of the lovely souls who are part of the community events – the Dagda, Witchfest, Artemis Gathering, Children of Artemis, Pagan Federation, Nottingham Pagan Network, Oakleaf Camp, Nottingham Goddess Camp, Empyrean, Pagan Pride, The Witches' Stitches, The Mystic Moon, Away With The Fairies, Indigo Forge, Fenix Flames.

About the Author

Moira Hodgkinson is a witch, author and public speaker. She runs talks, workshops and rituals, has worked with BBC Radio 4 as a witchcraft consultant, and writes regularly for pagan magazines, including Pagan Dawn and Witchcraft & Wicca. She has written numerous books including pagan fiction, paranormal fantasy and practical witchcraft guides.

Katy Hunter and the Magic Star
by
Moira Hodgkinson

A page-turning read full of mystery and magic for young readers – perfect for fans of Phil Hikes and Elly Griffiths.

Far away from everything familiar, Katy Hunter dreads the thought of spending six months in the sleepy countryside with relatives she barely knows. As she starts to settle in, Katy finds out that Clover Cottage is not as peaceful as it seems. Dark dreams, whispered secrets and mysterious midnight visitors fill her with fear in the dead of night. When she finds a silver star that belongs to a witch, Katy knows there's a mystery to solve.

But when trouble strikes close to home, how far will she be drawn into the magic and mystery?

One thing she knows for certain, her life will never be the same again.

At first I thought it was going to be a 'girly' book, but it's not! It's full of magic, it's really good and I felt like I was in the book.

Bentley (Aged 8)

Available from Fenix Flames Publishing Ltd
www.publishing.fenixflames.co.uk

Operation Cone of Power

by

Moira Hodgkinson and Philip Heselton

The summer of 1940 was a perilous time for Britain, particularly for the south coast of England, whose residents were under threat of imminent invasion.

It has long been rumoured that a coven of witches in the New Forest of Hampshire raised a psychic 'Cone of Power' in an attempt to stop the invasion.

This book, a dramatisation of those events, has been made possible by the skills of the much-acclaimed esoteric novelist, Moira Hodgkinson, and the extensive researches of the historian of witchcraft, Philip Heselton.

Real individuals and what they did are woven into this fascinating and exciting tale of commitment and sacrifice - the legendary 'Operation Cone of Power'

Available from Fenix Flames Publishing Ltd
www.publishing.fenixflames.co.uk

www.ingramcontent.com/pod-product-compliance
Lightning Source LLC
Chambersburg PA
CBHW071604080526
44588CB00010B/1015